FROM POWER TO PURPOSE

A Remarkable Journey of Faith and Compassion

SENATOR SAM BROWNBACK

WITH JIM NELSON BLACK

THOMAS NELSON
Since 1798

NASHVILLE   DALLAS   MEXICO CITY   RIO DE JANEIRO   BEIJING

Published in Nashville, TN, by Thomas Nelson. Thomas Nelson is a trademark of Thomas Nelson, Inc.

Thomas Nelson, Inc., titles may be purchased in bulk for educational, business, fund-raising, or sales promotional use. For information, please e-mail SpecialMarkets@ThomasNelson.com.

Scripture quotations marked NKJV are from THE NEW KING JAMES VERSION. Copyright © 1979, 1980, 1982, Thomas Nelson, Inc., Publishers.

Scripture quotations marked NIV are taken from The Holy Bible, NEW INTERNATIONAL VERSION. Copyright © 1973, 1978, 1984 International Bible Society. Used by permission of Zondervan. All rights reserved.

Library of Congress Cataloging-in-Publication Data

Brownback, Sam, 1956–
    From power to purpose : a remarkable journey of faith and compassion / Sam Brownback.
        p. cm.
    ISBN 0-8499-0398-X
    1. Brownback, Sam, 1956– 2. Brownback, Sam, 1956—Political and social views. 3. Legislators--United States—Biography. 4. United States. Congress. Senate—Biography. 5. United States—Politics and government—1989– 6. Presidential candidates—United States—Biography. 7. Presidents—United States—Election—2008. 8. Christian biography.
    I. Title.
    E840.8.B78A3 2007
    973.09'9--dc22
    [B]

2007016798

Printed in the United States of America
07 08 09 10 11 QW 7 6 5 4 3 2 1

*This book is dedicated
to those who cherish the hope
of a free and just society for
all God's people.*

CONTENTS

INTRODUCTION

AMERICA'S FUTURE

O ur goodness is our greatness. This thought was attributed for many years to the French statesman Alexis de Tocqueville after his visits to this country in the nineteenth century. The same basic idea was also expressed by Abraham Lincoln and more recently by Ronald Reagan. I've reflected on this idea, and I believe it's fundamentally true. No country has ever occupied so dominant a place in the world as the United States does today. But if we're to remain a great nation, we have to understand the providential role we've been given by history. We're the greatest nation in the history of mankind, but with size and influence comes responsibility. And that's our challenge.

We have 5 percent of the world's population, 20 percent of the world's economy, a third of the world's military budget, and a fourth of the world's research and development budget. As my kids would say, the place rocks, and it really does. Yet, if we want to maintain that American greatness, we need to remember that our greatness comes from our goodness. But we don't need to focus on the greatness. If we focus on the goodness, the greatness will take care of itself. It will naturally be there.

If we try to do what is good and right, we will be great. But if we only try to do what's great, then we will lose both the greatness and the goodness. The heart of the matter is the human heart, which is where human goodness begins. We need to be concerned for the well-being of others. We need to be logical, reasonable, and responsible, but we must also follow the dictates of the heart, which teach us to have compassion and to do unto others as we would have others do unto us. These are all lessons the founders of this nation understood, and I am convinced that's why the nation they created has achieved so much and risen so high.

I grew up in a small farming community immersed in the traditional values and beliefs of the American heartland. I was a member of Future Farmers of America and the 4H Club, and our values were based on fundamental patriotism and doing the right thing. I grew up going to Sunday school, and the America I knew as a youngster was a nation of basic Sunday-school values—nothing fancy about it. Work hard, treat your neighbors fairly, pitch in where you can when somebody needs help—whether it's a friend or a stranger—and do your best to be a good person.

I was raised in that tradition, and then later went off to college and law school, served in public office in Kansas, and eventually became a White House Fellow and a member of Congress. Today I'm in my second full term in the United States Senate, and the more I see, learn, and do in national office, the more I understand the importance of those home-grown American values. I believe they really are the secret of America's success.

America is not Washington, DC. It's millions of people making millions of decisions every day that determine the greatness of this country. That's why the culture is so important, because if our culture honors goodness, it encourages virtue and benevolence. If the culture silences goodness in the name of tolerance and celebrates vice instead of virtue, it enables and encourages wickedness. We reap what we sow.

President Reagan often spoke about American exceptionalism. This great nation, between two great oceans, made up of people from every country on earth, is a special place—a nation with a key role in the destiny of mankind. The success of other nations has often depended on America carrying out what we are called upon to do. These thoughts were echoed by British Prime Minister Tony Blair, when he addressed both houses of Congress in July 2003.

Mr. Blair has been a faithful ally of the United States for a long time, and during that speech he expressed a hope and belief for this country that I wish all Americans could grasp. At the end of his remarks, Mr. Blair said:

I know that . . . in some small corner of this vast country, out in Nevada or Idaho or these places I've never been to but always wanted to go, I know out there there's a guy getting on with his life, perfectly happily, minding his own business, saying to you, the political leaders of this country, "Why me? And why us? And why America?" And the only answer is, "Because destiny put you in this place in history, in this moment in time, and the task is yours to do."

In the aftermath of 9/11, the world recognized that America had been attacked because a group of barbarians feared our power. They feared our philosophy of freedom and democracy, and they feared our goodness and generosity, which is the fundamental threat to their desire for dictatorial control of, not just their own people, but the whole world. Recognizing that, Mr. Blair powerfully concluded his remarks by saying, "You are not going to be alone. We will be with you in this fight for liberty. And if our spirit is right and our courage firm, the world will be with us."

Another British prime minister, William Gladstone, who served in the late nineteenth century, said: "The problem of statesmanship is to find out which way God is going and to go that way." I think that's wise counsel.

In the pages that follow, I talk about many of these things, including the importance of renewing the family and rebuilding the culture. If we get those two things right, we'll be headed in the right direction. Much of what needs to be done in dealing with both of these issues is nonlegislative and can be handled best by citizens in cities and towns all over America. The values of America are still the source of our strength, and the more "we the people" become involved in solving problems at the community level, the faster and better the solutions will be. Politicians need to support those efforts.

My primary purpose in writing this book is to focus on the work that is needed in the world today. In these pages I'll be dealing with practical issues and everyday problems; but I also want to write about the challenges of citizenship and statesmanship and public service in a somewhat larger context. I focus on what I perceive to be some of the major challenges for our country, but I've tried to do it in a practical way and in terms that will be familiar to the readers.

Throughout most of our history, we've been able to count on a wonderful fail-safe device: the character and common sense of the American people. That's still true. We've seen it recently in the response to 9/11 and other disasters. But that reservoir of moral character and shared beliefs has been weakened over the past several decades by a breakdown of the family.

The American character may be struggling today, but it's still there, and it's especially exciting for me to see what's happening with the younger generation. If character and moral judgment can be awakened in the hearts of all our people, as it appears to be now in the hearts of many of our young citizens, we won't have to worry about what this new century may bring our way. The future of this great nation is as promising as ever, but we will need the dedication and perserverance of all our people if we're to achieve our true destiny and purpose. It's for all those who share this vision of hope for America's future that I've written this book.

PART ONE

A DOMESTIC AGENDA

★ 1 ★

THE CHALLENGE TO LEAD

There's an old saying that the apple doesn't fall very far from the tree. It means that the characteristics of one generation are often visible in the lives of their children and grandchildren, and I am convinced that's especially true for those of us who were born and bred in the heartland of America. Our ancestors were of hardy stock. They came here to farm and raise their families, but they were also fiercely independent people who were willing to stand up for what they believed in. For the most part, these early settlers were Christians who resisted oppression of any kind.

The American artist John Stuart Curry captured some of that spirit in a series of murals that now adorn the walls of the Kansas State Capitol in Topeka. The most famous mural in this group is a dramatic portrait of the fiery abolitionist John Brown, with his long hair and beard blowing in the wind. In the picture, Brown is holding high a Bible in one hand, with the letters Alpha and Omega written inside it. In the other hand he's holding what the abolitionists referred to as a "Beecher's Bible," otherwise known as a Sharp's rifle.

The figure of the wild-eyed abolitionist dominates the painting as he stands defiantly before a scene of armed combat on a Civil War battlefield. In the background a prairie fire is blazing away. The fire no doubt symbolizes the conflict that was sweeping the state of Kansas at that time.

According to one account, the abolitionists in the east who supported

Brown's war were eager to send rifles to aid the antislavery settlers, but they knew that the bushwhackers in proslavery country would seize those guns and use them against the abolitionists. So they shipped the rifles in boxes marked "Bibles," and addressed them to the "Beecher Bible Church." The church was fictitious, but the name clearly referred to Rev. Henry Ward Beecher, a renowned abolitionist, and his sister, Harriet Beecher Stowe, who wrote the antislavery novel *Uncle Tom's Cabin*.

Another of those famous murals by John Stuart Curry is a large portrait of the Spanish conquistador Francisco Vazquez de Coronado, who came to North America in the mid-sixteenth century searching for fame and fortune. The image of Coronado captured in that painting is of a rich and powerful conqueror on his majestic steed. In the foreground, walking beside him and almost unseen, is a diminutive figure in a brown robe. I remember looking at that picture several years ago and wondering, *Who is that person walking beside Coronado?*

I knew the story of Coronado and how he came as far north as the Kansas prairies looking for gold. He didn't find it, but he did find several tribes of Native Americans, and ultimately went home in frustration. The story of the man walking beside him was more interesting. So I did a little reading and found out that this was Father Juan Padilla, who had accompanied Coronado's expedition.

Several of the places where the conquistadors camped have been identified by historians and archaeologists. One of them is just outside of Dodge City, Kansas. Today the site is recognized as the place where the first Catholic Mass west of the Mississippi River was celebrated. Coronado crossed the Kansas River— which he named the Saints Peter and Paul River because it was near the saints' feast day when they arrived—and made his way farther north to an area near the site of Lyons, Kansas, where he made contact with the Quivira Indians.

Coronado and his soldiers stayed with the Quivirans for about a month before heading back south, disappointed that they hadn't found the treasure they were seeking. But Father Padilla found something more precious than gold—he found souls. He went back to Mexico with Coronado in 1541 but returned to Kansas in 1542, accompanied by three other Franciscans, to work among the Native Americans and spread the Word of God.

Padilla was well received and well treated by the Quiviran Indians. After some time he decided he wanted to meet with another tribe in the area. The best explanation of what happened next is that the Quivirans were afraid that Father Padilla would spread his good medicine to rival tribes, so on his journey to another village, a raiding party caught up with him and, on Christmas Day 1542, he was martyred while kneeling in prayer.

MIDWESTERN VALUES

As I reflected on the images in John Stuart Curry's painting, I was struck by the contrast between these two men who had come to America with such different goals. Coronado was after power and wealth, but he didn't find it. Juan Padilla came with a very different object in mind, to share the Word of God with others, and he found it. Even in martyrdom, Father Padilla left an important legacy to those that would come after him. In that light, I thought John Stuart Curry captured the characters of both men very well. On first glimpse, Coronado is the icon and the hero. It's only on closer inspection that Father Padilla stands out, and that's just as it should be.

When I first set out to pursue a career in public policy, I probably had more of the Coronado spirit in me. It wasn't the glitter of gold that I was after, but I confess I was drawn by the lure of notoriety and influence. It didn't take long to discover the emptiness of that track. It was only when I understood and followed my true purpose of service to God and my fellow man that I found what I was really looking for. Not power but purpose. That's the focus of my life and my work today in the United States Senate.

I'm a part of that large group of Americans that has been described by demographic researchers as "the pig in the python" moving through the system: the Baby Boom generation. Maybe you are, too. It's a group that has experienced a lot of life, but a lot of Boomers today are dissatisfied with what's become of it. Many of them have had financial success. They may be stable now, and the kids are mostly grown, but for some reason it's not satisfying. Things didn't turn out the way they expected, and a lot of Boomers are still looking for the meaning of life.

Many people in my generation have engaged in a selfish pursuit of pleasure, and they've found it. But they're not satisfied with that either. I can say that I've done that too. There were times when I thought that being comfortable and happy was all that mattered, but like so many of my peers, I discovered that pursuing pleasure alone is not satisfying. So now I'm after something better— I'm after joy. Even though pleasure and joy may sound like the same thing, they're not. Pleasure fades, but joy is constant and ongoing.

The entire Boomer generation of seventy-eight million Americans, born from 1946 to 1964, is now approaching retirement age. These men and women, between the ages of forty-two and sixty, are the largest, healthiest, and best-educated generation in American history. I believe that a lot of people in my generation have reached the point where they're searching more for meaning and purpose than pleasure. I believe my story is their story.

Our parents are aging, some of us are having health problems, and our kids may be going through tough times as well. Some of our classmates are getting cancer now. I've been down that road, and it's something I've thought a lot about. And 9/11 made a lot of us wonder what's going on in the world. Obviously something is going on, and we're finally getting the message that sooner or later we're all going to die.

No matter how much we want to live, we're beginning to realize that time is passing, and the prognosis isn't all that great. But despite the occasional fears, there's plenty of reason for hope, and that's really the best part of this story.

A Time of Transition

My motivation for going into public service had a lot to do with the economic crisis that hit Midwestern farmers back in the 1980s. I was born into a farm family, so that was something I understood and cared about. My dad farmed in partnership with my grandfather for a number of years, and then he went out on his own. Our farm was in eastern Kansas, about eight hundred acres of wheat, corn, and soybeans, as well as cattle and hogs. The Brownbacks had farmed in eastern Kansas for four generations. We're of German descent but long ago lost any connection with our German heritage.

We were farmers in a state that's known for farming. I was pretty sure that

I would grow up to be a farmer. It was a lifestyle I knew, liked, and was comfortable with, so I was fine with that idea. Dad was a hardworking man. He worked every day, even most Sundays. He'd ship the kids off to Sunday school in the morning, and we would take a few hours off for lunch and family time, and after that we worked.

That was a great way of teaching us the importance of work. The Protestant work ethic was a very real thing to us. You got up and you worked. My mother was a stay-at-home mom. She worked every day in the house and kept the farm records. There were four children: an older sister, an older brother, myself, and a younger brother. The community I grew up in, Parker, Kansas, was a farming community of about 250 people, where everybody knew everybody else—and most of everybody else's business. At one point we had a party-line phone of eight families, so we generally knew what everybody else was doing. There weren't many secrets in those days.

Looking back, I realize that it was a great incubator environment. Opportunities to get in trouble were limited, because if you did something bad, everybody in town would know about it before long. There was no hiding from it. There were aunts and uncles just a few miles away, and my grandparents on my mother's side were twelve miles away in the other direction. It was a stable environment. Broken families were rare.

As far as I knew, there wasn't anybody I went to school with—from first grade through high school—who was from a separated or divorced family. Of course, if you go to the same community today, I suspect you'd find that the numbers would be about the same as the national average. But when I was growing up, it was a stable, solid, peaceful community, and a pleasant way of life. Certainly we had problems. Alcoholism, abusive spouses, and rural poverty were present, yet it was mostly managed within the context of the family. Not perfect, but it did work.

I'm sure there are a lot of people who would call it a boring way of life, but I look back and think, *What a gift, to have a boring life in a setting like that.* Every morning we did chores and then went back to the house to get ready for school. I complained about it at the time. I would have preferred to go into town and play basketball with my buddies, but work always came first. My first real exposure to the outside world came through my affiliation with Future Farmers of

America. Without that I wouldn't have ventured out or explored very much. But the FFA was a door opener.

At that time I had a kind and gifted vocational agriculture instructor who encouraged me to get involved. I was active in district offices and contests and was eventually elected state president of FFA. That was the first time I'd met a U.S. congressman, and I thought, *You know, that must be a pretty interesting job. I wonder how you get to do a job like that*. That was my first contact with that level of politics, and it really looked interesting.

I hadn't thought much about college at the time. I assumed I would just continue working on the farm, but I won a National Honor Society scholarship my senior year in high school. It was only for a thousand dollars, but it would have been a shame to waste it, so I headed off to college. My parents agreed that it was the right decision. It was only later I realized that Dad never really expected me to be a farmer.

Dad knew that farming was a tough way to make a living, and he probably thought I could do better in some other line of work. He thought that college would be the best place for me to find a career. My older brother is a veterinarian with a practice south of Topeka, and my younger brother farms with my parents. I majored in agricultural economics in college, and I even came back after graduation and talked to Dad about working with him on the farm. But it was a short conversation. He just said, "Well, there's not room here." And that was it.

POLITICS AND RELIGION

There was no debate. I think Dad knew I was interested in other things, and he wanted me to know that I was free to pursue my goals. We were going into the 1980s, and there were many bankruptcies in farming at that time. If I had joined the family business, we would have expanded just in time for the high interest rates that hit in the early '80s. We would have been crushed. So Dad's words were a gift in many ways.

That sent me on to law school at the University of Kansas. Gifts come in so many ways. They're not always apparent, and sometimes you don't recognize them until much later. As a college freshman, a guy across the hall in my dorm was a Bible study leader, and he got me involved in the study. The state vice president of Future Farmers was a committed Christian, as well.

In those college years my soul grew in the most remarkable ways. It was only when I wanted to run for student body president at K State that I hit a speed bump. I had been a national officer for FFA. To do that you leave for a year and travel the country. I had a fabulous year. But when I said I wanted to run for student body president, some of my closest friends thought I should get more involved in the Bible study group. They said, "This government and politics stuff is not where you should be, Sam. Your soul is not going to grow that way."

I remember pondering that for a long time, because these were people I trusted and admired. Generally I thought these friends were right, but I prayed about it and decided, *No, this is what I'm supposed to do.* So I ran, I won, and that was my first taste of politics. I could see then how you could use an elected office to help others. I hosted a regular meeting with a group of ten student leaders—including the editor of the newspaper, dorm leaders, and a few others —and we discussed our challenges and the moral issues involved. This was in the late seventies, and I could see how a position of influence could be used to help people.

I worked for a time as a farm broadcaster after I graduated from college, and then I went to law school at the University of Kansas. I attended law school for very practical reasons and not from any idealism about the legal profession. At that time I still wanted to farm, and I couldn't see any way to support my farming habit other than by practicing law during the day and doing a little farming on the side. The farm economy was struggling at the time, but I figured I could practice law just about anyplace and still stay near home, so that's what I did.

I met my wife-to-be while I was in law school. We dated at that time and got married after we graduated. I discussed with Mary, my soon-to-be wife, that we could take a job close to the farm and I could begin farming, or we could move to Manhattan, Kansas, where I had an offer to join a small law firm. Mary didn't have any interest in farming, so she said, "Oh, I love Manhattan!"

So I joined the small practice and worked there for four years. You can learn a lot about people in a general law practice—I was doing criminal law, divorces, wills, foreclosures, trial practice, and just about everything involving the law in a place like Manhattan, Kansas. A lot of my work involved agricultural law, which I taught for three years at Kansas State University. I also coauthored two books on agricultural law.

After four years of law practice, I decided to apply for the position of Kansas secretary of agriculture when that office came open. Being a lawyer had its plusses, but I felt called to something else, so I applied and was delighted when I was appointed to the position by the Kansas Board of Agriculture. This was the job that really got me started in public service as a career.

UNEXPECTED CHANGES

The position of agriculture secretary carried a lot of influence in Kansas. We were in what became known as the "Farm Crisis." The farm economy was deflationary. No one was making much money in agriculture at the time. People were selling out or losing their farms to foreclosure. People in agriculture were looking for answers. They were willing to try a lot of different things, so I said, "OK, if it isn't working out for us now, let's find something that will work." So we looked at alternative crops and all sorts of things, including making food products, biofuels, and different technologies that were new at the time. In those first few years, we did what we could at the stste level to help the down market, instituting many forward-thinking programs.

During the middle of my term, I was notified that I'd been accepted as a White House Fellow, which meant that I'd be going to Washington as part of a class of young professionals who would be spending a full year learning about government, the executive branch, and the inner workings of government in the nation's capital.

This was during the first Bush presidency and in the middle of my term as agriculture secretary. It was an incredible opportunity to get an inside look at the way government works, and it seemed to me that being a White House fellow would be a good opportunity to learn about trade issues so important to Kansas agriculture, so I took a leave of absence in 1990–91 and went to Washington. Looking back, that was an incredible time for my family and me. It gave me a new appreciation for public service, as well as my first exposure to politics at the national level.

RUNNING FOR OFFICE

I wasn't thinking about running for Congress at that time. I was more interested in possibly running for governor. The year I spent as a White House Fellow was wonderful, but my family didn't want to be in Washington. They wanted to be back in Kansas, and I felt that I'd seen enough of the big city. I was anxious to get back home to my own state. Besides that, Republicans were always in the minority in Washington politics at that time, so why would I want to go back there and throw bricks? I wanted to do something constructive. I wanted to run for governor, and if I lost I'd go on and find something else.

But we don't always get what we want. My family and I prayed about whether or not I should run for governor, but we never had a sense of peace that it was the right thing to do. People were telling me, "Look, Sam, if you're going to do this, you'd better get in now. It's time to decide." I kept waiting. Then one day I received a call from the Democratic congressman who held the seat for our district. He was a good friend, and we had worked on some projects together.

He said, "Sam, I don't know if this has ever happened in Kansas politics, but I just wanted you to know that I'm going to give up my seat in Congress and run for governor." The implication was that if I had ever thought about running for Congress, now would be the time. I thanked him for his call and said I'd give it some thought. I had an instantaneous sense of peace about running for Congress. I knew then that it was the right thing to do—to get in the race, run for office, and see what happened.

That was in 1993 during the run-up to the 1994 elections. There was a lot of controversy across the country. It seemed as if a big shake-up of some kind was brewing. But even though I felt that I was supposed to run for Congress, I didn't want to go back to Washington. I didn't want to be in the minority party. I didn't want to be in the middle of all the in-fighting that was going on. Furthermore, my family didn't want to live there. More than anything else, they didn't like the fact that I would have to be away from home so much of the time.

It was a dramatic time. We had come out of the Reagan–Bush years and gone into the Clinton years. We had outspoken leadership in the House of Representatives, and conservatives were making waves and speaking out more than usual. Signs of change were becoming more and more apparent, but it wasn't clear what the changes would be. It was an important time, and the freshman class of 1994 was destined to make a huge impact on government. We didn't realize just how big an impact we would have.

I was determined to do a good job for my district in Kansas, but I had no idea what was about to happen. It never crossed my mind that Republicans would actually take control of the House in 1994. We would have ideological control, because there would be enough conservative Democrats who would find common ground with Republicans on key issues. With their help we could get some good things done, but I didn't anticipate the scale of the change that was coming.

There was a full-scale revolt taking place all across the country. People were upset about some of the over-the-top policies being pushed by the Clinton administration, nationalized health care being one of the most conspicuous. I campaigned almost every day for a full year, listening to the concerns of the people in my state—including door-to-door canvassing, public speeches, parades, and everything else you can imagine—and with all that I ran into five people who supported the Clinton health plan. Most didn't want it, and they felt that Bill Clinton was giving them the stiff-arm. He had run as a conservative Democrat and then governed as a liberal. People in our area felt betrayed.

A WORTHY HISTORY

The seat I ran for had been held by a Democrat for the past twelve years, even though the state of Kansas has deep historical roots in the Republican Party. Kansas became a state in 1861, the same year Abraham Lincoln was inaugurated. We came into the union as a "free state" under the terms of the Kansas-Nebraska Act of 1854. The history of that period is so important to who we are today that I feel I ought to recount just a bit of it here.

Events unfolding in Kansas in the middle of the nineteenth century would come to be seen as a major chapter in the sectional disputes that led to the Civil War. Stephen A. Douglas, the senator from Illinois who's best remembered today for his debates with Abraham Lincoln, had introduced the bill that divided a northern portion of the old Louisiana Purchase into two territories, known as Kansas and Nebraska. The slavery question was the burning issue of the day, and Douglas proposed to solve the problem through what he called "popular sovereignty." By that he meant that the people of those territories should be allowed to decide for themselves whether they would be "slave states" or "free states."

The bill passed and was signed into law, but it didn't solve the problem. Most people in Washington expected Kansas to enter the union as a slave state. But the Kansas territory had many passionate abolitionists, and they intended to keep it a free state. That's when the state acquired its nickname of "Bleeding Kansas." Many people fought and died over those questions. I'm proud of the strong stand against slavery that my predecessors took.

The area was ripped apart by skirmishes between proslavery and antislavery forces—the same forces that eventually led to the split between the North and the South. The Republican Party was born out of that conflict and Abraham Lincoln, who had debated Douglas over the slavery question, became the outspoken leader of the Republicans. In turn, he became the president who had the destiny of presiding over one of the bloodiest conflicts in American history. Kansas played a major role in that debate, and the citizens of our state have held strongly to their pedigree during most of our nation's history.

My mother was raised in Osawatomie, Kansas, where the notorious abolitionist John Brown had stayed when he was in Kansas during the 1850s. When John Brown's militia raided the federal arsenal at Harper's Ferry, he was known by the nickname "Osawatomie Brown."

Brown is a controversial figure, but one can certainly understand his motivation. He had successfully defended the free-soil settlement at Osawatomie with a party of less than two dozen irregulars against a force of some four hundred proslavery raiders from Missouri. One of Brown's sons had been killed just before the Battle of Osawatomie. It was there that Brown made the prophetic statement that there would never be peace in this land until the issue of slavery was resolved. The world soon discovered the terrible truth of those words.

That history gives a rich texture to the state and helps explain why Kansas has been in the forefront of so many moral issues. My seatmate in Washington, Senator Pat Roberts, has similar connections to this history. His great-great-grandfather came to Kansas as an abolitionist. His name was John Wesley Roberts—a great Methodist name—and he arrived at the community of Oskaloosa, Kansas, just north of Topeka, with a buckboard, a printing press, a rifle, and a Bible.

A Future and a Hope

Another strand of Kansas history is represented today by Judge Julie Robinson, the United States district judge for the District of Kansas, whose 2001 appointment to that position I was privileged to sponsor. Judge Robinson is a fourth generation "Exoduster," which has a special historical significance in the Midwest. "Exodusters" were African-Americans who left the post-Reconstruction South to move west in search of land and a new start in life. After the Civil War, African-Americans who had gained their freedom came to Kansas and established towns, farms, and homesteads of their own.

Benjamin "Pap" Singleton was probably the best-known leader of the Exoduster Movement. From 1877 to 1879 he brought hundreds of black families up from the South and helped them start new lives. For the most part, the Exodusters prospered in our part of the country, and they continue to make important contributions to Kansas life. Judge Robinson's ancestors settled in the northeastern part of the state, and her family is rightfully proud of that legacy.

If you understand the spirit that motivated Kansans in the nineteenth century to do those kind of things, then you'll understand the character of the state today. The men and women who settled the Kansas territory had a passion for justice and moral responsibility—views that were informed by their strong Wesleyan and Methodist roots. It's the same spirit that led them to speak up about the slavery debates, the prohibition debates of the early twentieth century, and other issues of social justice. Kansas has been a leading pro-life state, and we're still deeply involved in the debate of reforming prisoners while they are serving time for crimes they have committed.

If you read abolitionists' letters that were sent from Ohio in the mid-nineteenth century, and if you grasp the resilient faith of those people and their willingness to fight for what they believed in, then this state and the people of Kansas will make a lot more sense to you. The descendants of those hardy frontier people are the constituents I was campaigning to represent in Washington. When I entered the race for the U.S. Senate seat formerly held by Bob Dole, I understood that courage, tenacity, and accountability were prerequisites for the job. I soon discovered that it would take even more than that.

These are the values of the heartland, and my home state is at the center. We're geographically located in the heart of the nation, our politics come from the heart, and I think the values associated with the term "compassionate conservatism" apply to our beliefs very well. Our people have a passion for doing what's right, but that view is not unique to us. It's shared by millions of others, in every state and every community in America. That's our nation's real hope for the future.

In the chapters that follow, I want to talk about how that works and how we're trying to deal with some of the big challenges. I hasten to say that I didn't come to any of this on my own. I believed at one point that I could do it all myself. But God has ways of shaking things up, and that's an even bigger part of my story. I had tried to separate my faith from my work when I first started out, but all of that was about to change.

A GREATER PURPOSE

I arrived in Washington with the Republican Revolution of 1994. It had been a long, hard campaign. I was on the road for more than a year, often going door-to-door. I was a self-directed person at that time. I had been brought up with a Protestant work ethic, and I was going to do it all on my own, through hard work and self-discipline. I knew how to work, and I did. I went pillar to post every day. I was doing everything in my power to win that congressional race.

But since I was doing everything on my own, I couldn't sleep at night because I was always thinking about what I ought to be doing next. I wasn't thinking much about my family and wasn't much help as a husband and father when I was home. I loved my wife and three children with all my heart, but I was not there for them during that campaign, even when I was physically with them.

I ran hard and won the primary, but not by much. This primary race for the House of Representatives was the closest race I've ever been in, in terms of absolute votes. A sign of what was going on in the country was that another candidate ran to my right. The traditional way of running for office in Kansas was not to declare any firm positions on the big issues but to try to keep the tent as big as possible, so that's what I was doing. But in 1994, the voters wanted to know where the candidates stood on the issues. You could be right or wrong in their estimation, but they wanted to know what you were think-ing and how you would vote. I also knew that a candidate who came out strongly on the wrong side of the big issues could end up making many people angry.

I had watched the GOP machine for years. I had been an intern in Senator Dole's office as a young man, and I thought I understood how to play the game. So in the primary that's the way I ran, and I almost got beat. I had raised probably ten times more money than my rival, and I was much better known. But with all that, I still came close to losing the race.

I have always been pro-life but during the first few weeks of the campaign, I chose to focus on particular policies rather that broad principle. Instead I talked about where I stood on taxpayer funding of abortion, on the use of military bases for abortion, and things of that sort. All of that articulated a pro-life posi-tion, but I didn't want to irritate anybody, so I wouldn't come right out and state clearly where I stood, and that irritated many people in my state.

SEEING THE LIGHT

It was really my opponent in that race who taught me politics. He was a novice getting in, but he had a clear set of convictions, and he said, "Here's where I stand and what I'm going to do." I thought, *Wow, that's dangerous! There's not much wiggle room in that!* But I almost lost the election by thinking that way. Nevertheless, I won the primary, thanks in large part to name identification. In the general election I was running against John Carlin, a former two-term governor of Kansas, who was trying to make a political comeback. He had lost the race for a third term as governor, so he decided to run for Congress as a Democrat.

My rhetoric moved to the right in the general election, which is not the cus-tomary way of doing things. Most politicians tend toward the middle in order to reach the greatest number of voters, but my opponent in the primary taught me that I needed to be very clear about where I stood on the issues. As it turned out, 1994 was a good year to be very clear about where you were on the issues. Whether it was a reaction to the first couple of years of the Clinton term or something else, the voters wanted to know where I stood, so I left no doubt: yes, I'm pro-life; yes, I support tax cuts; and yes, I will vote to reduce the size of government.

I hadn't signed the *Contract with America* that Republican leaders had introduced—mainly because I had a different idea about how to manage welfare reform. Also I wanted to be an independent candidate and not simply as part of a machine. I made my principles and beliefs clear to the voters, and I did my best to assure them that I was a Reagan conservative.

When the smoke finally cleared, I was elected to Congress. The next day as I was reading the numbers and looking at what had happened around the country, I was stunned by the scope of the conservative uprising. When all was said and done, Republicans gained fifty-two seats in the House and eight in the Senate. Along the way they also managed to unseat several prominent Democrats, including House Speaker Tom Foley and the chairmen of two key committees.

It would be the first time Republicans controlled both houses of Congress since 1952, and the first time a Republican was chosen as Speaker of the House since 1953. Even the most optimistic Republicans had doubted that their party would ever be a majority party in their lifetime. But many people were deeply distressed by what they saw during the first two years of the Clinton administration. Two years of a Democrat-controlled White House and Congress were enough to shake the conservative nature of America awake. The 1994 midterm elections brought about a historic change of direction. I was in the middle of a conservative movement.

Democrats and many in the media had scorned the *Contract with America*, calling it a publicity stunt. But the voters were tired of vague promises and unmet expectations. As I had discovered in my own campaign, they were tired of equivocal answers to their questions. They wanted to know where the candidates stood on the big issues of the day, and clearly they found the Republican answers more agreeable than what they were getting from the Democrats.

The *Contract with America* included ten proposed reforms, including reducing the burden on taxpayers and shrinking the size of a bloated federal bureaucracy. For the first time ever, Congress would be required to follow the same kinds of rules that businesses were obliged to operate under. In addition, committees in both houses were required to reduce the size of their staffs and to eliminate expensive perks. Term limits were enacted for committee chairpersons. Even though I hadn't signed the *Contract with America* during the campaign, I realized that the policy objectives my colleagues were proposing were good ones. Over the next two years, we managed to pass nine of the ten pieces of legislation included in that document.

Some of the measures were eventually stopped in the Senate or the White House, where Democrats still had substantial power. But the people never lost faith in our reforms, and they continued to press for changes throughout the remainder of the Clinton years. If anything, the Republican base has only grown larger and more determined during the last ten years. Furthermore, I'm convinced that changes in the House and Senate in the 2006 midterm elections, which some would be quick to interpret as a repudiation of the GOP, are in fact an indication that the voters are finding their voices once again and demanding accountability and action in Washington. I'll come back to that in another chapter.

I called around to ask several friends and supporters what they thought of the 1994 election. They all agreed that it was hugely significant. I knew that going to Washington as a freshman member of Congress would be an important first step, but I really didn't know what to expect. Someone told me, "You'll never have more power as a group than you have right now at the very beginning." I thought, *What an irony! The most power we'll have is during the first few weeks after the election—when we still don't know how things operate!* I hadn't been in Congress before. I had never held elective office at this level. But I knew I had to hit the ground running.

THE START OF A NEW DAY

As it turned out, fully half of the freshman class of 1994 had never held elective office before. In some ways that was a good thing. We weren't frightened by anything and didn't know what was possible or impossible. We had to get ourselves organized quickly if we were going to be effective, so we immediately began contacting the more conservative members of that group to begin forming our coalition. Everybody was eager to get started.

We called ourselves "The New Federalists," and we began meeting twice a week. The group included Joe Scarborough (now an MSNBC commentator), David Macintosh, Mark Souder, Todd Tiahrt (also a Kansan), John Shadegg, Jon Christensen, John Ensign, myself, and others. At least forty members of Congress were involved in the group, and we quickly became known as the cutting edge of the cutting edge in the House.

We would meet with the leadership of the House and we helped move the Republican caucus in a more conservative direction. Some of the more established Republicans in the House weren't too excited about this conservative revolution business. So we pushed the Republican caucus to the conservative side and opened up the skirmish lines.

The leadership was glad to have us. We could help to ram through a conservative agenda because we had a third of the votes in the caucus in our class. We had the organizing force of the New Federalists. We wanted to take on the issues. Our big objective was to implement the *Contract with America* and to reduce the size, scope, and intrusiveness of the federal government. We even attempted to shut down four cabinet-level agencies (the Departments of Commerce, Energy, Housing and Urban Development, and Education).

REASSESSING PRIORITIES

We were on fire, but I soon discovered that my around-the-clock frenzy was taking a toll on my family life. In April of that first year, I specifically remember being in Pittsburg, Kansas, in the southeastern corner of the state, when I called home to talk to my wife, Mary. She said, "Sam, do you really need to be down there right now? You campaigned day and night for more than a year. Now you've been elected, and you're hardly ever home. I'm worried about the kids not knowing you as a dad." She may not have used those exact words, but that's the message I got. I heard her loud and clear. I didn't sleep very well that night. I was upset, but not enough to change my ways.

A couple of months later, we took the family for a short vacation and visited

Mary's brother and his family in Oklahoma. One night while we were there, Mary and I went for a walk; I was tanked up on the zeal of our cause. I told Mary about how well we were doing. We were changing the world, and we expected to get it done in six months. Mary listened patiently for a while, but when I paused to take a breath, she said, "That's great, I'm sure you're doing great things. But I just want your kids to know who you are."

That one scored. I knew she was right. She was hanging in there, but she was concerned that our kids weren't going to know their father. And before long they weren't going to care anymore. In 1995, our daughter Abby was nine years old, our son Andy was seven, and our daughter Elizabeth was five. I knew Mary was right, and I knew I ought to be paying more attention to my family, but I was running so fast in my political life that I didn't know how to slow down.

We knew that we would never have more power than we had at the outset, so we kept going around the clock for months. The lobby groups weren't organized yet to keep us from accomplishing our goals, so we started the session in early January and moved big bills in the *Contract with America* through the House. We were united and disciplined. We would hit a target, turn, hit the next one, turn, and just keep on moving. It was a heady time for all of us, and we were going at it full tilt, but I knew we couldn't keep going at that pace forever.

It was also a heady time for me personally. I was being quoted in the national media in publications like the *Wall Street Journal* and *Time* magazine. I was on the leading edge of the Republic Revolution. At first the Washington media, which is predominantly Left leaning, scoffed at us. Then they began to think that we might actually do something. I was thinking, *This is too good to be true! Here I am, a freshman congressman, and it feels like I'm in the Super Bowl of politics and they just gave me the ball!*

My year as a White House Fellow served me very well. I had already spent a year in Washington and knew to some degree how things operated. I wasn't afraid of the system. These are bright people, they're energetic people, but they're just people. Our advantage was in our numbers and in our fearlessness— a rare trait in politicians! We may have been green, but the key was to attack the system hard—and that's just what we did.

THE WHITE DEATH

During the August recess that year, I was invited to speak at Ross Perot's Reform Party convention in Dallas. Perot was big then, and I had been asked to speak about all the changes we were pushing through Congress. The media were everywhere. I was being interviewed on television, and my picture was all over the newspapers. I was calling for term limits, balanced budgets, and smaller government. The response was passionate. We were in a populist, conservative wave.

From Dallas I flew to Colorado to join my family on vacation. I soon realized that things weren't quite right. Mary and the kids were distant, and I wasn't feeling very good about myself. I pleaded with the Lord to make me different. All the world's accolades were coming to me, but my soul was empty. I was in line for some major soul surgery.

I soon discovered that I wasn't the only one who was going through an emotional realignment at that time. Of the seven men in the Bible study I attended in Washington—all of them members of Congress—three were in the midst of marital problems and would ultimately get divorced. I didn't see it at the time, but I was on track to become number four. I was thinking, *I'm saving the world, God! This is what you called me to do, so why don't I feel better about it?*

Shortly after that time I noticed a strange-looking mole on my side. I had it checked out, and the doctors were pretty vague. We let it go for a month or two and then they decided to do a biopsy to see if it might be something more serious. They should have removed it immediately. When the results came back they said it was melanoma. That was the first of September 1995.

I had always been a worrier, but suddenly I became a world-class worrier. It was a malignant tumor, and they were going to have to go back in and remove more tissue from my body and do further tests. I was devastated by the news. My dad had been diagnosed with colon cancer at a young age. He survived, but I knew that if melanoma goes long enough it can be very serious, even fatal, and that was more than I was prepared to handle.

They did the surgery and removed a hunk of flesh and muscle from my right side. The physical surgery had been simple. My soul surgery was just getting under way. I took some time off for recuperation and then returned to Congress a very different person. It's what the devotional writer Oswald Chambers called "the white death"—when you die to self and truly give your life to God.

It was during that time that I moved from the apartment where I'd been living in Washington to a group residence. I took a basement apartment, and that room became my spiritual Operating Room. I spent a lot of time during the next several months reforming my life and my focus. I was there alone each night during that time Congress was in session, often in prayer searching for answers and repeatedly asking God those unanswerable questions: Why me? Why this? Why now? The thought that I wasn't the person God wanted me to be was especially painful.

Yet during the day, when I was working on legislation, meeting with constituents, or participating in meetings and hearings on Capitol Hill, I don't think anyone could have imagined what was going on inside of me. In practical terms I was as effective as ever, if not more so, but I was on the ragged edge emotionally and spiritually.

A Time of Transformation

One day I was scheduled to attend a caucus meeting of Republicans in the House and Senate, and as I walked into the room I spotted Bob Dole near the front. I sat down beside him, just to visit for a few minutes. Bob was the majority leader in the Senate and the senior senator from Kansas. At one point he looked over at me and said, "You know, some of you guys in the House ought to be thinking about running for the Senate." I didn't say anything, but I looked at him and I thought, *If you knew my condition right now, Senator, you wouldn't be suggesting something like that to me.*

The thought of running for the Senate was the farthest thing from my mind. I was emotionally sidelined. I was still in the battle, technically, but I knew I had to start searching for better answers than the ones I'd found so far. I was looking for something that lasts, something I could hold on to.

At one point I visited the family farm, and I thought, *Okay, this at least will last. The farm and my parents, they'll always be here.* But then I realized, *No, that's not true. They won't always be here.* Days later I looked at my wife and my children and I thought, *Mary and the kids will always be here.* But I couldn't really say either; I didn't know what the future would hold. I hoped that Mary would always be there, but I knew the kids would all grow up one day and get married and have lives of their own.

So I just kept searching. OK, I had been secretary of agriculture in Kansas, and I had gotten some bills passed through the state legislature. They would be there, wouldn't they? But, again, I had to say, *No, maybe not. They could be changed in the next legislative session, and some of them have already been changed.* As I was thinking about all these things one evening, I had a visual image of a small car speeding up a small mountain—it was a mountain but not a very big one. There were gravel corners, and I was racing up this mountain as fast as I could go, sliding around those gravel corners and going all out with the accelerator to the floor.

Pretty soon I came to the top of the mountain and, sure enough, I won the race. But when I claimed my prize, it was just a pile of broken glass. It was pretty glass, bits of colored glass, but that's all it was. I reached out to take my prize, and then I died. I just accepted that. I wasn't emotional about it, but I looked up, thinking that I would be going up, but instead I was starting to sink. And that's the image that was passing before my eyes when I drifted off to sleep that night. A fitful sleep.

It was just a small mountain, but I had won the race. I did it all on my own. I won, but what did I win? That waking dream became very real to me during the next several days in my prayer time, and I realized I had to get off of the treadmill. Yes, I had been student body president, national vice president of the FFA, an attorney, secretary of agriculture, a White House Fellow, and now I was one of the leaders of the Republican Revolution in Congress. I had done all that. But what did it mean? I was just building my "City of Man."

That was St. Augustine's term for it in his classic work *The City of God.* When your only frame of reference is limited to the finite physical world, you're not living by any higher standard. You're living in the temporal and profane conceits of your own heart. I was doing pretty well at it, I thought. But all of that came crashing down, and I finally just gave up. One night I got down on my knees and said, "OK, Lord, that's it. I give up. It's all Yours. This life is Yours, and You can do with it whatever You like."

The winter of 1995–1996 was a time of transformation for me, and since that time, I'm happy to say, my life has never been better! Mary wasn't at all sure about the change in me for a while. Suddenly she was married to a guy who listened to Christian music, read his Bible, and prayed. She was used to the old Sam, and at first she had to wonder if this new Sam was better or worse. In time she realized that it was for real, but she still questioned whether or not this was the right thing for us. Like me, her activities and interests were mostly secular, and this was a dramatic change. Mary began doing some soul searching of her own.

CHANGING THE GAME

I realize now that through it all God was preparing me for the task ahead, which turned out to be a campaign for the Senate. That race was so different from anything I had ever done. Running for the House of Representatives, I was the odds-on favorite. I was the favorite of the political establishment in the state. I had raised a great deal of money for the race. I had a strong organization behind me and a strong political apparatus. I may have been a little too conservative for some of the party organizers, but they decided that, even so, I was better than the opposition.

But when I entered the Senate race in 1996, I was running against the political establishment. The Kansas GOP was backing Sheila Frahm, who was appointed to fill the Senate vacancy when Bob Dole stepped down to run for the presidency. They were supporting her to be elected in her own right. She was a moderate, appointed by a sitting Republican governor, who was also a moderate. Bob Dole had received the party's nomination for president at the Republican Convention in 1996, and the establishment leadership wanted to show a moderate face coming out of Kansas. They decided that Sheila Frahm was the way to go.

Consequently, I was running against the big-money crowd. I was running against the GOP machine behind Bob Dole. Yet because of the Lord's grace and mercy, I had a tremendous sense of peace because I knew this was the right thing to do. I was able to sleep at night. There was a time when my own polling numbers showed that I was down 19 points. I had to work hard, but I never let any of it get to me. The race started in May, and the primary would be in August, so we only had June and July to run the campaign. I would need to be going statewide by that time. I took up the challenge and moved ahead with a great sense of purpose and peace.

I was running against a popular incumbent who had been appointed by a popular governor, and despite all those challenges, I couldn't have been happier. When I announced my candidacy for the Senate, it was in the second year of my first two-year term in Congress. If I lost the Senate race I wouldn't be returning to Washington. But I had no second thoughts about it. When the Dole seat came open, I knew it was the right thing to do. When you walk by faith, it changes everything.

When I look back at the dynamics of that campaign, it's still amazing to me. In the general election the two candidates' campaigns only controlled about a third of the actual spending on broadcast advertising during the last two weeks of the campaign. There was so much outside money coming in, the market was flooded. Kansas is a relatively small state and a cheap market for the big-money promoters, so there was a huge amount of campaign activity and a flood of information going out that I wasn't in control of, but I was at peace through it all. It was a gift of grace. I believed we were doing the right thing, and we ended up winning by a double-digit margin in the general election.

I believe now that the difference in that election was the huge turnout of Christian conservatives and other voters who were motivated primarily by the sense that the nation was morally on the wrong course.

TRUSTING IN PROVIDENCE

I was elected in 1996 to complete the final two years of Bob Dole's term, which meant that I would have to run again in 1998, which I did. I won that race, and I won again in 2004. Today I'm in my second full term in the Senate.

Earlier in my Christian life, I had sought God so that He would bless me and my plans for my future. After the life-changing events of 1995, my focus shifted. This time around I was seeking God's will in my life, for His purposes and not my own. Running for the Senate I was just trusting that God's will would be done. Win or lose, I believed I was doing the right thing by running.

The week I announced for the senate race turned out to be a big surprise for everyone. Several months earlier I had set the date to announce my reelection plans. But then, the same week that I was going to say I would be seeking reelection to the House of Representatives, Bob Dole, announced that he was going to vace his senate seat to run for president. That was in May 1996, and the primary was set for August. So, Mary and i quickly compared notes on what I ought to do, and we made the decision to change from running for the House to running for the Senate. and by Friday of that week I was on the campaign trail, doing just that.

The political establishment in Kansas was not happy with this. They had other plans, and they had their eye on someone else. I had already scheduled my announcement tour, so I went to the Capitol in Topeka to make it official that I was running for the Senate. There was a room full of people when I arrived. As I made a quick scan of the room, I saw grassroots activists and people of faith. I saw moms, with babies, concerned for their futures. I saw people with heart. What I didn't see were people who could help finance a campaign. They held back, waiting to see how things developed.

My campaign chairman was there with me, but nervous. He knew the machinery in the state was going the other way. But what I saw were the people of Kansas who shared my values and who had supported me all along. Clearly these were conservatives. It didn't appear that many of them had the financial means to support a major political campaign, but they had passion, and they were all behind me. I couldn't ask for more than that.

When I prepared to make the announcement, I remember thinking, *OK, the financial people aren't here, but that's fine. This is the right thing to do, and these people are here because they believe in me and the cause. And that's enough.* That was a liberating feeling. This race was going to be about a cause bigger than me!

I would owe the good people of Kansas my faithful service and support, but we were going into the campaign relying on God. I was ready for whatever the hand of providence would bring my way.

★ 3 ★

TERMS OF ENGAGEMENT

I ran for both the House and the Senate on a three-word platform: *Reduce, Reform, and Return*. My purpose as a legislator was to reduce the size, scope, and intrusiveness of the federal government, reform the Congress, and return to the basic values that built the country. That was the theme of my 1996 Senate campaign. Kansas voters apparently approved of that direction.

When I returned to Washington as the newest member of the Senate, I had the advantage of being the senior member of my freshman class. I had been elected to complete the two remaining years of Bob Dole's term when he resigned to run for the presidency. I won that election in November of 1996, and as soon as I was certified, I was sworn in as a member of the Senate. There were nine members of my freshman class, but they weren't sworn in until January of 1997. Since I came into the Senate first, I was the senior member. By rule that meant I also had first choice of committee assignments.

At that time the Foreign Relations Committee was viewed by most members as a bad assignment. It was well known that a number of highly respected senators had lost their seats because the voters thought they were focusing too much on foreign affairs and neglecting the more important domestic issues. In particular, I remembered what had happened to Frank Church, who had served as chairman of the Senate Foreign Relations Committee. He lost the election because the voters back home in Idaho decided he was spending too much time on international issues and not enough time on the things they cared about.

When my time came to pick committee assignments, I took the Commerce Committee and the Governmental Affairs Committees as my first two choices. I still had another choice to make. I picked the Foreign Relations Committee at that point. The Senate rule is that members can only serve on one Super-A committee. Foreign Relations wasn't a highly sought-after committee, but it was nevertheless a Super-A committee, meaning that it was one of the four top-rated assignments in the Republican caucus. The other Super-A's are Appropriations, Finance, and Armed Services. I ended up picking two of the more popular committees first, and then I took Foreign Relations as my final choice.

FOREIGN RELATIONS

So there I was, the new guy, sitting at the end of the seniority bench on foreign relations, and happy as a meadowlark on a summer day. Before long, things only got better when, through an unusual set of circumstances, I was able to chair the Middle East subcommittee.

The conventional wisdom was that little would actually happen in this subcommittee. The executive branch handles all the high-profile issues of the Middle East. Little room exists for congressional action. So everybody ahead of me picked subcommittees with "potential"—they wanted Europe or Asia or Latin America. But I felt that this would be the right place for me. I asked to chair the Middle East subcommittee, and it turned out to be a perfect fit.

As a new member, I knew I'd get a chance to learn a lot about the region. I could hold hearings, travel in that part of the world, and educate myself in the process. I'd be learning about some of the most intractable problems we face as a nation. And that's what I did. We held hearings on all different subjects. I traveled in the region and got to know some of the leaders. The subcommittee also included India, and that put South Asia within my jurisdiction.

When we were dealing with issues in a regional hot-spot, we were able to schedule trips to that region after the end of the session—in November, December, or January. Occasionally we would schedule one-week breaks in

Congress and could make arrangements to go overseas during those times as well.

The world community has a long-standing interest in the Middle East, and by 1996 the situation in Israel was looking ominous again. When I met with voters in my home district and across the country, I found that the interest in Israel and the Arab world had intensified, particularly among Jews and Christians.

I remember one particular meeting with Madeline Albright, secretary of state in the Clinton administration. The State Department was holding talks about U.S. relations with Israel, and I was invited to take part along with six other senators—all of whom were Democrats, and all but one of whom were Jewish. I was the only Republican in the room.

As the meeting was getting started, I gathered that the State Department was planning to introduce a new diplomatic initiative in the region that would have a negative effect on Israel. This meeting had apparently been called to get a buy-in from the Senate. In other words, the Secretary had handpicked the group she wanted, knowing that most of them would eventually agree to what she proposed.

I sat there wondering why they had invited me to the meeting. They were sitting around talking strategy. I was a new member of the Senate, and everyone in the room had much more experience dealing with the Middle East than I did. They were talking about what they could to do to convince the Jewish lobby in Washington that what they were about to do was OK. They went around the room and each person at the table offered his or her opinion. Finally it came around to me, and they asked what I thought.

UNEXPECTED SUPPORT

I said, "Well, it's not only the Jews who care about Israel. Christians care about Israel too." At that point one of the senior Democrats barked at me, "Well, they didn't seem to care very much during the Holocaust in World War II." I replied, "A lot of Christians deeply lament what happened in the Holocaust and that Christians weren't more helpful." Then somebody else looked at me and asked, "Why on earth would the Christians care what happens to Israel?" I replied,

"Many Christians care deeply about what happens to Israel and the Jewish people."

Honestly, I was surprised by the remarks of my colleagues. It went back and forth like that. They kept asking what possible reason the Christian community could have for caring about Israel. A communication was started. More needs to happen, of course, but I think it particularly sparked an interest by Madeline Albright. She and I have worked together on several projects since then.

It was an eye-opening experience for me. It also gave me a better insight into some of the attitudes I would encounter in my work in the Middle East. Several years later, I had the opportunity to travel to Israel and speak in the Knesset, their parliament, to the Christian Alliance Caucus. I addressed the history of our relationship with the state of Israel, but I also wanted to mend fences. I took the opportunity to apologize for the poor relationships between Christians and Jews in years past. I said I wanted to do my part to see that those things never happened again. As a Christian, I wanted the people of Israel to know that Christians care very much for Israel.

It has taken a long time, but I think Jewish-Christian relations are much better and stronger now. John Hagee, who pastors an eighteen-hundred-member church in San Antonio, Texas, founded Christians United for Israel (CUFI). The group is made up primarily of evangelical Christians. More than thirty-five hundred people showed up for the big kickoff rally and banquet in Washington in July 2006.

I was invited to speak at that event, along with several other people and members of Congress. At one point in the evening, a rabbi who was seated at my table leaned over and said, "You know, my grandparents would never have dreamed of something like this." It was a mind-blowing experience for him, realizing that so many Christians would boldly stand up in support of Israel.

A LESSON IN HUMILITY

It's encouraging to see bridges being built between Jews and Christians all over the world. I can't help but be excited when I see committed people of faith working together on complex social issues. And I'm especially encouraged to see the strong bonds of friendship and mutual support that develop out of these working relationships.

A few years ago in Israel, I asked a group of five orthodox rabbis why we were seeing this reconciliation between Christians and Jews. There's no question that this is a remarkable thing. One of the rabbis said, "It's like we're both going up the same mountain, and we're looking up at the same light. And now we're finally getting up high enough that we can see each other." That created a beautiful picture and was a great way of putting it.

On several occasions I've met with former Israeli Prime Minister Ariel Sharon. I found him to be a thoughtful and courageous leader. We would often discuss the moral, even theological, basis for the Israeli society. Our time on earth is short but immensely significant. He clearly thought of the Jewish people in their historical context and security needs. He would not sit by while his people were being killed or threatened.

As chairman of the Middle East subcommittee, I was usually looking into some political or security issue when I met with the prime minister. We talked about the moral questions confronting us or the situation in the world today. He had a real sense of his place in history. On one of those trips, an American Jewish group said, "This is wonderful. We saw the prime minister right after your meeting, and he was reading the Bible. He won't read it for us!" I just laughed and said that I was glad I could do my part.

When I got back to Washington, I decided to move into shared quarters with my men's small fellowship group from Congress. We rented a five-bedroom house together. It didn't take long for me to discover that it's easy to get caught up in the trappings of power in Washington. I found that I needed to be on guard against the seduction of power and pride. I mentioned this to my prayer group, and they promised to pray for me in that regard.

I mention this story because my fellowship group had already been praying for my humility. They had seen how prideful I had become, going into the Senate. I had learned how dangerous pride can be and how easily it can permeate our thinking. It can be even more dangerous in a place like the United States Senate, where the dais is elevated, the walls are marble, and you're never wrong. At least according to your press releases.

Many people won't directly say to a senator, "You're wrong!" That's not so much a problem in the House of Representatives, where people are more inclined to challenge a congressman's remarks. I had been reading Russell Hittinger's book *The First Grace*, which notes that pride is the first sin and humility is the first grace. One of the things that opens the door to God's abundant grace is humility. Yet here I was in Washington, DC, in a setting that feeds pride and putting yourself first. I learned through that experience that you don't leave your Christianity at the doorstep. You have to embrace those principles and make them a part of your life, regardless of where you serve.

A CHANGE OF ATTITUDE

I should mention something that happened a couple of years later when I was asked to speak at the Senate prayer breakfast. I agreed to give a short talk but didn't give it much thought until the night before, when I sat down to collect my thoughts. I was considering what I should say when I confronted all the anger that I held for the Clintons. I thought, *I hate them for what they are doing to the country, and I feel justified in hating them for it.* That's a lie, of course, and bad theology too. That moment I became aware of that fact. We're never justified in hating someone in that way, regardless of how we appraise their actions, and I knew it. We are supposed to hate the sin but love the individual.

I reflected on all that, and I prayed about it. The next morning, when I spoke, I said I wanted to apologize for hating the Clintons. As I looked around the room, I saw Hillary Clinton. I spoke about my experiences in the House and how I came to Washington as part of the Republican Revolution. I also spoke about my spiritual journey and how I was changing. I said I was coming to grips with a lot of things that I'd done wrong, including my hatred for Bill and Hillary. At one point I spoke directly to Mrs. Clinton and said I realized that those thoughts of hatred were wrong. I apologized to her for them. I don't know what she thought, but I believe it made a difference.

Doug Coe, the head of the fellowship and organizer of the prayer breakfast, came up to me afterward and said, "Sam, you don't have any idea what you've just done. That's one of the most phenomenal things I've ever seen."

It hadn't been an easy thing for me to say, but I knew it was something I needed to say regardless of the consequences.

I know the Clintons could feel the hatred from conservative Christians during that time. They really didn't understand why so many people hated them. They thought they were doing the right things. We weren't just opposed to President Clinton's policies; we were full of anger and hatred toward *him*. I think my remarks that morning, and my sincere confession, were helpful in a number of ways, including increasing my ability to later work with Senator Clinton on plans for a National Day of Reconciliation.

A couple of months after the 9/11 attacks, Mrs. Clinton was my cosponsor in the Senate, with the biggest push coming from Congressman Tom DeLay, for setting aside the Capitol Rotunda for a time of prayer, just for members. We had a third of the House and a quarter of the Senate on hand at any one time, praying for the country. It's possible that, without the apology I had made, I don't think that sort of cooperation could have happened.

THE PIVOT POINT

I was doing a lot of learning and adjusting, but the pivot point in my understanding of my role in the Senate was a Bible study held by Lloyd Ogilvie for members of the Senate in 1997. Dr. Ogilvie was the Senate chaplain at that time, and ten or eleven senators regularly came to the meeting. On this particular day, Dr. Ogilvie looked at each of us and asked a simple question: "How many constituents do you have?"

If you're a member of the Senate, you know exactly how many constituents you have. We went around the room, and people said 2.4 million or 9.2 million or 3.6 million or whatever the numbers for their state happened to be. No one hesitated. We all knew the numbers. As a senator you not only know the total number of constituents you have, but you also know the interests they associate with. During the election cycle you're always trying to get to 51 percent, so you think, *OK, we've got this many farmers, this many vets, this many educators, this many professional people,* and so on. That's the way you think.

After we had all answered, Dr. Ogilvie said, "Thank you for those answers, but I'd like to suggest to you that each of you has just one constituent, and that constituent is God. If God is happy with what you're doing and the measures you're supporting in the Senate, then everything is going to be fine. But if He isn't happy, none of this is going to matter." That was an important insight. It had the ring of truth to it even though it was contrary to what many of my staff and political advisors would say.

Political activists would often say, *Look, Senator, you may be a good Christian, but that's not how you get elected. The way you get elected is by raising money, appealing to the voters, and assuring your supporters that you're on their team. If you don't do that, you won't be reelected, and if you're not reelected, you can't accomplish any of the stuff you want to do.*

When I left the Bible study that day, I was in agreement with what the chaplain was saying. I asked myself, *What would God be interested in? Well, He would certainly be interested in the poor and downtrodden, the weak and vulnerable, in those denied justice.* It crossed my mind that this had been the essence of a book I'd read about the great British reformer and abolitionist William Wilberforce, called *God's Politician.* From then on I was going to think seriously about that "constituency of one" in every decision.

This laid the foundation for much of my work in the Senate from then on. Some of it had already started. Along with Senator Paul Wellstone, I was working on the issue of the diabolical practice of human trafficking, of girls as young as nine years old being sold into prostitution. I was already working on the problems in Sudan with Representative Frank Wolf on the House side, but this gave me a philosophical basis for those policy matters. It also led me to reject the conventional wisdom in Washington—the idea that we're only here to get reelected.

I started working on those issues, and working on them more aggressively. After about six months I began thinking, *I wonder if you can get reelected with one happy constituent. He's a good constituent, and a key one, but is that really enough?* Somebody was polling the approval rating of various elected officials in Kansas at the time, and my poll numbers had gone up during that period. That information reinforced my thinking. Once again, the words recorded in Matthew 6:33 rang true: "But seek first the kingdom of God and His righteousness, and all these things shall be added to you" (NKJV).

WORKING TOGETHER

I've tried to operate that way ever since. I know the Lord is interested in the downtrodden. That has taken me into North Korean issues, to develop and sponsor legislation such as the North Korean Human Rights Act. I know the Lord is the author of life, and I've been pro-life for a long time, but I've become even more passionate about how we treat these innocent children and the impact on their mothers. I believe it's one of the key moral concerns of our day. This new understanding has led me to take on a leading role on reconciliation issues with Native Americans and African-Americans, getting together with representatives of those communities to coauthor important legislation, such as the new Smithsonian Museum of African American History and Culture and an official apology to Native Americans.

When I first got to the Senate, I encountered a deep root of bitterness from some people in the African-American community. Many had not been treated fairly. I asked leaders of the African-American community why they thought there was so much bitterness and a lack of reconciliation between the races. They told me how parents had been treated, how other family members had been treated, and how they had been treated. Many of those stories were heartbreaking. The bitterness and lack of reconciliation had a source.

Congressman Emanuel Cleaver from Kansas City spoke to me about this when President Bush signed the extension of the Voting Rights Act into law in the summer of 2006. His parents in Texas hadn't been allowed to vote. Honorable citizens, hardworking people, but not given the right to vote simply because of the color of their skin. It is obvious reconciliation is desperately needed.

Somewhere along the line it came to my attention that there had been many attempts to establish an African-American museum as part of the Smithsonian in Washington. Every attempt had failed. I felt a real calling to see what I could do to change that. I wanted to create not just a museum but a basis for reconciliation between the races. When my staff and I started doing the research, we discovered that there had been attempts for more than seventy years to put together an African-American museum. In each attempt something had happened: it passed the House but not the Senate, or it passed the Senate and not the House. There were always problems that would stop it.

I was convinced it was time for this museum to be established. I sought a Democratic partner for this project who was a member of the Black Caucus. Several members were possibilities, but the best champion was Congressman John Lewis of Georgia. John had marched with Dr. Martin Luther King Jr.. John is living history of the Civil Rights movement.

I didn't know John very well at the time. I talked with him previously when I was in the House, and he had seemed awfully fiery to me and an unlikely partner. But he was the right one to do this, having proposed the museum the last twelve years, so I went over to meet with him. Our first meeting was in his office, and I won't forget that day. He had a lot of memorabilia in his office. John had been one of the key Civil Rights leaders; he was the head of the Student Nonviolent Coordinating Committee, he was on the Selma march, and he was beaten to a bloody pulp while marching across the infamous Edmund Pettis Bridge on Bloody Sunday.

John had a huge pedigree in the Civil Rights movement. What really struck me was a book he showed me about lynchings in the United States. There were lynchings that happened in my state of Kansas as well as other places around America. The picture that stuck out in my mind was taken in the 1920s; it was a picture of a black man who had been lynched, and standing beneath him were two white children in straw hats. They were smiling as if they were at an exhibition. I thought, *How awful!*

A DREAM COME TRUE

After discussing the pros and cons, John Lewis and I became partners on the project, along with J. C. Watts and Jack Kingston in the House, and Chris Dodd and Max Cleland in the Senate. We also worked with Senator Ted Stevens, who chaired the Appropriations Committee. Ted, who was very supportive of the measure, wanted us to get an authorization bill put through. We did get an authorization bill moving, and some people talked about holding it up. Ultimately they let it pass on through.

I met with Coretta Scott King regarding this project. As the widow of Dr. King, she was a luminary figure in the Civil Rights movement. She was very supportive of our plans for the museum. Thanks to all the support we received, today that good idea is a reality. The official name, as part of the Smithsonian, is the National Museum of African American History and Culture. My name for it is the "Museum of Reconciliation." If we can put forward the stories of African-Americans, with their trials and triumphs, it will be cleansing for us all. It will be a museum of a lot of tears, but tears of reconciliation and commitment that a race of people will never again be so abused.

When I read Dr. King's speeches, I realized that many of them were about reconciliation. It wasn't just about civil rights; it was about reconciling. His most famous speech, the "I Have a Dream" speech, is about young black children and white children playing together. I remarked on that to his wife and told her Dr. King had been a prophetic voice to this land and that becomes very apparent when you read his writings. She agreed.

We were able to get that bill approved and signed with bipartisan support and the support of the black and the white communities. Public Law 108–184 was signed by President Bush on December 16, 2003. Over the next several months, a founding council was named. They held their first meeting in February 2005. Fund-raising is now moving forward—with 50 percent private and 50 percent public funding—and architectural, engineering, and other development plans are in the works. After looking at several sites in the District of Columbia, the regents of the Smithsonian selected an area of land known as the "Monument site," off of Constitution Avenue.

The site is adjacent to the Washington Monument and across the street from the National Museum of American History, which is a perfect place for a museum with such an important story to tell. We're moving ahead, and work has already begun. It's my hope that this will be a step forward in the process of racial reconciliation and healing in this country. People had tried for seventy years to get it done. A spirit of reconciliation and engagement helped make this dream a reality.

⭐ 4 ⭐

THE GOOD SOCIETY

When I first ran for Congress in 1994, I was pro-life, but I wasn't vocal about it. While campaigning one day somebody said, "I just want to give you the Scriptures on this. You can read it for yourself. Would you do that for me?" I said, "Sure." I had not done that before, so I went home and read the Scriptures about the sanctity of life. Afterward I thought, *Wow, this is very clear.*

God says, "Before I formed you in the womb I knew you; before you were born I sanctified you" (Jeremiah 1:5 NKJV); and the psalmist wrote, "For You formed my inward parts; You covered me in my mother's womb. I will praise You, for I am fearfully and wonderfully made" (Psalm 139:13–14 NKJV). In Luke's Gospel we see the angel's prophecy that John the Baptist would be filled with the Holy Spirit even before his birth. And in the letter to the Galatians, Paul said that God had "set me apart from birth and called me by his grace" (1:15 NIV). I thought, *How do you argue with that?*

I was convinced of the sacredness of every human life but not yet ready to make it a big political issue. That came after my cancer. During that period I read about the life of the great eighteenth-century parliamentarian William Wilberforce. When Wilberforce looked at the moral consequence of the decisions he was making, he had the grace to reconsider all his beliefs and to decide which were the central issues in his own life and times. He then dedicated the rest of his life to "one great objective," which was to eliminate the slave trade. It was certainly a daring challenge at the time. I'm sure he often feared that he would fail to achieve this objective.

During the last few years I've had occasion to meet with social commentators like Gertrude Himmelfarb, a scholar who serves on the Council of Academic Advisors at the American Enterprise Institute and has done extensive research on the Victorian era and how that relatively moral age contrasts with our own. During a meeting I asked, "Can a culture renew itself, and is it likely?" Her answer was that it's unlikely, mainly because not many cultures have renewed themselves. She said that the ones that have done it successfully did so through religious renewal. That was true of Great Britain and the "Methodist Movement" before the Victorian era.

She cited the pre-Victorian period, when men like William Wilberforce aroused the conscience of the British people over the issue of slavery. The changes that began at that time flowered during Queen Victoria's reign and gave the British new impetus. The spiritual support of that period grew out of the work of John and Charles Wesley, Gilbert Tennent, and George Whitefield, who aroused the nation during the Methodist Movement and helped bring about the Great Awakening.

THE GREAT AWAKENING

With God's grace, the ministry of John and Charles Wesley prospered. An evangelical awakening spread throughout British and American society between 1720 and 1750, and people of both nations were changed by it. Through faith they rediscovered the virtues that build great societies. They recommitted themselves to building strong families, strong communities, and a strong nation. They did it for God and country, not just for themselves. They were willing to sacrifice for the good of others, because they realized that this life is not all there is.

The founders of this country understood these things as well, and they were willing to put the welfare of the family, the community, and the nation above their own welfare. Unless you have faith in something greater than yourself, that's a very hard thing to do. Not impossible, but very hard. They did it, and they believed they were doing it with providential guidance and by God's design.

Most Americans support and understand what's required for the welfare of family, community, and nation. They care deeply about all three. They want to see the culture renewed. By that I mean a renewed focus on marriage, family, and children and a greater engagement of faith and patriotism. And like Wilberforce, they hope for a "reformation of manners" and a moral code that respects the dignity of every person.

During my reelection campaign in 2004, I traveled all over Kansas. Everywhere I went I saw people who were deeply concerned about where the country is headed. They said, "We've been praying for you, Senator, and we're praying for America." Frequently people said, "We've got a son in Iraq. We're very proud of him, and we're proud to know that he feels it's his duty and his privilege as an American to serve his country that way."

These people want the country to succeed, but they feel we're often not going the right way. Too often the mainstream culture seems to marginalize their faith, and that's a problem. We need more of God, not less. We need more and stronger families. We need more opportunities for our people.

AN EXPANDING BASE

People are beginning to realize that virtue can be a good thing, and that having a moral framework based on your religious beliefs is not as bad as they once thought. When I first entered politics, many people were saying that religious talk was bad. They said, "Christians do bad things. They think their way is the only way, and they're full of hate for people who don't agree with them. Besides that, Christianity is bad because it produces these wild-eyed people who do strange things."

OK, that can happen. But there are many, many more people of faith who are out there loving their neighbor, donating time and money to help the poor, volunteering at the local hospital or soup kitchen, and teaching their children to be good citizens and to love their country. They give of themselves for the sake of other people, without drawing a lot of attention to themselves. They're quiet about it, but people notice. I have often heard it said: "You know, I don't agree with your positions on abortion, same-sex marriage, and some of these other things. But there's no denying that it's often people of faith who are the ones reaching out the most to those who need help."

As I mentioned earlier, Pat Robertson's presidential campaign in 1988 politically activated many evangelicals, some of them for the first time. But whether it was because of that campaign or that this surge of conservative voters just happened to become active at that time, it's undeniable that "values voters" have become indispensable to conservative political victories.

Values voters are becoming better informed and more sophisticated in their political activism. They know what they believe and are becoming more engaged. Wherever I go these days, I see more and more people of faith politically activated. They're truly remarkable people. They're principled, purposeful, and politically well informed, and they're making a difference in the culture and in politics.

PERSON OR PROPERTY

Twenty years ago I think many faith-based conservatives felt they had to accept the idea of being marginalized as a subculture. That's changed now. These voters aren't intimidated by insults.

I'm a supporter and a true admirer of those with the energy and discipline to homeschool their children. But there are many families who either can't homeschool or feel called to take an active role in a traditional setting. Today we're also seeing a dramatic increase in the number of people of faith who are active and engaged in the mainstream culture. They're taking part in education reform; they hold important jobs in business, government, and academia. And some are even working in Hollywood and the media. We need more of them in every area of society.

But the issue in our day that's most comparable to the work done by Wilberforce and his associates is the struggle for the life of the unborn child and the inherent dignity and worth of every person, everywhere. I am pro-life and "whole-life" and am willing to confront the various life issues, including policies regarding destructive human embryonic stem cell research, human cloning, and assisted suicide. All of this can be tied to the abolitionist perspectives of the mid-1800s. The issues are so closely linked. The terminology in the slavery battle is closely linked to the terminology in the abortion debate.

The members of Wilberforce's group, the Clapham circle, had a Wedgwood ceramic pattern designed with the image of an African slave in chains. The legend underneath said, "Am I not a man and a brother?" You could use that same Wedgwood design with an illustration of a child in the womb. The slavery question was a debate about person versus property. Is the slave a person or a piece of property? For a long time people were quite willing to say that a slave was property, but eventually they had to admit that the slave is, first and foremost, a person entitled to all the respect of any other person.

I'm convinced that a good and just society is one that's based on what we know in our hearts to be true. I spoke about this at Harvard in April of 2005, as we were preparing for the congressional debates on destructive human embryonic stem cell research. When I finished my talk and called for questions, one student stood up and said, "Isn't this something that we really can't decide because we don't have a common set of beliefs? There's no agreed-upon standard of truth—you have your values and I have mine."

I said, "But we do have a common set of beliefs." There was a group of about 150 people in the room, so I asked, "Who in this room believes that you're not unique or special?" There were many bright people in that room, some with obvious talents, and others with equally obvious physical limitations. Yet nobody raised a hand. So I said, "You see, we agree on that. We agree that everybody is unique and special." And I would add, a gift of the living God.

The idea that everything is up for grabs is a fallacy that has been trumpeted by some for so long that it's now a commonly held belief. But it's a false belief. There are some things that are right and other things that are absolutely wrong. Murder, for example, is wrong, and there is universal normative agreement about that. The question then, as it regards controversial issues such as destructive human embryonic stem cell research, is: Does our respect for human life apply to the embryo or not? How we answer that question is absolutely critical. We may have difficulties discussing it, but we don't disagree in the belief that all human life is precious.

The task then was to decide how to deal with the issue in legal parlance. The Constitution declared that, for tax purposes and for purposes of congressional representation, the slave was equivalent to three-fifths of a person. The authors of that clause declared the slave to be a thing and not a citizen with equal rights. The same debate exists today with regard to the embryo. In our legal jurisprudence, everything is either person or property.

What is the youngest of humans? Is it a person with rights and human dignity, or is it a piece of property that can be disposed of as its "master" chooses?

That's how I started this debate on embryonic stem cell research. When I testified on human embryonic stem cell research, I started with that question: "Is the youngest of humans a person or a piece of property? That's the central question." The other side will not debate that question. They will not answer that question. They will not admit that their position unavoidably means the youngest of humans is treated as property.

During hearings I've asked scientists, bioethicists, and research scholars, "When does life begin?" They have said, "We don't know. It's a theological question. Christians say one thing; Muslims say another." And I have challenged them: "No, I'm not asking for a religious view. *Biologically*, when does life begin?" They quibbled and hesitated and tried to avoid dealing with the question directly. "Well," they said, "it depends on when sentience begins, and that's not at all clear." They didn't want to admit the simple truth that seems so obvious—that there is no other time for life to begin that at the beginning.

A FALLIBLE PROCESS

I was at a meeting with a large group of people, dealing with life issues, and a person became very upset with my position on stem cell research. I had said, "It's a question of person or property and when life begins." I looked at this man and asked, "Can you answer that question? When does life begin?" Then, as he was thinking about the question, I asked, "When did your life begin?" He looked at me and said, "I don't have any memories of my childhood until I was about four years old, so I guess my life began at four."

I said, "OK, would it have been acceptable to conduct research on you before you were age four?" He didn't respond to that, but I could see that he had never thought of it in that light. The other side doesn't want to answer the basic questions. They don't want there to be a distinction, whether it's a person or property. This is the issue, and it's precisely the same debate our ancestors had to deal with in the matter of slavery.

With my Kansas background and the work of abolitionists in my state, I realize that there's really nothing new under the sun. Unfortunately, after more than forty million abortions in the United States since 1973, we're still unwilling to settle this issue.

Some of this was galvanized in hearings that I held in the Senate. One important element of the discussion involved an elevator operator at the Capitol, a young man named Jimmy. Jimmy is a Down syndrome adult, in his midthirties, and by most counts he would be everybody's favorite employee in the Senate. He's a wonderful young man. Senator Orrin Hatch has given him neckties regularly and Jimmy wears them faithfully.

Sometimes Jimmy will give you a big hug on the elevator. He's a happy person. Recently, after the elevator door closed, he gave me a big hug, put his finger to his lips, and said, "Shhhh. Don't tell anybody. My supervisor told me I'm hugging too many people, so don't tell anybody I hugged you." I said, "Jimmy, that's not a problem with me." The warmth and sincerity and love that he has for people is very apparent. He's undeniably a very special person.

Not long ago I met a lady who told me about her experience having a Down syndrome child. Everyone in "the system" seemed to encourage her to abort the child. We started doing some research and found that today around 80 percent of Down syndrome children are aborted.[1] So 80 percent of the Jimmys are never born. If they somehow manage to get here, our laws, like the Americans with Disabilities Act, protect them and assure them of a certain level of accommodation by society. It assures them and their parents that we will help take care of them. It's one of the most highly touted pieces of legislation of the past thirty years. If you've got a disability, we want to help you.

The irony is that some people are working to make sure that babies with disabilities are never born. In effect they're saying that we'll kill you in the womb, but we'll protect you if you somehow get your feet on the ground.

That's such a shame. Many Down syndrome children are the centerpieces of their families. They have amazing gifts and are full of affection. But apparently society thinks nothing about their death in the womb. I raised this question with my colleagues; I've also raised it during hearings on Supreme Court justices. But there's still no support in favor of the life of a disabled child.

In legal circles they talk about the "effects test." What's the effect of the law? That's how people will judge the validity of a law. The effect of our abortion policy at this moment is that we are in the midst of a genocide of children with Down syndrome, cerebral palsy, and other in utero genetic conditions that medical analysis can detect. If we think there's a chance the child may have a disability, too often he or she is killed in the womb, and the system seems to push it.

The current system of analysis is a fallible process. Many times parents have been advised by their physician to abort their unborn child because the infant appeared to have a medical anomaly. I've had people tell me, "Our child tested positive for Down syndrome, but we went ahead with the pregnancy anyway, and it turned out he didn't have Down's at all." I think most people would be shocked to know this happens.

Teaming Up for Life

I was surprised to find out how intensely the system sometimes pushes for abortion. On one trip to California I had a series of not-so-productive meetings. I was at the end of the trip, preparing to leave, when a young woman and her husband came up to me and said they wanted to give me a book. It was about their Down syndrome child and the hurdles they had jumped just to have the baby.

These were young people. He was working, and she had decided to stay home and start a family. When she found out she was pregnant, she went to the doctor. He ran a test, and it said the child would have Down syndrome. The doctor told her she needed to terminate the pregnancy. He basically said, "Look, you're still young. You'll be able to have more children. But you need to terminate this pregnancy." She was torn apart. She was devastated and confused. She didn't know what to do.

The couple had a strong faith. As they prayed, studied, and thought about it, they realized that this was a special child. Yes, it would be difficult, but this was a special child. Incidentally, this is also the view of many people in Africa. I visited an orphanage in Rwanda in 2005, and they had a group of mentally and physically challenged children. In their view these were all children who had been specially touched by God.

This young couple told me they had to fight their way through the system. The doctor didn't want them to have the child, the hospital didn't want them to have the child, and they felt that the insurance company really didn't want them to have it either. The obstetrician wanted a child without "defect." In some cases doctors are afraid they'll be sued if the child is less than perfect by society's standards. And for their part, the hospitals don't want the risk of delivering a disabled child. The system is stacked against the parents of a potentially disabled child—to say nothing of the child herself.

When these issues came up in Senate hearings, I railed against the system that pushes this situation and the effects of the *Roe v. Wade* mentality that has created a modern genocide of mentally and physically challenged children. I've raised these questions with pro choice advocates, and they have no answer. Even now we have many more genetic screening tests for the child in utero. How many will be aborted simply because of their handicap, their condition, or the fact that they may present challenges? How can we tolerate such a system in the womb that is so abhorrent to us for children here on the ground?

We must be willing to say to the parents of a challenged child that we will help. It's not a unilateral issue, because these are more financially challenging and difficult situations. Because of that, I put together a bill with Senator Kennedy dealing with this issue, particularly involving Down syndrome children. The purpose is to require physicians to notify parents of the current information on children with Down syndrome. It also involves establishing a national network of people willing to adopt Down syndrome children. There are lists of people willing to adopt special-needs children.

The Shriver and Kennedy families and others have been great about establishing and supporting the Special Olympics and children with disabilities. Now we need to extend those benefits to children diagnosed with disabilities in the womb.

A PHILOSOPHY OF COMPASSION

Another aspect of the life debate has become what I would call the centerpiece of a bleeding-heart conservative philosophy. The bleeding-heart conservative philosophy is that every person at every stage of life is unique, sacred, and a child of the living God. Wherever they are and at whatever stage, they deserve to have protection, respect, and care. That extends to the child in the womb as well as to the child of a single mother in Washington, Philadelphia, New York City, or any other city or town.

It extends to the young person in Beverly Hills and to the refugee in Darfur. It extends to the student at Harvard as well as the man sitting in solitary confinement in a maximum-security prison. Each of these is unique, sacred, and a child of the living God, and must be treated as such. For anyone who believes in the doctrine of bleeding-heart conservatism, that must be our central thesis.

If we establish compassionate conservatism on that basis, how can anyone argue against it? I'm sure there are people who would argue that this doesn't necessarily apply to the man or woman in Darfur, or to the convicted thief in a prison somewhere, or to the child with Down syndrome. I would love to have that discussion with them. I have yet to hear anybody say, "I disagree with your premise." It is a consistent philosophy. I've found that you can build strong alliances around this thought.

Reverence for life starts at the very beginning, and it ends at the natural end. I believe this is a central debate of our time. Frankly, I don't think we've spent enough time looking at the impact of abortion on the mother. I've held hearings on the psychological, medical, and physical impact of ending a pregnancy by abortion. As others have said, "In every abortion there are two victims: one dead, one wounded." I met with a number of women in the Silent No More campaign, and I've worked with them in drawing attention to their concerns. They tell such sad stories of the emotional struggles they go through, particularly on the anniversary of their abortion or the day their child should have been born. In some cases they cry all day long, and the pain won't go away. Often it only gets worse over the years. In some cases they wake up with nightmares about their aborted child. Some self-medicate with alcohol or drugs.

Some experience unbearable pain and despair. These women deserve our sympathy and care.

One woman told me that she had tried to run from her pain by indulging in alcohol, drugs, and sexual promiscuity. For a long time she didn't really know what she was running from, but she was trying to deaden the pain. The Silent No More group, and others like them who are reaching out to women going through this struggle, are doing a wonderful service. They are willing to speak to other women in this situation, offering them consolation, understanding, and compassion. Too many people are carrying unbelievable levels of pain. It doesn't matter who the woman is or whether she's religious or not, many will feel the consequences of an abortion. It's wrong to deny that there's such a thing as post-abortion syndrome when so many women have personally experienced it. In addition to the psychological impact, in many cases there's also a medical impact that needs to be addressed responsibly.

I held a hearing with a leading researcher on the impact of abortion on women. She's a physician and scholar at the University of Michigan and by no means a pro-life advocate. She said that if you examine the current research on medical problems with a direct connection to abortion, you'll discover a clear medical impact, one of the leading ones being an increase in suicides.[2] This is yet another expression of the wound women suffer from abortion.

People who say that everything will be fine after an abortion, and that you can just go on with your life, are not telling the truth. They're misleading and possibly endangering the lives of women.

REWARDING GOOD BEHAVIOR

The law is a teacher. We can lead the nation in discussion and we can teach through the law. Our foundational ethic upholds the idea of maximum freedom. God is the author of liberty, and He has given us the incredible gift of freedom. This is something the founders understood, and it's why the government they established is unique in history. A free people are the most productive, even with the choice to choose something harmful. With liberty we can choose good or evil. We are not robots.

God has many attributes, but central to everything we know about Him is that God is Love. He loves us unreservedly. He loved us enough to give us free will, even though He knew that we would misuse our freedom and that a number of us would turn against Him and deny that He even exists. He was willing to do that because He wanted us to be able to love Him through our own free will and not because it was our only choice. He even prepared a sacrifice, in His Son, who would endure the punishment we deserve so that all who accept that free gift could live with Him and enjoy His love forever.

Our government is organized to follow this example of freedom—maximum freedom within perimeters of protecting the individual and society from those seeking to harm others or the society at large. Government ought to encourage what's good—or at least make sure not to prohibit it—and discourage what's bad—or at least not promote it. We should try to encourage marriage by removing the marriage penalty in the IRS code, and we should also remove the penalties in the welfare system for getting married. We discourage what's bad by raising the fines for obscene material on radio and television, and by increasing sentencing requirements for convicted pedophiles and human traffickers.

Government cannot command people to be good, but it ought to encourage goodness. The limits of the law are there to improve our chances of safety and happiness, not to punish us. But the law can be misused. When the Supreme Court "found" a constitutional right to abortion, it blocked state laws attempting to limit abortion and gave its approval to the destruction of innocent human life. That sent the message that killing an unborn child is acceptable. On a personal level, no matter how libertarian you may be, it's not fine. It is the death of a child.

A truism of public policy is that what government subsidizes we get more of, and what government taxes we get less of. We need to be judicious in what we endorse and what the government funds and try to use every bit of wisdom we can muster to encourage those things conducive to "life, liberty, and the pursuit of happiness."

A CULTURE OF LIFE

One good thing that has come from the tragedies we've endured in this nation since 2001 is that they've renewed our faith in American character. We were tested on 9/11, and we showed that we are people of compassion and resolve. We didn't cave in; we grew stronger. We were tested when back-to-back hurricanes devastated the Gulf Coast, and we pulled together to help the dispossessed and make life better but more still needs to be done. That's my hope for America, that we will face all of our challenges the same way and grow stronger through them.

By any measure the human toll of death and despair unleashed by the Supreme Court's *Roe v. Wade* decision in 1973 has been staggering, not just in this country but around the world. How do we recover from that, and how will we ever change it? Now we're seeing part of the impact of the regime of legalized abortion in the industrialized world. Russia is on a trajectory to go from 150 million people to 100 million by the middle of the century. Nations like Russia and France are paying women to have children. They're doing it for practical reasons. They've come to the realization that life matters and abortion robs countries of their best hope for the future. Abortion is not the only problem affecting our future, but it is a major one.

Thanks to their forced abortions policy, China has a huge demographic problem, with a current male-to-female ratio of 120/100 in live births. That gender disparity causes problems in many ways. As just one example, North Korea is in political and social chaos, and thousands of men and women are risking their lives to escape from North Korea to mainland China. We're beginning to allow North Korean refugees to immigrate to this country, and I've spoken to some of those people.

The women who have made it out of North Korea tell me that all of the women who cross into China are captured like wild animals and sold into some type of sexual bondage. In some cases they're sold as wives, but more often they're sold as prostitutes or sex slaves. Part of the problem, I suspect, though not proven, is that the gender ratio is out of balance because of the one-child policy and forced abortions, where more girls are aborted than boys. This is one of the awful consequences.

The Chinese person who captures these women on the border implies to them, "If you don't do what I say, I'll turn you in to the authorities, and they'll send you back to North Korea. And you know what they'll do to you. They'll send you to the gulag for trying to escape, and you know what happens there." If they decide to cooperate, they'll be sold to some man in China who will say the same thing: "If you don't do what I say, I'll send you back to North Korea, and you know what will happen to you there." All sorts of terrible abuse takes place in that environment.

DANGEROUS ABSTRACTIONS

People need to realize that the suffering doesn't end with abortion. The misery continues in many other forms. Under the delusion that we're so modern, scientific, wise, and in control of our world, society has been trying to play God, and we're paying a price for that. People's lives are being destroyed every hour of the day, and that story is not getting out. We've got to tell it, and we've got to tell it even in the most difficult cases.

I hear people say, "I'm pro-life except in the case of rape, incest, or the life of the mother." What does that mean? There are very few hospital room emergencies where the mother's health requires that lifesaving measures be taken that result in the death of the unborn child. While I support a "life of the mother" exception, still, our fundamental principle is that we should try to avoid intentionally taking the life of an innocent person. Our fundamental principle—that we can never intentionally take the life of an innocent person—is not violated.

Rape and incest are different matters. Yes, those are horrific, tragic circumstances. But what has the child done wrong? I have a friend who is the child of a rape victim. What did he do wrong? Should he have been aborted? If you want to know, ask someone who is the child of a rape. People have told me they're glad their mothers chose to go ahead and give birth to that innocent life.

These are all tough points in the debate over abortion, but I think we have to be logically and philosophically consistent. We also need to be biologically consistent. The bioethics point of this debate is where the battle is taking place today. Many just want to talk about human embryonic stem cell research, cloning, and the creation of human-animal hybrids in the laboratory. It's much easier than talking about the killing of an unborn child, but there's really no difference. Every one of these questions involves the taking of human life and the compromises we're willing to make with human dignity.

Stem cells are undifferentiated cells that have the ability to develop into any of the cells that make up the tissues of the body. The laboratory practice needed to isolate embryonic stem cells involves the destruction of a living human being at the earliest stage of development for the purposes of medical experimentation. Cloning is the manipulation of human eggs and DNA in order to create, in essence, a duplicate copy of an existing person. And human-animal hybrids, referred to as chimeras, could be created in the future in the laboratory by combining genetic material across species. Each of these raises serious ethical and biological concerns that science and law are just beginning to grapple with.

Some argue from the standpoint that the younger the person, the less human it is. Or at least, it's harder to identify an embryo as a human, so they argue that it isn't fully human but merely a mass of cells. But from biology, not theology, we know that human life begins at conception, that it is a genetically distinct life, and if you kill it then, it will not mature to adulthood. The American public is opposed to killing innocent people. When the facts are presented fairly, they agree that an unborn child is still a child, and the child in the womb is a human being who deserves respect and protection as does any other child.

STANDING ON PRINCIPLE

We've got to keep standing on the side of life, as President Bush did when he vetoed the bill that attempted to expand federal funding for destructive human embryonic stem cell research. On the stage behind him, when he announced his decision to veto the bill, was a group of "snowflake babies." These were children born from tiny embryos that had been frozen and stored in the laboratory. They were all children adopted as embryos from in vitro fertilization clinics.

We had several people testify before our subcommittee about the successful treatments they've received through various kinds of adult or umbilical cord blood stem cell therapy. Many of these were, frankly, miraculous. In one case a three-year-old child was successfully treated for cerebral palsy through a transfusion of cord-blood stem cells. A man named Keone Penn testified that he was cured of sickle cell anemia by the same type of procedure. And a man who had been given only months to live without a heart transplant, because of congestive heart failure, was treated with his own adult stem cells and no longer needs a transplant.

We heard about patients who have been successfully treated with adult stem cells for a variety of ailments, including one patient who testified of his successful treatment for Parkinson's disease with adult stem cells drawn from his own body. Actually we had trouble getting this man to come in to testify because he was on an African safari after his treatment. Five years after undergoing adult stem cell therapy, however, he began showing new symptoms of Parkinson's disease. More research on adult and cord blood stem cells is needed.

One young lady from Illinois came to Capitol Hill to share her amazing story. Paralyzed from the waist down after a car accident when she was in high school, she received an adult stem cell treatment into the spinal cord where it was severed. Now in her college years, she is experiencing increased feeling in her legs and can walk short distances with braces. This is truly amazing, and there is real hope that she may be able to regain more mobility through rehabilitation and additional adult stem cell treatments. We want her to walk and run again. These miracles don't get press coverage, but they are real treatments happening to patients today. They're treatments that don't require the destruction of innocent human life.

FUTURE PROMISE

I believe that within five years we'll be seeing many more miraculous treatments using the patient's own adult stem cells or cord blood or from the stem cells found in amniotic fluid. For the person who is seriously injured in an automobile accident and loses the use of his arms or legs, physicians will immediately begin harvesting his adult stem cells. Scientists can then grow and multiply those cells outside the body so that the doctors can inject a sufficient quantity into the affected area to induce healing. The sooner that treatment begins, the quicker the recovery can begin. This may become standard practice for many more medical procedures in the near future.

It's becoming more and more common for doctors to collect and save the cord blood of newborns. Public and private cord-blood banks are now in existence to store cord blood. There are a growing number of instances in which one's own cord blood can be used to treat a disease, injury, or disability. A young woman from Ohio told us the story of her daughter, who began to exhibit troubling symptoms before the age of three. She wasn't growing properly, and her limbs seemed to be shriveling. The doctors who examined the child concluded that she was in the early stages of cerebral palsy. Her mother was devastated.

She tossed and turned in bed that night and couldn't sleep. Suddenly she remembered that she had saved her daughter's cord blood. It had been sealed and stored in a medical facility. She felt that her best hope was for the child to get a cord blood transfusion. The first thing the next morning she began calling around to find a physician to do the procedure. To her amazement, she couldn't find a single doctor who would agree to give her daughter the transfusion of her own cord blood. Eventually, through a series of referrals, she found a doctor who would perform the transfusion.

The doctor said the worst that could happen would be nothing, because it was simply a transfusion using the child's own blood. They scheduled an appointment and made the trip to the medical center, where the procedure was carried out. Today that youngster is almost back to normal, running and playing. Her favorite activity is bugging her older sister. When that mother tells her story, she cries, thinking what could have happened but for the cord-blood stem cells.

When I see cases like this, I have to wonder why it's so hard to find doctors who are willing to try these new techniques. The man who had the heart condition had to go to Thailand to find a doctor to carry out the stem cell therapy. The young woman recovering from a spinal cord injury had to go to Portugal for treatment. Some of these techniques were developed in the United States, but the standards are slow to develop, and many doctors will only take the patients with the best prognosis for a full recovery. We need to be doing more adult stem cell research and treatments here in the United States, rather than losing our edge to overseas researchers.

I know there are many doctors who are concerned about the exorbitant costs of medical insurance and the litigious atmosphere surrounding practically all medical procedures these days. I'm sorry to say that Congress hasn't spent enough time looking at this aspect of it. We need to make sure the law intended to protect patients doesn't work against patients who need these treatments. These are not standard techniques and there are risks. But they hold such promise for medical breakthroughs, if we can only get the researchers and doctors to use them.

REVOLUTIONARY RESEARCH

The debate on issues such as human cloning, embryonic stem cell research, and other types of genetic experimentation has proved to be highly controversial and a major critical ethical challenge of our day. Many people first became aware of this area in 1997 when successful cloning of Dolly the sheep, by researchers in Scotland, made headlines around the world. It seemed like a medical novelty at first, but scientists quickly understood that if they could clone a mammal, such as a sheep, then they could clone humans.

Scientists had known about embryonic stem cells in laboratory animals for many years. Stem cells had been discovered in mice, and then embryonic stem cells were isolated from primates back in the early nineties. But it wasn't until a researcher at the University of Wisconsin–Madison published his studies on the isolation of human embryonic stem cells in 1998 that the subject entered the mainstream and became an important public policy debate.

That started the push we've witnessed since that time, which has a segment of society believing that embryonic stem cells are the ultimate cure-all. Some of the media reports seem to imply that medical science can fix every part of your body that starts to age and that the new science will be a veritable "fountain of youth." This term has actually been used. Some people promote embryonic stem cells as a cure for Parkinson's, Alzheimer's, multiple sclerosis, and other illnesses. The sacrificial young human embryo, after all, is so small and seems to pose no ethical problems.

Since that time it has moved from the cloning of Dolly the sheep and embryonic stem cell research with monkeys to the point where scientists say they need to destroy larger numbers of human embryos for stem cells. At that point others began saying, "Wait a minute! We've found adult cells, and they work much better." These cells are like janitorial cells that go around and fix things that are broken. If you have a need of some kind in the body, adult stem cells can migrate to the source of the injury and help facilitate the healing process. If you break your spinal cord, the janitor comes around and says, "Uh, oh. That's too big for me. I'll need more help to do this job."

When scientists isolated these adult stem cells and were able to grow them in large quantities in the laboratory, they could then inject them directly into the affected area of the body. So what one janitor couldn't do, five thousand could. As of this writing, we now know of more than seventy human maladies that have been effectively treated with adult and cord-blood stem cells. Despite all the outcry from the mainstream media, this is not the case with embryonic stem cells. What we're finding is that embryonic stem cells are often uncontrollable and that in many cases they create tumors and other serious anomalies that, rather than saving life, would actually endanger the life of the recipient.

At first the conversation was about embryonic stem cells. Then adult stem cells entered the discussion. Some researchers and bioethicists said that adult stem cells didn't have the flexibility needed for genuine medical cures—meaning that stem cells from the bone only worked on bones, and stem cells from fat only worked on fat, and so on. This turned out to be false, however. Adult stem cells do have plasticity.

Then the scientists found stem cells in cord blood, which is the blood contained in the placenta and umbilical cord of newborns. These proved to be malleable and easy to collect and work with. They were in many ways more useful than stem cells previously collected from bone marrow. We suddenly had three competing areas for stem cells: embryonic, adult, and cord blood. Now we have even found them in the amniotic fluid surrounding a baby in the womb.

We were able to acquire useful blood products for adult and cord-blood research through blood banks and other readily available sources, but the other side in this debate decided to fight us on the decision to restrict use of human embryos for research purposes. As we've argued from the start, an embryo is a person at the earliest stage of life, and the science needed to extract the necessary components for stem cell experimentation kills the embryo.

STAYING THE COURSE

That's where the debates have been most intense. They have been difficult debates, but in some ways they've also been helpful in discussing with the public whether the human embryo is a person or a piece of property. Previously the abortion debate had been exclusively about the mother's right to choose. That was the issue that always colored these debates, and it was never about the question, "What is the embryo?" But now *that's* the question. Today we're debating the status of the embryo and whether it is person or property.

The discussion is taking place in the public arena. My own line of reasoning is still the same. It's legal for independent researchers to conduct these experiments. I believe it is wrong, but it is still legal. We do not support taxpayer funding to destroy human life. That's immoral, and it's in the law. Society has always regretted, sooner or later, when it's taken advantage of weaker humans for the benefit of stronger humans. People have done that throughout history, and they've always regretted it. Furthermore, embryonic stem cell research is not necessary. We're getting positive results with adult, cord blood, and amniotic stem cells. It's unnecessary to use embryos for these purposes.

The debate began in 2000 and is still ongoing. It has gone from destructive human embryonic research to human cloning, and today it's moving into human-animal hybrids—the crossing of the species with human and animal. Today in the United States the creation of human-animal hybrids in the laboratory is legal, as is human cloning. There are some states that are funding human cloning research. There is also federal funding for human embryonic stem cell research using stem cell lines that were already available at the time this issue came before President Bush. We've tried to ban human cloning, but so far that hasn't succeeded, and cloning research remains legal for now.

This will continue to be the debate, but I fully believe that the science will overcome the debate. Embryonic stem cell research will go the same way fetal tissue research went in the early 1990s. That was going to be the fountain of youth, and it turned out to be disastrous. They tried putting young cells into the brains of people with Parkinson's disease, and they made the patients worse. Embryonic stem cells can create tumors and can't be turned off once implanted in a patient.

Some researchers are admitting that embryonic stem cells are not the magic bullet they had been hoping for. Now they say the object is not curing people but learning how the cell works. Certainly that has more scientific plausibility. But it doesn't sell as well with the public if all we're doing is learning. There's also the fear that they're simply using humans as guinea pigs. I think science is going to bypass cloning as well. Why do we need cloning if we have adaptable stem cells in our own bodies and they're a perfect genetic match? The only reason to clone is to produce cells that will match. So that step is no longer necessary. Plus, we've banned fetal farming, a bill passed through the House and the Senate and signed into law by the president. So now it's illegal to grow a young human for replacement body parts. That's a bigger issue than many people realize. We stopped a hideous practice before it started.

The third issue is the issue of human-animal hybrids. This is the one that, technically at least, could work. It's a process by which researchers take genetic material or cells from one species and combine them with another species. The idea to treat certain diseases in humans by introducing genetic material from an animal that has an innate resistance to the condition you want to eliminate. It may mean genetically altering the sperm or the egg and creating a hybrid creature, but this includes at least the prospect that the particular hereditary characteristics may be passed on for generations.

If that research has the potential of being passed on generationally and changing the species in some fundamental way, then I think that's dangerous and must be thought about for a long time. If, for example, you need an artificial hip and a new joint can be created from an animal part, that's fine. We know of cases where organs from pigs have been used to create new heart valves for humans who would have died without the treatment. That's great, and a good use of science.

We get into trouble when we change or alter the species. At that point we will have reached what the English writer C. S. Lewis called "the abolition of man." When we change the species either by introducing foreign materials or by selectively destroying those with "undesirable" traits, that is a big issue and not something to be taken lightly. I fear we may be approaching that point with some of today's testing, where doctors can test for as many as 120 medical issues in the unborn child. How many of those children will be discarded because the parents fear the child may have a propensity for cancer or heart disease or even something as simple as obesity?

REVIEWING *ROE* AND *DOE*

I can't overemphasize the dangers to society if we aren't cautious about how we proceed with experimentation in these vital areas. For perspective, we ought to remember that the same thought that is pushing for unrestricted experimentation with human embryos, human cloning, and human-animal hybrids, is the basis of the thought that led to unrestricted abortion on demand, and that a young human is property, not a person. We know now that not only millions of human lives have been destroyed, but also the whole fabric of the legal battle that led to *Roe v. Wade* in 1973 was based on lies.

Norma McCorvey was Jane Roe in *Roe v. Wade*, and Sandra Cano was Jane Doe in *Doe v. Bolton*. These were the two Supreme Court cases that led to the legalization of unrestricted abortion in this country. I met these ladies and asked them to testify before a Senate subcommittee about their cases. Both women testified that the factual bases of their cases were false. And they said it without hesitation in open Senate testimony.

In the original case, Norma McCorvey stated that she had been raped, and she even said in her signed affidavit that this is what happened, but it wasn't true. She wasn't raped. Sandra Cano's testimony in the other case was even more striking. She told us that she didn't even want an abortion when her case was filed. She had simply gone to talk to a lawyer about getting a divorce, and the attorney turned the lawsuit into a test case for abortion. Her case made its way to the Supreme Court before Mrs. Cano discovered that it was her case.

The factual basis of the two pillar cases of the abortion debate, and the constitutional basis for the Supreme Court's finding in two of the most controversial cases in American history, were based on lies, very costly ones. The constitutional basis of abortion in America, by which more than forty million American children have been killed, is the result of fraud and manipulation. I find that very dramatic, especially because I live in Topeka, Kansas, which is the town where *Brown v. Board of Education* (1954) began.

That decision ended the practice of segregating black and white children in separate schools, and it's recognized today as one of the pillars of the Civil Rights movement. Many people have said that was the case in which the Court became activist, and they point to the good that came out of the decision. I agree. Ending legal segregation was a good thing. I can take you to the school where Linda Brown was denied entrance in 1953, and you can see the white schools she walked past on her way to Topeka's black-only school. You can see the evidence upon which that monumental decision was based, and you can see that the argument was factual and true. The end of legal segregation has brought great blessings for all our people.

You can't say any of that for either *Roe v. Wade* or *Doe v. Bolton*. Both cases were built on falsehood and deception. And just think of all the death and despair that have come from those two decisions in the years since 1973. Today both women are attempting to have their cases reviewed, since both decisions were based on fraud. To date, the courts have denied their requests to reopen the cases.

THE SORCERER'S APPRENTICE

I'm hopeful that we will find cures for all diseases, but is it worth killing a child? I would hope that people on all sides of these issues will be willing to discuss and debate the facts, particularly the risks involved in the medical use of human-animal hybrids. Scientists are already using these techniques in animals and plants. Farmers are using hybrid techniques in crops such as soybeans in order to make them resistant to certain types of insects and plant diseases. They understand the science, but when it comes to humans, I'm afraid we're racing far beyond our ethical understanding in the area of genetic reaseach, and we need to pause and consider where this may lead.

At the very least, we should pass laws to stop federal funds from being spent on these types of research. We aren't talking about stopping private researchers from experimenting with them. Some of this is going on now in research laboratories around the country. Still, now is the time to pause and seriously consider the consequences of these actions.

Once we allow scientists to take those steps, what happens when someone else comes along and says, "I can make sure that every child born from this day forward will have a high IQ"? Or what about, "I can give everybody a luxurious head of hair that will never fall out"? Or "I can extend human life by ten, twenty, or thirty years, with little or no serious illness"? We would enter into it with the best of intentions and the most altruistic motives, and the debate would be very difficult. But where would it lead?

Will it be like *The Sorcerer's Apprentice*, unleashing dangers in the laboratory or society that no one could have anticipated? Will it be a research scientist's nightmare, with unanticipated results and dangerous side effects that may inflict chaos upon the society for generations to come? This is a very serious debate.

The other issue that will need a great deal of thought and study is the end-of-life debate and how we deal with individuals who, either through advanced age or illness, have come to the point where the manner of death is of concern. Since 1973 when *Roe v. Wade* established the right to unrestricted abortions, there has been a major change in the public's attitudes about abortion. I think we're winning the beginning-of-life issues, and the country is now pro-life. A majority of young people under the age of thirty are instinctively pro-life, and national polling data show that most people agree it is a child in the womb from the moment of conception, and that it should not be killed.[1]

The focus in the near future, I believe, will be on the end-of-life issues, such as doctor-assisted suicide and euthanasia. Oregon has already passed the first assisted-suicide law in this country. Some European countries have implemented assisted-suicide laws.

We must engage the public in a discussion about end-of-life issues and why life is sacred even when it is incredibly difficult. We must help people at the end of life deal with pain, despair, and depression. We must offer them our care and compassion and love. We also must be clear that the truth of the natural law in the commandment "thou shalt not kill" includes taking your own life.

★ 6 ★

MODELS OF COMPASSION

The term "compassionate conservatism" was popularized in 2000 by a book of the same name written by Dr. Marvin Olasky, who was an adviser to President Bush in Texas and in Washington. During his presidential bid, Mr. Bush adopted that phrase and made it a key part of his domestic policy agenda. I think that was a good decision, and I've supported the president's policies whenever I could. I would have to say that my interest in compassionate conservatism goes back even further, to my study of two pivotal figures.

The first was the English parliamentarian William Wilberforce, who devoted his life to abolishing the slave trade in Great Britain. The second was Mother Teresa, who worked with the poor and downtrodden in the slums of Calcutta and around the world. I became interested in the life of Wilberforce many years ago when a good friend introduced me to his story and the various books written by and about him. Those works helped me to understand the integration of faith and public service.

There's a great biography written by John Pollock entitled simply *Wilberforce*. I took that book with me on a trip to Central Asia. I met with many leaders in the region; then I had to make the long flight home. During the return trip I was reading Pollock's book on the plane and came to the part that described Wilberforce's conversion to faith. He was a handsome, talented young parliamentarian, a singer, and a gifted public speaker. He was very popular in

British society, and almost everyone believed he would become prime minister one day.

One of his closest friends was, in fact, William Pitt, who later became prime minister. Pitt referred to Wilberforce as the most eloquent speaker in the House of Commons. While Wilberforce was on an extended trip in Europe during the summer of 1784, he became engaged in a long debate about religion with his traveling companion. He was shocked to discover that the young man was an evangelical Christian. Wilberforce was witty and urbane, and he was determined to prove that his friend's religious convictions were silly and unrealistic. But despite many attempts, he couldn't refute the other man's logic. Eventually he accepted Christ, and his life was dramatically changed.

When he began to think about what this new Christian worldview would mean for his career as a politician, Wilberforce thought he would have to give up politics and go into the ministry. The House of Commons was a secular, sometimes vulgar and profane, place. Wilberforce feared that his friends in Parliament would think it was strange if he showed up one day and announced that he had become a Christian.

Before he took that fateful step of leaving Parliament, he had a meeting with John Newton, a former slave trader who had converted to Christianity and had become a dynamic preacher and strong abolitionist. Newton was the author of the hymn "Amazing Grace" and a man who was greatly admired. When Wilberforce told Newton that he planned to give up his seat in Commons, Newton said he must not do that. He told him that politics was the vocation that God had given him, and surely God had put him there for just such a time. If Wilberforce wanted to have an influence for good, Newton explained, then he should do so where God had placed him—in Parliament.

A PASSION TO SERVE

As I was reading that chapter, I couldn't help but think of my own situation. Here I was, a young politician who had been reasonably successful in winning elections and enacting legislation. When I thought about the things I had done, particularly in comparison with what Wilberforce accomplished in his lifetime, I felt it was of little value. It was mostly for earthly things—the accumulation of power and prestige. I felt I'd been wasting much of my time. At best I had wasted my own time; at worst I may have hurt other people.

That was a very emotional experience. I was deeply moved by the descriptions of Wilberforce's life and work and how he had sacrificed everything for the cause that God had given him, which was first to abolish the slave trade and second to seek a reformation of culture. It was a difficult task, since so much of the commerce in Great Britain at that time was involved in some way in the trafficking of human flesh.

Wilberforce spent decades at that task. He sacrificed his reputation and his health in the process, but he eventually accomplished his goal. The news came to him on his deathbed that Parliament had finally passed the law abolishing slavery in Great Britain. He lived long enough to celebrate the wonderful news of the emancipation of all of Britain's slaves in 1833, and he died just three days later.

When I put down the book I had tears streaming down my face, in part because of the power of that story, but also because of the feeling that I needed to rededicate myself to the mission God has given me. As those thoughts were running through my head, I leaned over and looked out the window of the airplane and saw green fields below us. We had left Central Asia and flown to Germany. And now we were on our way back to America, but I was curious to know what country was down below.

When I asked the flight attendant, he checked his map and said we were over England. That was a bit of a surprise, but the fact that we were directly over the place where William Wilberforce had done all of that magnificent work reinforced what I was feeling. It was a sort of confirmation of the new sense of purpose I felt. I'll never forget that moment.

I eventually finished the book, and I was challenged to focus on things that would have lasting importance. On several occasions I have heard Wilberforce referred to as "God's politician." What a great title! He is the model of a leader who sought to use public life to serve the weak and to do God's will of caring for the downtrodden.

Reading about the life of Wilberforce had a major impact on my thinking. He was a man of faith and action. He prayed every day. He had a group of loyal friends, known as the Clapham Circle, who lived near each other as a faith community and planned their tactics for ending the slave trade and social action. They picked their targets wisely, stirring the public's indignation by showing them the evils of slavery. They were also concerned with what they called "the reformation of manners," which was the term in those days for renewing the culture.

HEROES FOR TODAY

Wilberforce's England is my America. By that I mean that both nations were at the pinnacle of power. In the early 1800s, Great Britain had no peer. It was a powerful nation, but signs of cultural decay were showing. Our battle today is similar to theirs. Our battlefield is the fight for life. The core question is, do we believe in a culture of life or not? We certainly need a renewal—a reformation of manners—in contemporary culture.

The Methodist Movement of Wilberforce's day was led by men such as John and Charles Wesley. When Wilberforce was first elected to Parliament, there were few if any active Christians in the ranks. By the time he died, in 1833, there were many who professed their faith, and many more who, though of little or no faith, nevertheless advocated for moral and social reform within the government. These men helped usher in the Victorian Era and a period of spiritual renewal in that nation. I think it's fair to say that these cultural influences kept Great Britain strong for many years to come.

I believe we're at the same cultural moment in this country. We can see difficulties in American society—the breakdown of the family, out-of-wedlock births, teen suicide. We are the greatest nation on earth, with no peer in terms of economic or military might. But which way will we go? Will we turn toward a moral and spiritual renewal and revive the culture, as happened in Wilberforce's day? Or do otherwise? I'm convinced that the key to our future prosperity is to rebuild our family structure, renew our culture, and revive our soul. We've got to have our own reformation of manners.

I identify with that time period and all that was happening in the life of William Wilberforce and the Clapham Circle. This also seems to connect well with the other person I have come to admire so much, Mother Teresa. I have read a great deal about her. She said some of the most incredible, pithy, and clear spiritual truths I've ever heard. They weren't lengthy. Usually just a sentence or two that was a jolt of truth. I have several of her sayings posted on the walls of my home and my office.

She said, for example, "I pray that my love for the poor never gets in the way of my love for God." We must all love the poor, but we cannot let our work detract from the way of our love for Christ. She also said, "If you're too busy judging people, you don't have enough time to love them." That's a message we all need to hear. And she said, "At the moment of death we will not be judged according to the number of good deeds we have done or by the diplomas we have received in our lifetime. We will be judged according to the love we have put into our work." That says it all. She also said of others' religions, "I love all faiths. I am in love with my own."

Once I recognized the spirit of this remarkable woman, I began to follow what she was doing and saying. She was very critical of the West, particularly because of our culture's compromise on abortion and sexual ethics. She gave a moving speech at the National Prayer Breakfast in 1994, speaking clearly about the need to protect the unborn. Her Nobel Peace Prize speech was one of the strongest pro-life messages I've ever read. Her consistent, compassionate witness to the cause of life was a gift to the whole world.

During my first two years in the Senate, I worked on two Congressional Gold Medal awards: one for Billy Graham and one for Mother Teresa. Billy Graham made the trip to Washington and gave a very strong speech on cultural renewal. Mother Teresa was very ill when the presentation was made and it was uncertain whether or not she would be able to come to Washington to receive the award. But she did come. She was only with us for about forty-five minutes, but I was captivated by her strength of spirit and her lifelong testimony of faith in action.

A LIVING MEMENTO

Mother Teresa's visit was very touching. She was elderly and frail. Nonetheless she came all the way from Calcutta to speak to us and offer a challenge. Even before she came, her order of religious women, the Missionaries of Charity, were calling to ask if they could melt down the medal for the gold and sell it to give the money to the poor. She was much more concerned with feeding the poor and using the award to help them than she was in receiving personal honors. We told her it would be better to auction off the medal, if that's what they wanted to do, than to melt it down—they would get more for it that way than by selling the gold.

Material possessions meant nothing to her, and anything the order accumulated was used to help the poor and dying in India, and in many other places around the world where the Missionaries of Charity have established houses. Today the sisters minister on every continent and in many cities around the globe, including Washington, DC. The only thing she asked for at the ceremony was that we would pray for the sisters.

She said repeatedly: "Pray for the sisters." I thought that was an odd request. Why didn't she ask for a billion dollars? Wouldn't that be the thing to do in Washington? But I realized that she was asking us for the most powerful thing we could give, which was our prayers. She said in one of her books that the reason for her order's success is that they pray. Saint Paul said that we are to "pray without ceasing," and to give thanks in all things because that's God's will for us. Mother Teresa had obviously taken the apostle's challenge to heart.

After her speech, I walked her out to the portico, held her hand, and helped her into the car. The thought ran through my mind: *This is a great person and a true saint, but I caught her on the downhill side.* This is an awkward example, but I thought it was like Joe Montana when he played for the Kansas City Chiefs. At the beginning of his career, when he was with the 49ers, Montana was unstoppable. Crisp passes, great moves, impeccable timing. When he played for the Chiefs, he was slower, the passes were just a little off, and the magic was fading. You could still see the greatness, but he was on the downhill side. That's the feeling I had as I stood there helping Mother Teresa into her car. But I was looking on the outside; Mother Teresa's beauty was on the inside.

She looked up at me, grasped my hand in her warm hands, and she said three words four times: "All for Jesus. All for Jesus. All for Jesus. All for Jesus." I thanked her again for coming and closed the car door. As they drove away I thought: *You know, I've been looking for the wisdom of the ages, and I just got it.*

Taking all of her years of service and prayer, and the constant struggle to demonstrate God's love to "the least of these," she had boiled it down to those three words: "All for Jesus." And she lived it every day. Her life, as she would say, was a pencil in His hands. She did everything for Him, so that His love for all poeple would shine forth.

Mother Teresa helped me most with her thoughts on how to frame our own souls and by speaking about the time she would spend in prayer. She was weak and frequently ill toward the end, but the strength she demonstrated when she spoke about the poor, the hopeless, and the unborn was truly amazing. It amazed me how she could reach out with love to her detractors and to those who disagreed with her.

PRACTICAL COMPASSION

Coming into contact with that kind of love has helped me to reach out to my own political and ideological adversaries, and it also helped me to consider getting involved in areas of law and jurisprudence that I might not have considered previously. The example of those two models of compassion, Wilberforce and Mother Teresa, made me more determined to find common ground with people who don't share my beliefs or my political philosophy. I disagree with those on the other side of the aisle on many things, but if they don't see compassion in me, where will they see it?

This was Wilberforce's model, too. He didn't care who he worked with so long as it moved the issue forward. On many occasions I have consciously followed that model—the further left, the better in some cases, so long as we're in agreement on the central issues. This attitude has taken me into some unusual issues and unusual coalitions. One of the most important of these is the area of prison reform and reducing recidivism rates for those who have committed crimes. We must stop the cycle!

My interest in prison reform started when I was a young lawyer in Manhattan, Kansas. Going into law practice in a four-man firm, in a town of about thirty-five thousand at that time, I had to learn the basics in a lot of different areas. Lawyers were general practitioners in that town, and each lawyer in the bar was required to take a certain number of indigent criminal clients. If an individual was charged with a crime and couldn't afford an attorney, then we each had to take our share of those cases.

Since I was the newest member of the firm, the senior partner gave me his indigent criminal cases, too. I had double duty on those cases. It was a challenge. It was also a good way to learn about a segment of society that I had not previously encountered. Growing up, I had a great respect for the law and a tremendous fear of ever doing anything that would land me in trouble with the law. I wasn't generally around people who had committed a serious crime. Not many felons lived in farm country in those days.

But now I was representing people who had committed a number of felonies in their lives. This was a big eye-opener for me. I took an aggressive stance in these cases. I said, *OK, let's try these cases and see how we do*. I would meet with my law partners every day, and we would have coffee and talk about some of our cases. As I brought these cases up, my partners always commented, "Oh, yeah. I represented this guy before." Or "I represented his uncle twenty years ago" or "I represented his son last month." I realized that when a person goes into that lifestyle—committing crimes—too often he or she tends to stay in it, and it tends to spread within the family. It seemed odd to me, but the criminal mentality was often multigenerational.

Later on when I entered the public policy arena, I discovered that statistically this is the case. Once a person goes into that lifestyle, his or her children are five times more likely to be involved in crime. And a person who commits a crime and goes to jail, two-thirds of the time he or she will likely end up going back to jail. One report said that more than half of all ex-offenders are back in prison within the first two years. Sadly, the criminal lifestyle seems to permeate their souls, and it becomes a part of them.

In 1980, there were over five hundred thousand men and women in federal, state, and local prisons and jails; today that number stands at 2.1 million. Statistics show that two-thirds of those who are released from prison will be arrested and again be incarcerated at some point in their lives. The statistics are very clear: we have a problem with our prison system that needs to be addressed.[1]

There's hope in the midst of these dire statistics, and this hope can be found in programs that not only nurture education and job-training skills, but nurture the soul of the individual as well. Today, in prisons where mentoring programs and faith-based initiatives are operating, the recidivism rate is under 10 percent. Why? Because while the body may be locked up, the soul of the inmate is free, and that freedom of the soul can lead to a reformation of life—a life that is rooted in the assurance that there is a life beyond that of poverty, drug addiction, or crime. It's a ray of hope that anyone can embrace.

Programs rooted in faith are designed to restore the individual's sense of self-worth, with respect for his or her human dignity and effectively reducing crime at the same time. Instead of treating prisoners as disposable, they're treated as persons with dignity. They must pay for their crimes, but in the process the goal is to change each individual for the better on the *inside*, so that we're all better off when they're back on the *outside*.

Change from the Inside Out

As a young congressman in 1995 and 1996, I represented a district in Kansas where the Leavenworth Federal Prison is located. Leavenworth was the first federal penitentiary and one of the premier penitentiaries in the Bureau of Prisons system. We also had a state penitentiary in my district, a disciplinary barracks for the military, and a privately run prison. So in my district we had a lot of prison space and many prisoners.

I toured each of those facilities, and one of the things that was striking to me was that we had an extremely high recidivism rate—prisoners were being released and then ending up back in prison a short time later. We were just warehousing these people, knowing that the majority of them were going to be released back into society. They were going to be living in our cities and towns, and we weren't attempting to help them make the adjustment back to a normal life and become productive members of society.

As I looked into the history of prison reform, it seemed to me that back in the late 1960s we had some well-intentioned but soft-headed policies on prison reform that had failed miserably. We were letting people out early, and they were returning to our communities and committing more crimes. Soon the country said, "That's enough!" Then the mantra became "You do the crime, you do the time." In fact, one of the ads I used when I first ran for Congress in 1994 used those very words.

Then the popular idea became to lock them up and throw away the key. Forget reform, just give them the punishment they deserve. The problem was that they were doing this to living souls. No matter how dark the heart of the criminal, and no matter how terrible his crime, he has a soul that is precious in the sight of God. The other problem was that in most cases these individuals were likely to come out of prison at some point, having paid their debts to society. They were going to come out unskilled, untrained, and angry. They were often already mad at society and socially dysfunctional. For anyone who bothered to pay attention, it was obvious there had to be a better way.

As I was pondering these matters, I learned about Chuck Colson's prison ministries programs and his organization, Prison Fellowship. Chuck Colson had been the chief legal counsel to President Richard Nixon during the Watergate era, and he was sentenced to seven months in jail. He had been "Nixon's hatchet man," a man who would "run over his own grandmother," and he was ruthless with political opponents.

During the course of his highly publicized trials and public humiliations, Colson met with Doug Coe, Tom Phillips, and other Christian leaders in Washington and accepted Christ as his Savior. The transformation was so radical that no one believed him at first. Reporters and broadcasters claimed his conversion was a trick, an appeal for sympathy. Over time, however, even his enemies had to admit that the change was genuine and Chuck Colson was a new man.

The fruit of Colson's new life was everywhere and certainly could be seen in the ministry that he launched after his release from jail, working with prisoners and preparing them for rehabilitation and their return to society. It is an important ministry, but it is in an area of social justice that we've had great difficulty dealing with. We're used to working with prisoners strictly on a physical basis, and we're even willing to train their minds to some degree. But we haven't known where to begin to touch their souls with reformation. Yet that's the most powerful part of who each of us is.

Society couldn't do that, but Prison Fellowship found a way. I began working with them, supporting the faith-based prison that was being established in

Kansas. The first one was operated in Winfield, Kansas, and later moved to Ellsworth, Kansas. The system is modeled on the successful program that Prison Fellowship established in Sugarland, Texas, when George W. Bush was governor. That program had a recidivism rate of less than 10 percent. Fewer than one in ten individuals who came out of that institution returned to a life of crime when they returned to the community.

Prison Fellowship's InnerChange Freedom Initiative (IFI) is a faith-based reentry program for prisoners. It started in 1997. In 1999, IFI became a separate 501(c)(3) organization that contracted with Prison Fellowship for staffing and support services. Today there are IFI programs in Texas, Minnesota, and Arkansas, as well as Kansas. The state of Florida has announced plans to convert one of its prisons into an IFI facility. There's a growing demand for prison programs that work, and this one has proven to be very effective. It has been an uphill battle to convince bureaucrats that this passes the separation-of-church-and-state test, and to allow these faith-based programs to do what they do best, so the matter is still being litigated.

FAITH BEHIND BARS

The Texas Department of Criminal Justice and the University of Pennsylvania have conducted studies that show that IFI graduates are far less likely to return to prison after release than prisoners who don't go through the programs. The University of Pennsylvania found that only 8 percent of IFI Texas graduates returned to prison within two years of release, whereas in the control group that didn't participate, 20 percent of those prisoners were back in prison within two years. And the percentage of recidivism increases dramatically over longer periods of time for those who don't participate in the IFI program.

To understand the program better, I volunteered on one occasion to spend the night at the IFI prison in Ellsworth, Kansas, and I have visited that facility on two other occasions. I also spent the night at Angola prison in Louisiana, which is a model prison for sucessful faith-based initiatives. The key, which the IFI program has used so effectively, is to engage the totality of who a person is and build relationships with them. These people need relationships with other people outside of prison that last when they get out. They need a group of friends, and they need mentors. They need people who care about them and who care about the nurturing of their souls.

When those men or women get out of prison, they're going to have problems just like the rest of us. The key is to make sure they don't return to their old habits and bad company that took them down the wrong path in the first place. We need to see that they have a new set of guidelines and new relationships. We need to make sure that they have a relationship with someone who understands and cares about their rehabilitation. IFI does that, as do a number of other programs.

The value of faith-based programs cannot be overestimated. Statistics compiled by governmental and nongovernmental organizations paint a somber picture of today's prison population. In a typical year six hundred fifty thousand prison inmates and more than ten million jail inmates are released back into society. Nearly 97 percent of all prisoners will return to the community at some point. Three-quarters of these will have a substance abuse problem, and one out of five will be infected with HIV.

According to a 2004 Re-entry Policy Council Report, more than half of those currently incarcerated (55 percent) have children under the age of eighteen, and only about 27 percent are participating in vocational training to improve their chances of a successful return to society. The remarkable thing is that programs like Prison Fellowship's IFI have been extremely successful in restoring human dignity and building a sense of accountability in those who complete the program. It's hard for me to imagine that anyone would want to stop it.

I had an opportunity to spend the night in a homeless shelter in Washington, DC, in the spring of 2006. I spent much of the early part of the evening talking to the men staying there. I asked them, "Why are you here? And how did you get here?" They shared a fairly consistent pattern. They had been involved in a series of relationships—family, a spouse, maybe a significant other—but they had all been involved in a community of sorts. Then they started to isolate themselves, generally through drugs and alcohol. At that point their spouses would kick them out of the house, and they would begin wandering. They would lose jobs and become even more isolated. Then they would turn to crime to pay for their habits.

One gentleman at this shelter in Washington told me about something that happened to him in jail that made him realize he was going to have to make a decision one way or the other. He was lying in his prison bed. He was addicted to drugs—they could get drugs in the prison he was in. There was a man on his left shooting up with heroin and a man on his right reading the Bible. He said he looked at both of those men, and he told me, "That was the moment I knew I had a choice to make. Either I could go on using drugs and being strung out until I dropped dead from an overdose, or I could get my act together and turn over a new leaf."

Fortunately, he chose the better option. He came to faith in Jesus. He said he felt an immediate sense of peace, and his drug addiction broke immediately. He did lapse back into drugs several years later but this time he knew there was a better way. He is now a productive member of society.

A MODEL OF REFORM

There is a way to reduce this terrible recidivism rate. It's through compassionate engagement on a personal level, with faith. It's one-on-one, soul-to-soul work that's needed. It's new relationships, and it's helping people while they're still in prison and after they come out. Thanks to programs like Prison Fellowship and a number of others that understand this challenge and minister to the individual through God's love, many inmates are receiving that kind of attention.

I've coauthored a bill—the Second Chance Act—with Senators Arlen Specter of Pennsylvania and Joe Biden of Delaware, that has strong bipartisan support. The program would give a series of grants to state and local governments and nonprofit groups with the goal of reducing the recidivism rate of the individuals they work with in the program by 50 percent over five years. I believe that's a realistic goal, so long as the groups are free to offer inmates the kind of help that will lead to real and lasting change.

This can be done through mentoring organizations, which are often faith-based groups that engage the soul of the individual. They work to keep people on the edges of our community from becoming loners, separated from culture and society. This could be one of the great compassionate conservative achievements, on a par with welfare reform. It recognizes the dignity of the individual so that people are treated like the beautiful souls they are, not like animals.

This model for the reform of prisoners is something we should engage aggressively and with honor—on a par with any of our finest achievements. It's a proven system for working not only with the prisoners but also with their families, to break the chain of bondage that they are in. It's precisely the kind of work William Wilberforce and Mother Teresa would approve of.

BUILDING BLOCKS OF
A HEALTHY SOCIETY

I would never have thought when I ran for the Senate in 1996 that one day we would be debating the definition of marriage. When I debated my opponent during that campaign, the issue of marriage never came up. And it did not come up in my run for reelection in 1998. You could have asked me at that time to name the top one hundred topics we were going to deal with in the United States Senate, and I wouldn't have listed the definition of marriage as one of the topics.

We were at the point where a number of people were deeply concerned about the breakdown of marriage in American society, and they were talking about the need to strengthen the institution of marriage. Things such as the marriage penalty tax debate were very lively topics. We were able to remove the marriage penalty from the tax code because we wanted to encourage couples to get married, and many people were concerned about the decline in traditional marriage. But never in our wildest dreams did we think that the definition of marriage would become an issue.

In my campaigns for both the House and the Senate, I talked about my proposals to Reduce, Reform, and Return. That was my theme in each of those races. As I said earlier, that meant reducing the size, scope, and intrusiveness of the federal government, reforming the Congress, and returning to the basic values that built our country. In that last category, of course, was the belief that marriage is incredibly important and, sadly, under serious attack. If you look at the statistics, you can't deny it. In the city of Washington, DC, 63 percent of all children born in the District are born to single mothers.[1] We have a marriage crisis. There are many single parents who struggle heroically and do a wonderful job, but we know in our hearts (and it's supported by the social data) that lifelong marriage between a man and a woman, bonded together for life, is the best place to raise children. It is not the *only* place, but it is the *best* place. That's the way civilized societies have been doing it successfully since the beginning of time.

Some people looking at this modern phenomenon of single parents and children being raised in single-parent homes, tend to believe that this is just the way it is and things will always be this way. I don't believe that. This is a recent phenomenon. If you look at what was happening in the 1960s, you'll see that it was generally a stable marriage environment. In 1960, only 9.2 out of every 1,000 women over the age of fifteen had been divorced; by 2000, that rate had quadrupled. Today's marriage and family crisis is a recent phenomenon. And that's basically happened with my own generation. It's the people in their forties, fifties, and sixties who have produced this enormous change.

There are bad marriages, and I'm sure there are marriages that simply cannot work. But there are many situations where people opt for divorce simply because they're unhappy or they feel they're not getting their needs met by the other person. That thinking is tragically flawed, and society has paid a terrible price for it. We need more committment to marriage, not less. Divorce is never easy, and it's almost never good for the children who are affected by it. Recognizing that the divorce rate is far too high is not a matter of condemning anyone but a matter of trying to create a culture of strong families in which to raise our children.

STRUGGLING WITH DYSFUNCTION

There's a famous Harvard study that followed two groups of people who were going through conflict in their marriages. The first group divorced, and the second group worked through their problems and did their best to stay married. When the researchers interviewed both groups five years later, they found that those who stayed together were happier and better adjusted, while those who divorced were generally unhappy and were still searching for someone to fulfill their needs.[2]

Those who stayed married didn't have it easy, it's true. Some of them had to fight their impulses and ignore a lot of distractions. They may have had to put cotton in their ears to be able to stand each other. But even if they had to do that, five years later they were happier, and they were uniformly glad they had made the effort to keep the family together.

As I mentioned earlier, I grew up in the town of Parker, Kansas, population 250, and I went to a consolidated high school serving seven small farming communities in the area. During all my years growing up, I can't remember a single classmate who came from a divorced family. Go there now, however, and the statistics would be essentially the same as in any other town in America. That shows how much things have changed. But my point is that this is a one-generation shift, and if enough people care about this issue, I believe it can go the other way. I've worked with groups like Marriage Savers that do a nice job of counseling couples before marriage and mentoring them during marriage. This program works because it helps couples to put more effort into their marriages.

We were able to eliminate most of the marriage penalty in the tax code, and we're now beginning to look at making changes to the welfare system in order to get rid of the rules that discourage marriage. But it will take some work.

Today the welfare system pays people *not* to get married, and it penalizes them if they *do*. A woman on welfare can lose up to 88 percent of her monthly payment if she decides to get married, and that's a terrible disincentive for her. During the summer of 2006, I met with a group of single mothers in Washington, DC, to hear their concerns. These were all women on public assistance. All of them had children, and I wanted to know about their experiences with the welfare system and why they chose not to get married.

When I opened the meeting, I told them what I was hoping to learn, and they reacted strongly. I could see that the question upset them. Just asking why they didn't get married was upsetting, but their answers varied. One woman said she didn't want her children's father coming around the house. Another said she just wanted her own private space. And another woman said she couldn't find a man at her income level who could provide for her and her children.

What struck me was that, culturally, none of these women saw marriage as a legitimate option. They all said that at some point they had dreamed of having a husband to share their life with, to help raise the children and make a home together. But that was just a dream. None of them saw marriage as a realistic option.

ENDING DEPENDENCY

One woman that I had met earlier had taken advantage of the Marriage Development Accounts created by Congress. This was an initiative supported by both Left and Right to encourage more mothers on welfare to get married. Her answer to my question was perhaps the best reason I've heard why many people don't get married. She and her boyfriend had been living together for twenty years. They had four children together, and they decided to get married using one of the Marriage Development Accounts.

As she was telling me about her experience, I asked, "If you were together for twenty years, why didn't you get married before?" She told me, "It's something you think about from time to time, but you don't really know how reliable that man's going to be. He can just up and leave one day. But you know how reliable the government is going to be." Then she said, "You know, I'd be willing to risk losing my benefits if it was just me. But with my children, I'm not willing to risk it."

She made a good point, I'm sorry to say. Under the welfare system, single mothers get health benefits from the government and other kinds of assistance. So even if she were willing to walk away from all that, if it were for her own benefit, she said, she wasn't willing to do it at her children's expense. I thought, *How do you argue with that? From a mother's perspective that's absolutely rational thinking.* For millions of mothers in that situation, who can't depend on a husband to stay with them and look after the family, the government has now become the reliable provider.

In one of my first meetings with Mayor Anthony Williams in Washington, DC, I brought up the issue of family formation. I expressed my concern that family formation wasn't happening in DC and asked what he was doing about it. He said, "Yes, I know it's a terrible problem. We need to do something about it, but what can we do?" So we began working with him and others in his office, and that's when we first came up with the idea of Marriage Development Accounts.

For each dollar put into the program by government, the private sector puts in two dollars, and the couple who wants to get married puts in a dollar. So that couple will be getting a three-to-one match for their investment. There are certain income restrictions for couples to qualify for these grants, but the object is to encourage more people on public assistance to choose marriage.

The mayor supported the idea, as did a number of think tanks and research groups on both the Left and the Right, and the congressional delegate from DC, Eleanor Holmes Norton. Now we're taking it to the next level, by going to the welfare program and saying that any couple that takes the marriage option will be at the top of the list for public housing. In addition, they can continue to receive direct payments from the government—without penalty—for up to three years, so long as they remain married.

This has the possibility of having some real impact. When I mentioned this plan to the women in the focus group, they responded very positively. They liked the idea of being held harmless on welfare payments for three years if they would go ahead and get married. That's one reason I feel so strongly that these kinds of programs can work. I'm convinced that the government cannot be the father in these homes. So we need to use the tools at our disposal, and we need to reengage with these issues before we lose yet another generation.

THE DEFINITION OF MARRIAGE

The second part of this debate on marriage is the definition of marriage. It's been a difficult debate, but it has taken a different twist than many people expected. This issue first came up in the courts in Vermont, but it wasn't until the case in Massachusetts made headlines that most people became aware of the controversy over the definition of marriage. The idea of a court forcing a state to redefine marriage didn't go over very well with the public, but using the courts to change the culture has been a standard tactic of the Left.

We saw it happen in 1973 with the abortion debate. But unlike that case, where the country sat on its hands while the Supreme Court gave its imprimatur to a controversial policy that could never have made it through Congress, the fight over the definition of marriage brought the nation to its feet. The rest of the country was activated, and when they saw what was happening in Massachusetts, the American people said, "Enough is enough!"

I have discussed these issues with Dr. Bernard Nathanson, who was an abortionist, cofounder and first president of the National Abortion Right Action League, and one of the leading voices pushing for unrestricted abortion back in the 1970s. He told me that the first lawsuit on abortion was filed in 1968. Five years later, thanks to the tactics of litigation, they had abortion-on-demand and the fight was over. That wasn't about to happen with the marriage debate. The people said loudly that they were not going to allow the courts to redefine this fundamental institution of society. So Congress quickly passed the Defense of Marriage Act (DOMA) that said one state could not be forced to recognize a same-sex marriage recognized by another state.

There were warning signs that this issue would be coming with the case of *Lawrence v. Texas* (2003), in which the Supreme Court ruled that state laws cannot outlaw sodomy, even though twenty years earlier, in *Bowers v. Hardwick* (1986), the Court had said they could. Many wondered what had changed in the Constitution during those twenty years. Obviously, nothing. Liberal voices on the Supreme Court had decided that cultural norms needed to change. As Justice Scalia said in his blistering dissent in the *Lawrence* case, it's obvious that "the Court has taken sides in the culture war."

A CONTEST OF WILLS

I was active in the marriage debate and encouraged my colleagues to take the issue very seriously. The only way we could do something to protect traditional marriage after passing the Defense of Marriage Act (which, incidentally, a number of scholars had told us wouldn't pass muster once the courts got involved), was to enact a constitutional amendment to define marriage as the union of a man and a woman.

We held many meetings about this issue, and almost everyone agreed that it would be a good idea to put the measure through, but they also agreed that it would be next to impossible to get two-thirds of the House, two-thirds of the Senate, and three-fourths of the states to ratify any amendment, particularly one that would be vigorously challenged by the Left, the mainstream media, and others on that side of the issue.

Many people needed to be convinced that it was important enough to go to the mat for. We heard from some people who said, "Yeah, I don't like same-sex marriage, but is it really that big a deal?" Others said, "Same-sex marriage doesn't hurt my marriage." The problem is, it does. We now have a lot of social data from countries that have passed laws that allow same-sex marriage.

In Scandinavia, for example, we have ten years of sociological research, and it shows that very few same-sex couples get married. Because that society has adopted an ambiguous definition of marriage, fewer heterosexuals are bothering to get married either.[3]

Here you have a foundational institution that's already in trouble, and on top of that you take the sacredness and uniqueness of marriage away. The result is that the marriage rate plummets further and faster than anyone could ever have imagined. In some of those countries, traditional heterosexual marriage is fading away.

Eighty percent of the first-born children in one county in Finland are born out of wedlock. And that's a racially homogeneous country. It's also a small country with few of the social concerns of the United States.

In Europe, same-sex unions have been associated with a weakening of traditional marriage. With the advent of same-sex unions, parents in Sweden and Norway have increasingly given up on marriage altogether, no matter how many children they may have. And unfortunately, unmarried parents split up two to three times more often than married parents. In some parts of the country, two-thirds of all children and four-fifths of first-born children are born out of wedlock. At this pace, marriage may disappear.

The Netherlands provides an even clearer example of the negative effects of same-sex marriage. Dutch marriage was actually quite strong before the passage of registered partnerships in 1997 and formal same-sex marriage in 2000. But since that time out-of-wedlock childbirth has increased more sharply in that country than in any other western European nation. This means more instability for Dutch children, and a wide range of social problems.

Some African-American leaders have argued that homosexuality is not a civil right. Rev. Walter Fauntroy, a member of the Alliance for Marriage and a former aide to Dr. Martin Luther King Jr., has campaigned for a constitutional amendment to define marriage as the union of a man and a woman. And others, including Bishop Wellington Boone, Rev. Jesse Lee Peterson, Bishop Paul Morton of New Orleans, and Rev. Talbert Swan of Massachusetts, are among a growing number of African-American leaders speaking out about this issue, working to prevent promoters of same-sex marriage from hijacking the Civil Rights movement.

After considering all of these issues carefully, I got busy and worked with my colleagues to put together a constitutional amendment. We experienced great difficulty during the process. The other side would not debate with us on the merits. Instead, they would say we shouldn't be wasting our time on the issue. As we say in the Senate, they would just "vote no and go." They didn't say much about it, but they refused to debate us. They've tried to characterize it as a states' rights issue or have said that we shouldn't write discrimination into the Constitution. But the American people understand what's at stake with this issue.

A RACE AGAINST TIME

The definition of marriage in this country is still an important and ongoing debate, and the state courts have been energized on this issue. In the weeks and months surrounding the 2004 general election, fourteen states passed laws in support of traditional marriage, and by the 2006 midterm elections, twenty-six states had voted to incorporate language into their state constitutions affirming that marriage is the lawful union of a man and a woman.

We have a string of legislative precedents at the state level to protect traditional marriage. The state can do whatever the state wants to do, and those who disagree can take their complaints to the courts. But, in any case, the voters are letting their voices be heard.

Unlike the life debate, however, there's a generational divide on this issue.

The older generation supports the view that marriage is the union of a man and a woman. But it appears that the younger generation is much less committed to that view. A majority of college-age young adults have no problem with homosexual relationships, and many more are in favor of same-sex marriage.

A study by the Higher Education Research Institute at UCLA, which compiled results from 393 schools, found that 61 percent of incoming freshmen in 2006 agreed that same-sex couples should have the right to marry. This was 3.3 percent higher than the previous year.[4] The figure was 56 percent in 2000 and 50.9 percent in 1997. Clearly this number is on the rise among young people. A 2003 Gallup Poll reported that six out of ten Americans feel that same-sex relations between consenting adults should be legal. On the marriage question, the individuals surveyed by Gallup were about evenly divided. Clearly, we're in a race against time with this issue.

The challenge for our generation is to renew the institution of marriage. So many of our young people have grown up in broken homes. These young people are justifiably skeptical about the value of marriage in the first place. The fact that many young adults will never marry, preferring to live with someone for years without the benefit of marriage, tells us they're afraid of what they perceive as a traumatic and potentially harmful institution. This, in turn, leads to a general ambivalence about the issue of same-sex marriage.

Somehow we have to renew the sanctity of marriage. Marriage has been so weakened during the last forty years that it has been devalued as an institution. This is apparently true whether or not the person is religious. Some current research suggests that divorce among church members isn't noticeably different from divorce in any other segment of the population. I would say parenthetically that when the Lord took me through a period of sanctification, my own marriage became better—because then it wasn't only Mary and me working at the marriage. Our faith became engaged as well. God does love to give us joy!

COMMITTED RELATIONSHIPS

It's disconcerting that this generation of young people in the prime of life, when they should be finding their life partners and making plans for marriage and children, are often headed the other way. They have witnessed so much brokenness and difficulty that they're scared to consider a long-term commitment. In some cases their parents had such difficult relationships that they want nothing to do with marriage, and that's truly tragic.

My own experience has been that marriage brings out the best in each partner and gives them the freedom to grow and thrive as intended. Children bring new challenges along with new opportunities for growth. By every measure—statistically, historically, and morally—marriage is an essential building block of a healthy society, and for any society to function well, young men and women need to pursue and honor this essential institution.

Several of my young staff members in the Senate are either engaged or in the process of getting married, and they're going about it in a great way, by taking marriage training and counseling. One person told me that in one of the books they're working through, the author said, "Marriage isn't to make me happy. Marriage is to make me better." If what you're looking for in marriage is to find someone who can make you happy, you may be disappointed. But if you're willing to go into it with the idea that you've become a team and you're committed to living and working together, then it can be fantastic.

Money, health, career options, child rearing, and many other things will challenge you at various times. That's a tough standard, and five years down the road you can easily feel that this other person isn't making you happy. If you can go through the struggles and maintain your commitment to the other person, your strength will be multiplied immensely. Putting faith in the center of your marriage adds strength, durability, and joy as well.

We have so many people hurting in this country, and for many of them the source of their unhappiness is a difficult family situation. We need to emphasize family formation, and once we form families, we need to support them. They need to be growing in their love for each other and God. I believe that for our country right now, this is an area we really need to think about and talk to each other about much more.

In too many ways we've allowed, even encouraged, the decline of the family unit. We need to do more than say, "We're creating a new type of family." And we can't let the culture redefine the family for us, so that the family is any group of people who happen to live together. We need to look at what the studies are telling us. It's important that children be raised in a stable setting. It's very important for children, and it's also beneficial for the adults.

That's what all the studies are saying. Go to the social data. It says that kids from stable families are less likely to commit crimes. They do better in school. And it's a whole litany of things that we ought to understand better than we do now. Children can be raised well in single-parent households, but it is much more difficult.

THE BLESSING OF ADOPTION

There's another important aspect of family formation that I want to mention, and that's the blessing of adoption. Our family has been blessed by it, although there was a moment when our older children didn't see it that way. Mary and I had three children—Abby, Andy, and Elizabeth—when we decided to adopt Mark and Jenna. When we talked to the older children about the idea, they were initially opposed. They liked our family the way it was. That lasted about a day when we adopted Mark, who was the first one. They fell in love with him right away.

Actually, I would say that Mark and Jenna recentered our family. There are so many forces in society that are centrifugal, that tend to pull the family in different directions, but these two children have helped to restore our family focus. They're eight years younger than our oldest child, and they've pulled the older kids back, to the point that when our firstborn went off to college, she didn't want to go too far from home because she wanted to be close enough to see Mark and Jenna grow up. When our son Andy went off to school, he said much the same thing.

The second adoption was a little harder for them. I think they thought that four children was enough, and when we adopted Jenna in China, it was a bit of a load for them. Mark and Jenna are about the same age, so when they first came to live with us, it meant we had two two-year-olds at the same time—twins, in effect. And anybody who has raised a two-year-old can imagine what that was like.

I think I first saw the need for adoption when I began traveling in other countries. When I traveled in Azerbaijan, China, or Africa, I saw many orphaned children who needed a home. We estimated that there are twenty million AIDS orphans in Africa alone. There are thousands of orphaned girls in China. The situation is very serious in virtually every country I've visited. And many of the kids are in poor condition. We also have many children in America in foster care just waiting for a home.

When I looked at those beautiful, innocent faces, I said, "I can't do everything, but I can do something." Mary and I both felt a deep calling to adopt, and after we researched what was involved, we made arrangements to adopt Mark in Guatemala and Jenna in China. I highly recommend it to everybody interested. A child is a precious gift, and an adopted child is a gift to the entire family.

An Option That Works

The problem, however, is the expense of adopting. We need to do something to reduce the cost. Mary and I contribute to an adoption fund that has helped several families adopt. The up-front cost is so high that many families who would otherwise like to adopt simply can't do it. They can handle the day-to-day expenses of raising a child, but they can't come up with the twenty or thirty thousand dollars—or more sometimes—that it takes to begin the process.

Many organizations are involved in helping American parents adopt. They cover legal fees and adoption agency fees, which can be quite high. In the case of an overseas adoption, it can be even higher because of all the arrangements that have to be made through different governments and several different agencies. Every organization in the process has some fee or assessment. The cost can vary greatly, so anyone interested needs to do his homework and shop around.

When we adopted Jenna, I gained great respect for the women who refuse to have abortions. In China, with the one-child policy, coerced abortions and sterilizations continue to happen. We've held hearings on this, and it's a sad thing. I've often gone into Jenna's room at night, looked at her sleeping, and thanked God for the woman who fought the system to have her. It would have been much easier for that mother to have gone another way, to have taken the state-funded abortion, but she chose life for her child. I urge women who find themselves with a difficult situation to consider the route of adoption. I know there are mothers who find themselves in situations that would make raising a child very difficult, or they may fear that the child may have a physical or mental condition that they believe is beyond their ability to handle. But the worst decision would be to kill the child! Instead, how much better it would be to take the life-affirming step of having the child and then putting that little life up for adoption.

There are thousands of couples who are unable to have children of their own and are eager to adopt. There are waiting lists for handicapped children and Down syndrome children and other children with special needs. These are homes where the parents have been sensitized to these special little miracles of God, and they want to give them a loving home.

My wife is an active volunteer with the Building Families Foundation and helps with a fund to assist families with the up-front costs of adoption. It's one of the best things we've been associated with. I love hearing the stories from the families as they go through the process and bring home a child they have adopted. I know there will be problems in some cases. Raising a child is not sunshine and roses all the time. My experience has been that, first, you can do it. And, second, it's well worth the effort.

I remember when we picked up Mark in Guatemala. We met him at the airport with people from the orphanage. He looked at us and started crying, and we looked at him and started wondering, *What are we doing?* Then after flying back to Topeka, friends who met us at the airport were asking, "What on earth are you doing?"

We were in our forties when we adopted, and at one point a friend came up to me and said, "Sam, when you're having a midlife crisis, you buy a motorcycle. You don't adopt a child! You can always sell the motorcycle, but the kid is for life!" I understood the humor, but we were convinced it was the right thing for us. Despite a few misgivings at first, it has been an awesome experience for our entire family!

★ 8 ★

LIBERTY AND JUSTICE FOR ALL

To whom much is given, the Bible says, of them much is required (Luke 12:48). There is much required of us, and I'm convinced we can do it. I have seen this passion to make the world a better place among the young people of America wanting to help in Darfur, Sudan. I have seen this spirit in young people advocating for the release of child soldiers in northern Uganda. I've seen this spirit in the committed young men and women standing in front of the United States Supreme Court for more than two years now, praying for an end to abortion in America. I have seen it in our troops in Iraq and Afghanistan.

Life and liberty are central concerns for us. We're involved in a life-and-death struggle against terrorism. We're deeply engaged in bringing relief to those struggling under the thumb of oppressive regimes and circumstances of severe deprivation in Africa. And we're working in Congress to stop the trafficking of humans in many parts of the world—which is one of the most grotesque forms of slavery imaginable. There are still many problems to be solved, and I've already talked about several of them in this book. But I'm optimistic about the passion to do the right thing that I see in people all across America, and I'm encouraged by the essential goodness that continues to emerge in many places throughout this great land.

We've made progress in establishing a culture that respects the dignity of human life, but we have more work to do. I'm convinced that my generation will be judged by our success in the ongoing struggle for the dignity and worth of every individual. We must defend the weak and defenseless. We must reach out to the poor and dispossessed, offering hope without fostering dependency. We must never treat any person or any group as someone of less worth than another. And we can't afford to look the other way in the defense of life, whether it's here in our own neighborhoods or in some remote corner of the world.

PRESERVING CULTURAL FOUNDATIONS

Those of us who take the pro-life position need to understand that we are defenders of human life in all its forms and at all stages. The life of the unborn is a vital concern, but being pro-life doesn't end there. Our culture must be strong, but it also must be compassionate, and our character must be based on the pursuit of what is just and right for all our people. These are time-honored truths, but they're also part of the unending struggle for justice and righteousness that has challenged every great society.

In the aftermath of recent national disasters, we've seen both tragedy and hope. We've shared in the heartbreak of those whose lives were shattered, and we've witnessed the incredible bravery of those who rushed in to help without concern for their own safety. We've heard it all too often lately, but the expression, "Where do we get such people?" really expresses the sense of awe we feel when heroes emerge from our ranks. And we have many of them.

There is also another side to the drama, a side we were forced to acknowledge in the aftermath of Hurricane Katrina. As the storm waters subsided, the nation saw something in the faces of those living on the edges of society. We saw people who had been living for years in poverty. We saw many bound by chains that they couldn't break without help. We must help them. But we need to do it in ways that lead to self-sufficiency instead of dependency.

Ron Haskins, a scholar at the Brookings Institution in Washington, recently offered a practical assessment of what's needed in his testimony before a Senate committee. He said, "There are only two ways known to man and God to reduce poverty: number one is work, and number two is marriage." He also said, "If the single most potent antidote to poverty is work, marriage is not far behind."[1]

As I've said in previous chapters, the honorable institution of marriage is in sad shape in America today. The marriage rate has plunged 48 percent since 1970, and half of all new marriages end in divorce.[2] One result of the weakening of marriage is a rise in the poverty rate among single-parent families. Forty years after Senator Daniel Patrick Moynihan's famous warning about the emerging crisis in the family, the percentage of out-of-wedlock births is now approaching 40 percent of all births in this country. As Ron Haskins pointed out, statistics show that if we returned to the marriage rate of 1980, "we could reduce child poverty by almost 30 percent."[3]

Children of single mothers are five times more likely than other children to be poor, and nearly 80 percent of all children suffering long-term poverty come from broken or never-married families. Let me say clearly, you can raise good children in single-parent households, but it's much more difficult. Much of the crisis of poverty in this century is a crisis of marriage. Marriage has the effect of lifting children and their parents out of poverty. After the birth of a child out of wedlock, only 17 percent of poor mothers and children remain poor if the mother marries the child's father.[4] Not all people in this setting are able to get married, but clearly more could.

Stage one of the welfare reform package passed by Congress in 1996 was directed at eliminating the disincentives to work. By creating new incentives and giving those in poverty a new sense of worth, those reforms helped people transition from public assistance to gainful employment. By cutting the welfare roles in half, millions of men and women were able to participate in the "dignity of work."

Our job isn't finished. Stage two is to eliminate the disincentives to marriage that are still contained in some benefits programs. It's wrong to penalize women and their children for the mother's decision to get married. A compassionate nation will work to eliminate the disincentives that still exist in our laws, and compassionate people will work together to restore America's families. And that means restoring the institution of marriage as the backbone of the family and of this great nation.

FOUNDATIONAL TRUTHS

Alexis de Tocqueville's oft-cited, though most likely apocryphal, observation that a nation is great as long as it's good includes an implicit warning that if the nation ever loses its goodness it will inevitably lose its greatness. And that has happened throughout history. The cultural foundations of a society are fragile. History teaches us that a similar fate could befall us here as well. And it's not an idle fear.

At our best we have done truly great things, and at our worst we've done some very bad things. But thanks to the American spirit and the legacy of our forefathers and mothers, we still yearn for the good and strive to be a nation worthy of our high calling. We've shown that as a nation we're willing to change the wrong and do what's right.

I've seen the spirit of those who take part in public issues and contribute to charities and other important causes. Donations to relief efforts for the victims of Hurricane Katrina, the 9/11 families, and survivors of the tsunami in Indonesia rival the best that government can do. According to one report, private contributions to the Katrina relief effort totaled more than $4.2 billion. Obviously a lot of people want to help make things right. We want to see wrongs righted and problems solved. At the inner core of the American character, there's a heart that not only wants to do justice but knows righteousness. Righteousness is the plumb line, and justice is the level. Righteousness is the knowledge of the difference between good and evil, and justice is its application.

Bishop Harry Jackson, who is the pastor of Hope Christian Church in College Park, Maryland, and chairman of the High Impact Leadership Coalition, gave me something to think about in that regard. He said that Republicans get the righteousness idea better, knowing better the difference between right and wrong, good and evil, and that's important. But we're a little slow in the justice stuff, which is in its application. Democrats, on the other hand, have more trouble with righteousness. They don't want to think about right and wrong, good and evil. To them, it's difficult to discern. So everything moves to being an issue of justice. The problem is that righteousness and justice are inseparable in a healthy society. They travel together. Alone, they don't function properly. Righteousness is how we live before God, but justice serves and benefits others.

Righteousness without justice leads to being a hypocrite at best and a menace to society at worst. Justice without righteousness means there are no standards, just do what you want. A society loses all its bearings. Under that system, anything goes.

We'll be a great nation as long as we're good. If we ever lose our goodness, we'll soon lose the greatness. There's nothing to be ashamed of in standing up for what's right. I'm pro-life. There's no problem with standing up and saying not only that you're pro-life but also that it's the right thing to do. There's no problem with saying that this is a nation that has been blessed by God and that the words "In God we trust" are the motto of this land. There's nothing to be ashamed of when we invoke the blessings of heaven on our nation.

Some people may object to that, but I see no reason to hide from these fundamental truths. There's no honor in being noncommittal about what we know to be true and right. The national motto and the beliefs of the American people are woven into the fabric of our nation. Even if the fabric sometimes seems a bit tattered, it's still there.

WRITTEN ON THE HEART

The issues that are most challenging today are those that involve the law written on our hearts and how our society will deal with its most basic customs and beliefs. Think for example of marriage. We all know in our hearts that the best place to raise a child is in a home with a mom and a dad—a woman and a man, bonded together for life in marriage. The studies all point to the truth of that, but we don't need studies to understand it. We know it in our hearts. We do have normative agreement on such things, but sometimes we have to remind people and work from the basis of what we know by basic human reason to be true.

From the beginning of human civilization, the tradition of raising children in a two-parent home with a mother and father united in marriage has been the norm. Yet today some believe that we can simply rewrite these ancient laws of human nature. If we do so, we do it at our own peril.

One of the real culture warriors of the last century was Senator Daniel Patrick Moynihan, a Democrat from New York. He was a wonderful man who nearly lost his position in the Johnson administration for speaking out about cultural issues in this country. I was very interested in cultural issues, so I made an appointment to visit with Senator Moynihan and talk to him about it. I wanted to pitch the idea of organizing a bipartisan, bicameral commission to deal with cultural concerns. To some people that apparently sounded as though I was pushing for a "culture czar" or a "secretary of culture," and they didn't like that idea. But we had many cultural issues to discuss, and I felt they needed to be discussed in a bipartisan forum. So I approached Senator Moynihan about it.

He was in his last term in the Senate, but he was still quite active. He was from the old-school, liberal, Catholic tradition and understood the central importance of the family. I met him in his private quarters in the Senate. He had one of the best hideaways I've ever seen. Being a junior member of the Senate, I didn't have one at all, so I was impressed. During our time together, we talked about the cultural initiatives I had in mind. He said he supported my idea of a cultural commission, which encouraged me. But too many other people were against it, and ultimately the issue failed. In hindsight I can see why it failed, but it was a good idea that never gained much traction.

We were aiming at a way to deal more effectively with the problems that were showing up with greater frequency in the morning headlines, especially involving young people. The level of teen suicides was rising; we had kids killing kids in the schools; video games were becoming more and more violent; and children in this country were being raised by televisions and computers rather than by their parents. The breakdown of the family was in full swing, and it was high time we started doing something about it.

The collapse of the traditional culture was our main concern, and the loss of a moral standard was clearly one of the biggest problems we faced as a society. A few people, like Senator Moynihan, were saying that strong families are a key to stability and prosperity in society, and if we get that part right, we will be well situated for whatever happens in the future. But if we get that part wrong, then we're going to have even bigger problems in the future.

If the children are not properly educated in the values of the nation and the common culture, then they are vulnerable to being misinformed and misled.

We ought to be very concerned about what our children are being exposed to and why. We need to make sure that all Americans in every generation learn about the history and culture that has contributed to America's greatness. We all need to understand that without a personal commitment to goodness, no nation can long survive. And sometimes that means crossing fences and mending fences, to join hands with those whose view of the American experience may be vastly different from our own.

Mending Fences

For some Americans, the dream of a better life has been a struggle. This is particularly true for a group of people in my home state: the Native American population. As a congressman and as a senator, I've traveled to all parts of Kansas and tried to meet with as many groups as I could, in order to hear firsthand what they had to say. The Native Americans who live on tribal land have their own governments are part of this country, too, so I have made it a point to meet with them whenever possible.

The first few times I did this, I was surprised by the anger they expressed toward American society. The reaction was stronger in Kansas, I suspect, because of our history and the way the lands of Kansas and Nebraska were used by the federal government for relocation of the Indian tribes from other parts of the country. My visits to the tribes weren't always easy ones, and the conversations were often difficult. But I've learned a lot from them, and I think what I discovered tells of a need for reconciliation.

The Kansas Territory was the traditional home of the Kansa Indians. There were also Arapaho, Comanche, Kiowa, Osage, and Pawnee tribes in the area during the first half of the nineteenth century, and a half dozen other tribes were brought in and housed on government reservations. To entice these tribes to agree to the government's conditions without a struggle, they were offered treaties. In the first one, they were to be given the whole state of Kansas. Before long, however, the government decided that was too much, so in the second treaty the Indians were given a smaller portion of land, along with some livestock and equipment.

The third treaty was for even less land but more livestock and equipment. The policy, quite clearly, was designed to encourage the Indians to settle down and become farmers, but the promises made by the government continued to get smaller and smaller over time.

When I was brand-new in the Senate, I met with some of the tribes. I was elected for the entire state, so I went to the reservations, as well as Haskell University, which is one of only two universities for Native Americans in the country. When I met with the students there, some were obviously angry about something.

As I began digging into it, I could see that there was a deep root of bitterness in some of the students and tribal members. The broken treaties, the taking of the land, the bloody battles, and on and on, had left deep scars that needed addressing and healing. That prompted me to research the issue of reconciliation. I read John Dawson's book *Healing America's Wounds* and later talked with him about his research on reconciliation and healing with Native Americans. At that point I realized that none of our government programs were addressing the root problem. Money, assistance, education, and all those things were fine, but unless we could address that root issue, we were not going to heal the breach between Native Americans and the rest of society.

NATIVE AMERICAN CONCERNS

A minister from Colorado brought a group of five Native Americans to my office in Washington to talk about the need for reconciliation between Native Americans and the nation. One lady in particular impacted me when she talked about the bitterness that she held toward whites for taking away the Native American culture and their children, and for all the treaties that America had broken with her people.

She was a beautiful lady, yet the root of bitterness was deep and clearly painful for her. I couldn't help but feel sympathy and compassion for what they told me that day and decided I ought to help do something about it. If this woman, a Christian with a strong faith, felt such deep and powerful emotions about these issues, I had to wonder what kind of emotions other Native Americans must be feeling in dealing with their hurt and pain.

My staff and I took a look at this situation, and we began researching an official apology to Native Americans for the way they had been treated over the years. A major step was to find a cosponsor on the other side of the aisle, but when I learned of the failure of similar measures that had been considered in previous terms to formulate an apology to African-Americans for the institution of slavery, I began to wonder if a bill of this kind could ever pass the Senate. I began to wonder if I was going to run into the same thing with the bill aimed at reconciliation with Native Americans.

I sat on it for a while. One Sunday I was home in Topeka (the name Topeka, by the way, is an Indian name), and I had taken my children to a place where they liked to play—a place with a lot of history, built by the Baptists in the mid-1800s as a school for Native American children. As I sat in this park, I became strongly convinced that I ought to put this bill forward. When I got back to Washington, I spoke to Senator Inouye of Hawaii, at that time the ranking Democratic member of the Indian Affairs Committee, and he agreed to cosponsor the bill with me.

Senator Ben Nighthorse Campbell, from Colorado, was chairman of that committee, and I talked to him about the bill a number of times. Ben is a Native American, so he didn't feel he should be the one to introduce the bill, and I agreed. It could have appeared self-serving. I introduced the bill, and it was well received overall. We've put the bill forward a couple of times now, and it has made it out of committee, but it's being held up by some senators who aren't convinced yet of the need for it. So I know that more work is needed.

The point of the Native American Apology is to acknowledge that one of the key things we need to do is to reconcile. No matter how many millions of dollars you put into something, you must still deal with the heart. In the process of studying and researching this issue, I came to a much better understanding of the great need we have as Americans to reconcile among all of our citizens—between groups and individuals. Because of this, I often say, if you are at odds with someone today, go to him or her and resolve the issue that is at the heart of your dispute. It will be a gift you give to that person and to yourself!

RESPECT AND RECOGNITION

Through the years I've made it a priority to work on African-American issues as well. I helped propose and secure funding for the new National Museum of African American History and Culture in Washington, which I mentioned briefly earlier. I believe this will be a step in the process of reconciliation and healing between the races in America. When it's completed it will recognize the culture and the achievements of African-Americans. The elegant new National Museum of the American Indian in Washington, just a couple of blocks from the Capitol, serves a similar purpose—to encourage healing, understanding, and reconciliation, and to let it be known that all Americans deserve respect.

I'm convinced that one of the things we need to do to restore broken relationships is to face up to the wrongs we've committed and ask for forgiveness. That's the only way to move forward. I've had meetings with my colleagues to discuss their reservations concerning a formal apology to Native Americans. If we could get it to the floor for a vote, it would pass with a strong majority. But some people have said, "OK, I agree. Bad things were done, but they weren't done by me." Others have said, "OK, but what about all the pioneers who were killed by Indians?" So the controversy continues.

Think about it. If somebody has done something wrong, and he comes to you and says, "You know what? Ten years ago I did this thing, and I know it hurt you, and I want you to know that I'm sorry about that. I want to apologize to you," how would that make you feel? If you accept that apology, and you should, it may very well make you want to apologize for the bitterness and anger you've harbored over that incident.

Whether or not that's the case, that's how you start the process of reconciliation. One party has to start that ball rolling. Sure, it's a risk. You may not really trust the other person (or group of people) but you're willing to take the first step. Until you do that, there is little chance of healing those old wounds.

The Dawes Severalty Act, signed into law in 1887, required Native Americans to give up tribal lands in various parts of the country in exchange for individual land grants. The legislation was put forward by Senator Henry Dawes, with the hope that the bill would make it easier for Indians to enter the cultural mainstream. By helping establish farms and homesteads of their own, the act would make Indians part of the community and the economy. But in fact it reduced the amount of land owned by Native Americans even further, and made it easier for whites to settle on land that had once belonged to the tribes.

It's no wonder that acts of this kind by the Congress created hostility among the tribes in Kansas. We have conducted a congressional Civil Rights tour for groups of congressmen and senators to Selma, Alabama, and other places where the early struggles for racial equality took place. The organizers of the tour believe this is an important way to help legislators understand the depth of emotion and history involved in the Civil Rights movement. I think they're right, but I suspect we also need a congressional "Trail of Tears" tour to help us come to grips with the suffering of the Native American community and the contributions they've made to American culture.

QUESTIONABLE RESULTS

Undertaking this initiative has also built my relationship with Senator Campbell. There were many nights Ben and I would sit together in the Senate while bills were being considered. On one occasion I told him I was curious to know more about what's happening among the Native American communities. Along the way, he shared many stories about how and why the hostility has increased on the reservations toward the majority culture. Many of those stories were shocking, and some of them broke my heart.

The basis of the bitterness is impossible to deny. But I believe this is a problem that we can remedy. First, we have to admit that wrongs occurred. Not everything was bad, and Native Americans committed atrocities too. But federal laws and practices were put in place that caused great suffering by the Native population. We need to acknowledge the wrongs, and we need to apologize for them. For the good of the nation and for our own well-being, we need to say we're sorry for the wrongs that occurred and take steps toward restoring our relationships.

Some people have expressed their concern that an apology of this type is simply a first step toward reparations or some other welfare scheme. The bill

I've submitted specifies that the legislation does not address any property issues, property rights, or any other material concerns. The bill simply says that these things happened, they were wrong, and we apologize.

SETTING A HIGH STANDARD

As a final note on this area of concern and engagement, I think it's appropriate to mention the work of a woman who had a profound impact on Native Americans in Kansas and the Midwest, in a very meaningful way. Near where I grew up, in eastern Kansas, not far from Mound City, a woman named Rose Philippine Duchesne, who is one of only a handful of saints who have been canonized by the Catholic Church from this country, came to work among Native Americans for a year in 1841.

Mother Duchesne spent her entire adult life in Christian service, and she did many amazing things. She made what many people, myself included, would call her most lasting contribution among the Native Americans who came to Kansas on the "Trail of Tears." She ministered to many whose families and children had died along the way. She had made a vow when she was just a girl growing up in France that one day she would go to America to serve the Native Americans. The mission she started in Kansas was the fulfillment of that promise.

By the time she finally made it to Kansas, she was already seventy-two years old and had lived a very full life as a sister of the Society of the Sacred Heart. The other sisters wished her well when she set out for Indian territory. Mother Duchesne took a paddle wheeler up the Missouri River and arrived at Westport, Kansas, in 1840. From there she took a buckboard to Sugar Creek, where she began her work among the Potawatomi Indians, who had been resettled there.

Even though she never learned English and couldn't speak any of the Indian languages, she ministered to the Indians, and they came to love her, referring to her in their native tongue as "woman who prays always." Her custom was to spend hours in prayer day and night. The natives at Sugar Creek were deeply touched by the compassionate heart of this woman. The Indians would lay twigs or leaves on her dress at night to see if she moved during her all-night prayer time. They were surprised to see in the morning when they came back to check on her that nothing had been moved. She had prayed all night for them.

Mother Duchesne had said that God told her that her greatest work would be accomplished through failure, and in fact she felt she was a failure in the mission at Sugar Creek. After a period of time she returned to St. Charles, Missouri. She had a passion for teaching children on the frontier, and she set up schools in Missouri and Louisiana. There are still many schools named for her in those states. In many ways, the story of this woman who shared the gift of compassion and concern with the native people of our state reminds me of Mother Teresa.

Both women had been born into comfortable circumstances in Europe. They could have married and lived quite comfortably, but they chose to give their lives to God, to be a blessing to others who desperately needed their help. They did it as service to God and their genuine love and concern for their fellow humans. What a beautiful model of compassion, and what a high standard they set for the rest of us to aspire to.

CLEANING UP THE CULTURE

One of my first meetings when I entered the Senate in 1996 was with Bill Bennett, who had served as secretary of education in the Reagan administration and as drug czar in the first Bush administration. I had been an admirer of his work on cultural issues for a long time, and Jack Kemp and he had recently founded Empower America to work for economic and social reform. As far as operational politics, I viewed myself as a Kemp–Bennett Republican, pro-growth and pro-cultural renewal. Jack had the economic issues, and Bill had the family issues, and between those two, that was a key set of domestic agenda items for me.

Empower America had done some great work on cultural issues such as song lyrics and the impact of popular culture on young people. Bill Bennett was dealing with that from a conservative perspective, which was not so much legislative as talking to the culture and saying, "Look what we're doing."

This all tied into what the late Democratic Senator Daniel Patrick Moynihan had been talking about for some time. He captured it in one of his books when he said that the central conservative truth is that it is culture, not politics, that determines the success of a society. The central liberal truth, he said, was that politics can change a culture and save it from itself. He was right. What you honor and dishonor as a culture is very important, and government does help shape the culture.

Bill Bennett was a leading culture critic at the time. I wanted to get his counsel on what we could do and what he thought were successful strategies to address cultural issues. That started me on the track of looking into the effect on our young people of hateful, sexually graphic rock and rap lyrics. I was ready to go after the piece of the entertainment industry that used these harmful approaches. One tool we had available was that the entertainment and media giants that used public airwaves had agreed in their licenses to use them in the public interest and for the public good. The airwaves are public property just as the national parks are. The license to use the airwaves is extremely valuable, but one of the conditions for obtaining a license is recognition that overtly sexual or violent material is not for the public good, and violation of those community standards could lead to fines or even forfeiture of the license.

We started going after the industry, at first trying the route of shame. What could we do that would shame this industry into doing the right thing? We held hearings initially with the recording industry regarding the lyrics they were using, and the lyrics were vile. If I had said any of those words in public, I would have been drummed out of the Senate in a heartbeat. But instead, the words were being target marketed to our kids. I thought it was crazy. They were words that are vulgar and offensive by any measure and could not be spoken in polite company, but the recording industry was pouring millions of dollars into advertising campaigns to mainline that stuff into impressionable young minds. How could this be?

This industry said, "Oh, these words have no impact. People don't listen to the words of this music. All we're doing is reflecting the culture; we're not making culture," all of which was clearly false. Why would they be spending millions of dollars in advertising if they didn't think they were shaping minds and buying habits of teenagers? Obviously they were having an impact. And as far as not hearing the words, if you listen to a piece of music hundreds of times—and that's not unrealistic—after a while you pick up the words pretty well, even if you don't hear them in the beginning.

OBSTINATE RESISTANCE

I remember the time Hillary Rosen came in to testify on behalf of the Recording Industry Association of America (RIAA). She's now a Democratic consultant, but at that time she was defending the use of these lyrics as free speech and saying they had no impact. I handed her the lyrics to a set of current top songs. They were all hit songs at the top of the charts, and I said, "I'd like for you to read these lyrics for me." She refused to do it. I said, "Ms. Rosen, these are top songs. They're sponsored by the companies you represent. So why won't you read them?" And she said she wasn't willing to do that.

I said, "You mean, you will target these lyrics to our teenagers but you won't say them here in a Senate hearing?" and she refused to even answer the question. She knew where she was, and she knew she couldn't say those words that denigrated women and talked about rape and murder and the most evil things imaginable. She wouldn't do it, but my point came through loud and clear, not only to her but to the men and women in that hearing, and even to the mass media who were following the hearing.

I began traveling to Hollywood and New York early in my years in the Senate to meet with entertainment industry executives. I would take lyrics of the most popular songs along with me. I took them into meetings with the presidents of the companies and asked, "Do you let your children listen to these songs?" Many of them said they didn't. So I asked, "If you won't let your own kids listen to this stuff, how can you justify marketing it to everybody else's kids, all across America?"

Sometimes they would go back to the free speech argument, but at the end of the day they would suggest something like this: "Look, my duty as CEO of this company is to maximize profits for our stockholders. I don't like all that we present, and I don't let my own kids watch [or listen to] it. But my job is to maximize profits for my shareholders, and this stuff sells."

At that point I began thinking, *OK, how do we change their shareholders? Or how do we get the artists to think about the impact of what they're selling?* I went to some of the artists, and they would say that this is artistic liberty and we're just reflecting the interests of our fans. Then I went to the writers, and surprisingly they were the most introspective of their responsibility of the whole group. In many cases they would say, "You know, I don't like this trash either. We know it's not imaginative. We could do much better, but we can't sell it, and the producers keep asking for edgier stuff. This is what I have to do."

In the end it was all very unsatisfactory. The public knows that the culture is coarsening, and they generally reacted to all this, but I could see that we needed to be able to prove cause and effect. We had to be able to show that the coarsening of the culture was having a detrimental effect on the health and well-being of our children.

We had literally hundreds of psychological studies proving that if you watch violent, vulgar, sexually explicit entertainment, you're more likely to be violent and vulgar and engage in earlier sexual activity. Psychologists on the other side would say, "Those are just behavioral studies, and correlation does not prove causation." I would come back to the question, "Then why do people advertise?" Again, they would throw up smoke screens and try to deflect the logic of our arguments.

Everyone knew what was going on. The public knew it, and the industry was profiting from the violent, sexual material they were producing. We finally came up with two approaches that worked. One was getting the Federal Trade Commission to conduct a study as to whether or not the entertainment industry was target marketing children with products they had rated as inappropriate for children of that age. In other words, were PG-13 movies being target marketed to ten-year-old boys? Or were violent video games rated "M" for "mature" being marketed to teenage boys?

Taking Positive Steps

We commissioned and required the FTC to report to Congress annually on whether or not this was taking place. This was built off the "Joe Camel" model, where the tobacco industry was target marketing kids with products that were inappropriate for minors. We went that route, and they found that it was true. The companies had been doing focus groups with ten-year-old boys on R-rated movies. And the movie industry had been advertising in teen magazines for R-rated movies.[1]

The industry knows its business very well. They know exactly where to advertise to get people to watch their productions. They were doing it, and we finally shined a light on it. We held a big hearing in the Commerce Committee, and a number of top executives from the entertainment industry came forward, and they had to admit, "Yes, we do this. But, no, we won't do it in the future." There has been some marketing change as a result.

The next big step came with the Janet Jackson episode in the 2004 Super Bowl, when the singer exposed herself during the MTV-sponsored halftime entertainment. I had been pushing the Federal Communications Committee (FCC) for some time to go after companies that use the public airwaves for broadcasting violent and overtly sexual material in violation of their license. The FCC had been hesitant to do anything, because it's difficult to prove that public standards have been violated. The industry doesn't like the idea of regulation, and it was presented as prudish to try to punish producers for using these images. After all, community standards are always changing, they said, and it's too subjective on our part to keep insisting on restrictions. They resisted us every step of the way.

Then Janet Jackson's halftime episode at the Super Bowl galvanized the public reaction, and everything changed after that. People were saying, "Look. This is a family event. It's supposed to be wholesome and safe for adults and children. Parents don't want to have to guard their children's eyes from obscene material while they're watching the Super Bowl." Before long the overwhelmingly negative public reaction created such an uproar that the industry had to respond. That was the galvanizing event that brought the first real changes.

Out of that episode we were able to get a tenfold increase in the fines for companies that violate standards of decency over the public airwaves. It took two years to get it, but a number of companies have been penalized. Even the so-called "shock jock" Howard Stern left the public airwaves and went to subscription-based satellite radio. We started getting serious about enforcing those standards.

Another big event that helped bring about change was the tragedy at Columbine High School in Colorado in 1999, when two teenage boys went on a wild shooting rampage, killing twelve fellow students and one teacher, and wounding two dozen others before committing suicide. Unfortunately, the phenomenon of horrific violence in our schools has not gone away since then, evidenced by the tragic events at Virginia Tech University in April 2007, which claimed thirty-two innocent lives.

DESENSITIVITY TRAINING

In the aftermath of Columbine, it was discovered that the two boys, Eric Harris and Dylan Klebold, had spent months training for that day with video games. Some of the men and women who testified before our subcommittee told us that the games the two boys had used were similar to training films employed by the military to train soldiers to kill the enemy. It depersonalizes the enemy and desensitizes players to the act of killing.

Particularly in World War I, the military had a hard time getting young recruits to pull the trigger and kill enemy soldiers. One of the experts who testified in the subcommittee told us that in the first year of the war, approximately 83 percent of the shots fired by American soldiers missed the target. This, he said, was primarily because our soldiers were reluctant to shoot to kill. It may have been a German soldier on the other side, but he was still a human being. You don't win wars by missing, so the military set out to train our soldiers to shoot better and hit the target more often. They did that by using techniques that desensitized them to the humanity of the enemy. This went on for more than forty years, and by the Vietnam War the percentage of rounds fired that actually hit the target went up to 60 percent or higher.

Now, obviously, the accuracy of the weapon was much higher as well. In war we want our weapons to be effective in stopping the enemy. The video games that Harris and Klebold used to desensitize and practice did the same things, so they were able to go into Columbine High School and mow down their classmates without hesitation or remorse. Games like that are still being sold to teenagers all over the country today. The video games did not make them want to kill their classmates—that was already in their heads—but it likely helped train their actions, and allowed them to repeatedly visualize the atrocities.

This is still an ongoing struggle, I'm sorry to say, but we're now getting information from brain-mapping studies that tell us what parts of the brain are being stimulated by violent entertainment. It turns out that these images are stored in parts of the brain where instinctive reactions are located. For example, most of us remember exactly where we were when the planes struck the Twin Towers on 9/11. Those of us who are old enough also remember exactly where we were when we first heard the news that John Kennedy had been shot. Those thoughts are stored in a particular part of the brain, and that's the part that's activated when a child watches violent material on television or in a video game. This is the "fight-or-flight" area, an area of long-term storage of data regarding the intuitive response reaction.[2]

This means that the connection between physical violence, increased and earlier sexual activity, and the fight-or-flight reaction are being stimulated by images created by the entertainment industry for profit. Now we have situations where a kid who has been playing violent video games goes out to the playground and sees something that stimulates that part of the brain. Instinctively, he reacts in a violent way. He isn't processing information in a rational manner; his emotions and cognition aren't fully developed, and his instincts tell him to react. Consequently, his behavior may be wildly inappropriate to the actual provocation. This doesn't happen to all children, but it does happen to some.

Over a long period of time, these things can change the culture in very disturbing ways. The cultural atmosphere is all around us, like the air we breathe. If the air is polluted, people are going to get sick. The younger the person taking in the pollution, the more vulnerable he or she is going to be. There's no doubt that the cultural atmosphere is troubling. It is clearly too sexual and too violent. It's going to take a major effort by all of us to clean it up.

PORNOGRAPHY AND OBSCENITY

All of this ties in very closely with the epidemic of pornography in contemporary culture. On one occasion I attended a Promise Keepers rally in Kansas City. Promise Keepers was a great way of getting men back to their families. People have questioned the movement, but it instilled in men from all walks of life the central importance of being a good husband and a good father. What really got my attention was that at least half of the men who were in attendance at that

Promise Keepers rally held up their hands and confessed that they had a problem with pornography. I was astounded.

I thought, *These are guys who are committed in their faith and serious enough about it that they're willing to come here and spend a couple of days listening to speakers talk about the issues that will affect their lives. They want to be better husbands and dads. But at least half admit to having problems with pornography! How can this be?*

The problem of pornography addiction is not a small one, in large part because pornography is a multibillion-dollar industry that is fiercely defended by all sorts of associations and business interests. As long as they can cast it as a "free speech" issue, lawyers have been able to protect their turf through the courts. When it can be shown that this is really an issue of community standards, it's a different story. Communities have the constitutional ability to limit the pornography sold in their communities. This is the place to start.

COURAGE TO SAY NO

The Supreme Court has ruled that pornography is a protected form of expression, but cities like Cincinnati, Ohio, have been able to go after smut merchants and prosecute them on the grounds that they're violating community standards. That's what we have to do. We have to go after pornography at the local level. We need active local groups to take up the fight to drive pornography out of town.

We brought in some of the people from Cincinnati and other places that had been successful in stopping the pornography incursion. They met with members of the Values Action Team (VAT), which I chair in the Senate. They explained how they've been effective. One of the most important observations was that you need lawyers who know how to prepare the cases. These community groups hired lawyers with experience in pornography cases, because they know how to counter the defense tactics of the other side.

We also need prosecutors at the local level who know how to prosecute the cases. I met with Attorney General Alberto Gonzales, and he wanted to take this issue on as a Department of Justice initiative. He has appointed a national task force to look into it in greater depth. There are also books on the subject that are helping to wake people up to what's really going on.

This is an issue of human dignity. It has become a human tragedy because of its impact on families—divorces, individuals whose lives have been shattered by it, and thousands if not millions of men who can't free themselves from the addiction. It's targeted and pernicious. It's well known that with any illicit drug, the user has to have more and more to get the same level of euphoria, and pornography is the same.

Hard-core users keep going further and further into the abyss in search of gratification, and the Internet is custom-made to deliver it in ever more intensified doses. Whatever it is you're looking for, and however disgusting it may be to anyone else, it's there, and it's easy to find. But it's dangerous and very expensive, and it takes more and more each time to feed the craving. Which is one of the best reasons I can think of for activists to get involved.

The pornography industry has had an extraordinarily dark and negative impact on families and the culture as a whole. Obscenity is still against the law on a community standard basis. This is why we have to appeal to community standards to win these cases in the courts. We need more communities to step up and do it. Some are. In Abilene, Kansas, the citizens shut down a XXX-rated video and bookstore on Interstate 70. And in Cincinnati, Ohio, the effort to keep pornographers out of the city is effective and ongoing.

In some places citizens have come together to put up large billboards along the highway near adult bookstores. These signs are intended to remind people what's really at stake when pornography seeps into the community. I recently saw a billboard in Kansas City that said, "Pornography Destroys Families." That's certainly a true statement, and the men and women paying for that sign out of their own pockets care enough for others to say so in a clear way. They're simply using their free speech rights to point out the dangers and to remind the people who patronize those places what they're doing.

In other places citizens have purchased signs near strip clubs with a more religious message. One sign in Texas quotes a Bible verse: "The wages of sin is death.—Romans 6:23 [NIV]." These are just some of the ways that people have responded; there must be hundreds more. My own experience has been that if you can get ten people locally who will become active on an issue like this, they can change the community. The key is finding people who have the moral courage and enough concern to stand up and act.

★ PART TWO ★

AT HOME AND ABROAD

☆ 10 ☆

ENDING EXPLOITATION

The head of International Justice Mission (IJM), Gary Haugen, came to see me in the late 1990s to familiarize my staff and me with his organization and what was happening regarding sex trafficking and the exploitation of women and children in this country and abroad. When he came in, Gary had a padlock with him. It was an old, rusty lock that looked as if it had been made in the fifties. He handed it to me and said, "We took this lock off of a door in a brothel in India, and behind it was a young girl, no more than eleven years old, who had been taken out of Nepal and trafficked into India as a child prostitute."

That poor child was in despair, Gary told me. She had no hope, and if she didn't perform for her clients, she was beaten. She knew that escape was not only impossible but it would do no good. If she went back home to Nepal, she would be an outcast and would likely face even worse treatment there. Chances are she had already contracted TB and AIDS and one or more sexually transmitted diseases.

Gary and his colleagues at IJM set up a raid with the reluctant help of the local police, and they busted the brothel and shut it down. Gary and his coworkers then took the girl to a safe place where she described the nightmare she had endured. She was regularly beaten and abused by her clients. By any measure, her life was a living hell. That story and the other information that

Gary shared with me that day was one of my early introductions to the horrors of sex trafficking and the work of courageous groups like IJM to stop it.

Hearing about that situation once again reminded me how important it is that we do whatever we can to stop exploitation in any form. At the time of Gary's visit, I had daughters just a few years older than that little girl, and the thought of what had been done to that poor child from Nepal made me angry. My first inclination was to simply discount what Gary told me. I thought, *OK, this is one of those big stories we're often told in Washington. We're a long way from that here. It's graphic, but it's probably not as bad as all that. And I'm sure it's very rare.* Actually, I didn't want Gary's story to be true. But as I began looking into it after that meeting, I discovered the exploding sex trafficking business—a sick underside of the increase in global travel and economy.

In the weeks following that first conversation with Gary, I met with Holly Burkhalter, who was U.S. Policy Director of the advocacy group Physicians for Human Rights. She told me about the current research on the routes used by traffickers and the huge number of people involved. Generally, she said, the women who are snatched from their homes are trafficked from poor countries to richer countries. Organized crime is very much involved.

Her organization, working with local law enforcement, had determined that trafficking is one of the largest sources of income for organized crime in the world. Through our investigations and subsequent testimony in the Senate, we found that it's the third leading source of income for organized crime, behind drugs and gun running. It's the fastest growing of the three, a product that criminals can sell repeatedly by moving their victims from one brothel to the next, and highly profitable.

GETTING THE FACTS

I was in research mode on the sex trafficking issue for several months, and fortunately I had a staff member who cared deeply about the issue and helped me accumulate a lot of important information. At that time I also met with Kevin Bales, who wrote the book *Disposable People: New Slavery in the Global Economy*. He told me that the modern slave trade is larger than the African slave trade at its height. Even worse, today's slaves are considered disposable and easily replaced.

That ten-year-old-girl from Nepal has no value after she contracts AIDS or some other serious disease. When she's used up, her captors just throw her out into the street and leave her there to die. There's an almost unlimited supply of women and children to replace her—thus, the title of his book, *Disposable People*. I was truly shocked by what I read in that book, and I asked Kevin Bales to testify before our committee. I know now that trafficking in humans is a ghastly global epidemic.

Researchers tell us there are more than 27 million slaves in the world today. That's nearly ten times the population of my home state of Kansas, more than the combined populations of the states of New York, Massachusetts, and Rhode Island, and more than the combined population of the countries of Australia and New Zealand. Through his research, Dr. Bales documented sex trafficking in South America and India, with victims being imported into the United States. It's a pernicious, ugly, and apparently very profitable form of human bondage. It's critically important that we do something to stop it.[1]

As this issue was beginning to stir public concern, the government produced a number of studies on trafficking, and one of those showed that at that time as many as fifty thousand people were trafficked into this country each year. And millions more are being trafficked internationally. The problem is very real and very disturbing, and when I saw the information, I knew I needed to get involved. About the same time, Senator Paul Wellstone's wife, Sheila, mentioned that she had been noticing something very unusual in Minnesota where they lived. She said there was a growing number of Ukrainian women showing up at the shelters for battered women, looking for help.

When she spoke to some of the women, she discovered that they had been brought to this country by trickery. They were promised jobs as nannies or domestic workers, but when they arrived, they were forced into prostitution. Sheila told her husband what she was seeing, and they discovered a systematic pattern of trafficking and slavery in that area. Subsequently, he put forward a bill in the Senate in 1998 to halt sex trafficking in this country. The next year, Paul and I put together a bipartisan bill to stop trafficking. The bill would create a special department to monitor kidnapping, hostage taking, smuggling of aliens for prostitution, forced labor, and the enforcement measures for stopping the illegal immigration that supports trafficking. Before long a broad-based coalition was coming together from both the Left and the Right.

There's also an important historical connection that ought to be mentioned. After the Berlin Wall fell in 1989–1990, there was a sudden loosening of national boundaries. It was as if a signal went off around the world that people were free to move from one place to another and cross borders. This meant, in turn, that traffickers could begin expanding their operations into previously unknown markets. The Left began seeing the problem at women's shelters. The Right was hearing about it from groups like IJM and other Christian organizations that were going abroad to combat illegal prostitution. So we were picking this up and coming together from all sides.

Consequently, I believe that the steps we've taken to stop sex trafficking in this country, as well as the actions we've taken to try and stop it abroad are some of the most important pieces of legislation I've been involved in during my service in the Congress. With the help of people who were outraged by what they were seeing, we were able to put together a remarkable coalition. If you can imagine it, we had people such as the head of Prison Fellowship, Chuck Colson, working together with feminist activist Gloria Steinem to pass this legislation. So this was definitely a broad coalition of people from both sides of the political spectrum who were ready to do something about the problem.

Changing the Laws

There were times when the Left wanted to include provisions in the legislation that we couldn't agree with, and there were times when we would put forth a counterproposal that they couldn't agree with. But because both sides cared deeply about this issue, we reached a point where they were willing to compromise with us on certain issues, and we agreed to leave off things that the other side wouldn't support. We came up with a bill that rated countries on their effectiveness in combating trafficking. It had a spotlight, it had funding, and it had law enforcement associated with it.

This was toward the end of the Clinton administration, at a time when typically very little legislation gets through. It wasn't a very bipartisan time, but this bill moved because people instinctively understood the evils of human slavery and sex trafficking. And when they saw that both Chuck Colson and Gloria Steinem were behind it, they understood that this was a revolutionary opportunity. It was through this action that the Department of Justice set up the Involuntary Servitude and Human Trafficking Initiatives.

As we were getting these measures through Congress, I began traveling to different places around the world and meeting with groups that work with women who have been trafficked. I met with them in Nepal and on the Thai-Burmese border. I met with them in Israel and the United States, and I have to say that during my travels I've seen some of the most ghastly things you can imagine.

The experience that was most disturbing to me was in Katmandu, Nepal, in a women's shelter for those who had been trafficked and who had returned from brothels in India. The woman who took me around pointed out the girls, many of them no more than fourteen or fifteen years of age and in the prime of their youth. They had been trafficked and used up. They were coming home to die.

The folks in this shelter were caring for those young women and giving them the respect they deserved but had never experienced. As my guide took me around, she would point to one person and say, "That girl has AIDS. She's dying." And she would point to another and say, "This one has AIDS and tuberculosis, and she's dying." Over and over, as we walked from one place to the next, she was saying, "Dying, dying, dying." It was heartbreaking.

They were all beautiful young girls and it was hard to imagine that any of them were under a sentence of death. I bought some gifts in the little shop they ran to help support their work, and there were tears in my eyes as I walked out. I thought, *How can people do this to other people? How can humanity allow such evil things to happen?*

I met with the prime minister of Nepal in early 2001, and he was very noncommittal. "Yes," he said, "I see what you're saying, Senator. I know this is a problem, but it's just one of the hundreds of problems that I have to deal with in my country." And this was the same response I got wherever I went in South Asia. Of the one hundred most important issues they were dealing with, this one ranked about ninety-nine.

Even though the leaders I spoke to didn't say any of this in so many words, the language they used and their gestures told me that this was exactly what was going on. It was as if they were saying, "Sure, we know all about it, but there's nothing to be done. So why are American officials coming over here and causing so much trouble? This is really none of your business." I traveled there to let them know that it was very much my business—and everyone's business—when human dignity was violated, and human lives were being destroyed in such hideous ways.

A Global Epidemic

When I was on the Thai-Burmese border, I met with some of the Karen people who had been run out of Burma and were forming settlements on the Thai border. What was happening was so ugly. I was told that the hotels in that region have pictures of girls for their guests to look through, so they can choose the ones they want for sex. Some of the pictures are marked "virgin" or "very young" or some other feature. So when the client picks one of those girls, the hotel sends out a runner on a motorbike to find that girl in the village and bring her back.

The horror is that in most cases these were simply young girls in poor families, still living with their parents, struggling to survive. This is just one example of the horrors the Karen people are living with, day in and day out. These are historically Christian people who have been run out of Burma, which is run by a repressive Communist regime. The Thai government tolerates them, but nobody is providing support or protection for them. They're truly a people without a country.

What typically happens anywhere in the world when you have a group of people in that condition—such as the North Koreans in China or the Karen people in Thailand—is that they are victimized by the local inhabitants, and they become subject to predators on the fringes of society. That's what was happening in those places. In some cases the Karen girls would be taken to Bangkok and sold to brothels.

I met with a Christian group in Bangkok whose mission was to rescue these girls and try to restore them and, if possible, to return them to their families.

While I was there, some of the girls sang a song for us, and it was very moving. I asked the administrator what they were saying, and she told me the song says, "You can sell my body, but you can't sell my soul." It was beautiful, but it was also tragic, and all the more so because so many of them were so terribly abused at such a tender age.

A few years later, in 2003, I was on a trip to Israel and met a group of older women who had been trafficked. The U.S. Embassy had helped fund a group of women who were returning from being trafficked. I hadn't visited the country specifically to meet with them, but when I heard that the women were there, I asked to meet with them. In one of the places where they were living, I met with a group of fifteen to twenty women from the former Soviet Union. They were all between eighteen and thirty years of age, and they had been tricked into going to Israel as domestic workers.

They came from Uzbekistan, Kazakhstan, Ukraine, and other former satellite countries, and they understood that they were going to be smuggled into Israel illegally. But the criminals who were running this operation had told them they would be paid four or five times more money than they had been earning in their home countries. The women thought this would be their chance to break out of the difficult and often dead-end situations they were in and begin a new life in another country. But that's not at all what happened. They were beaten, stripped of their passports, and sold into sexual slavery.

They told stories of being sold from one brothel to the next. As I looked around the room, full of women who all shared similarly terrifying stories, I saw faces that were vacant of emotion. For the most part, they had lost hope— their souls were so damaged that life had been stripped of all meaning for them. When I had seen those young girls in South Asia, defeated and dying, I thought that was tragic. But here I was seeing older women who had endured much the same torture, and I realized it was tragic for them as well.

THE SCOPE OF THE PROBLEM

Trafficking and sexual slavery are still an enormous problem, although more and more nations beginning to deal with it. Unfortunately, it's a growth industry among the criminal element that feeds on poor and vulnerable peoples. It's a modern form of the slave trade that's still growing, and it has many tentacles. But at least we're beginning to deal with it on an international basis.

Until I got involved in this issue, I had never associated this kind of trafficking with what's happening in North Korea. I knew that men in North Korea were being trafficked for their work value, but I learned that an even greater problem is the number of women from North Korea who are being trafficked and sold into slavery.

There's a direct link between human trafficking and the so-called "sex tours" in which foreigners and even some Americans are taking charter flights to parts of Asia to see. This involves the sexual exploitation of both boys and girls who have been taken and used in this way. It involves fake "mail-order brides" who are bought and sold as sex objects and, in many cases, as sex slaves. There are people who've tried to defend this practice, saying that there's a long-standing historical basis for arranging brides from other countries. We're trying to limit the practice now, particularly as we've found evidence that some of the male clients have been ordering three or four brides a year.

I also worked with Senator Maria Cantwell, a Democratic senator from Washington state, on a case where a mail-order bride had been beaten and killed. We invited a couple of women who had been mail-order brides to come in and testify for a committee hearing, and we discovered that most of these women are abused in very disturbing ways. Yet the practice is still going on, and there doesn't seem to be any lack of women who are willing to take the risk.

I asked one of these women why they would do this, and she said that for her it was the money. She had been told that she would have a much better life in America and that the economic opportunities here were so much better than in her native country. Another woman said, "Well, you know American men still have a good reputation in my country." That was a sad and ironic commentary, since we were holding hearings about how badly the women had been treated in this country.

And worse yet, we're hearing reports of the involvement of the pornography industry in the exploitation of women who have been trafficked in this way.

Now it's going global, so it's happening in places where there's not much supervision. Since it's getting harder to traffic women into the United States for sexual exploitation, these unscrupulous filmmakers are now working in Third World countries in Africa, South America, and certain former Soviet republics, where they can make arrangements with thugs—sometimes with the local police or even with government cooperation—to provide the women. And the filmmakers don't have to get involved in trafficking at all. The corruption takes place and the pornographers get what they want, and when they're done with the women, they toss them out in the street.

COALITION BUILDING

The good news is that this issue is helping us to build a Left-Right coalition to fight for stronger laws and better enforcement, here and abroad. The Left increasingly and certainly the Right see that pornography takes a very dark view of women, treating them as sexual property, and a libertarian view of such things can only lead to even greater tragedies and worse forms of exploitation

We began running across this when we held hearings on the impact of pornography across the United States. Several witnesses told us that pornography is the most addictive substance in America today. It's pervasive, it's targeted, and it's very difficult to escape. If a man gets hooked on drugs or alcohol, we can put him into treatment—there are programs to help him dry out. But with pornography, it's very hard to get it out of his mind. Once the images are in there, they won't come out. They're seared into his memory, and those who become addicted will have cravings that are insatiable.

When you realize that there are probably millions of otherwise moral, law-abiding men who are addicted to pornography in some form, you know how insidious it really is. I've heard many sad stories from family men and even pastors about their struggles with pornography addiction.

There's no telling how much money is made each year through pornography, because much of it is either disguised by the pornography industry as something else, or it's simply not reported. The profits are in the tens of billions of dollars worldwide, and it involves magazines, books, films, the Internet, adult bookstores, gentlemen's clubs, brothels, and just about every kind of media or communication you can imagine. Slavery and prostitution may be the dark side of the sex industry, but they're no longer rare, and the impact they're having on our society is dangerous and growing.

According to the most recent reports that I've seen, the sex industry in this country generates more than 12 billion dollars per year, which is more than the total income from professional football, baseball, and basketball combined. By some accounts, the global tally is at least five times that high. It's estimated that fully a fourth of all search engine requests on the Internet are pornography-related, and 12 percent of all Web sites on the Internet are pornographic. Even worse, there are a hundred thousand Web sites on the Internet that include child pornography, and they generate more than three billion dollars in illicit profits each year. These are alarming numbers, and they're part of the reason why both the Left and the Right are beginning to work together for changes in the laws that regulate such things.[2]

In 2005 a young woman named Pamela Paul testified before our committee. She wrote the book *Pornified: How Pornography Is Transforming Our Lives, Our Relationships, and Our Families*, published by Times Books, one of the *New York Times* companies, and she told us about her research on the impact of pornography on society. She said she had interviewed a number of pornography addicts, and many spoke to her about pornography's negative impact on their marriages, their work, and their lives.

EXPRESSING OUR CONCERN

Parents are justifiably concerned for children who are exposed to the worst kinds of pornography on the Internet, and there's almost no way to prevent them from stumbling onto these Web sites by accident. Children are naturally curious about sex, and they're mesmerized by these images when they come across them. Most of them have never seen or imagined such things, so they're led innocently enough further and further into it. A predictable percentage of these kids will find ways to sneak around, to explore these Web sites. Boys are especially vulnerable to this kind of seduction.[3]

It's important that we find ways to block these images so that children aren't exposed to salacious material in this way. It's just as important that we counsel our kids if we find that they've been exposed to it. We want to help them understand that these images are unhealthy and unnatural. Pornography exploits both women and men in the most vulgar ways. It treats them as meat, to be bought and sold and manipulated. That in itself is offensive.

It's almost impossible to keep our children from running into pornography on the Internet these days. Some media networks on television play on these types of images. They call it "pushing the envelope" of entertainment, but it's little more than rank sexual exploitation, and I'm afraid it's destroying the minds and souls of many, particularly the young.

11

A LIGHT IN AFRICA

Early in my first term in the Senate, a staff member told me something that initially I didn't believe. She said, "People are still being sold as slaves in Africa. It's happening in the Sudan." That got my attention. Slavery, as I've said repeatedly, is horrific. The battle to stop slavery in this country escalated in "Bleeding Kansas" and in the struggles of abolitionists like John Brown during the pre–Civil War era.

Abolitionist history is important to me, so when the subject of slavery came to my attention in 1997, I was a bit skeptical. But I thought, *If this is true, it's bad, and we must do something about it.* That's when I started digging into the topic. One of the first things I did was to meet with John Eibner of Christian Solidarity International. He was well informed on what was happening in southern Sudan, and I wanted to get more information on this topic from someone who had seen it with his own eyes.

During that meeting Dr. Eibner gave me names, dates, and places. He told me his main mission at that point was to raise money to buy Sudanese slaves out of slavery. He was going around the United States and Europe, raising money, and I thought, *I'm finding this hard to believe—that slavery still exists in this day and time.* But my colleague from northern Virginia, Congressman Frank Wolf, who has been a leading light in the House of Representatives, had been involved with this issue for years. He had traveled to Sudan and was very aware of the tragedy that was taking place there. I talked with Frank about it, and he assured me that the situation in Sudan and other parts of Africa was every bit as bad as John Eibner and my staff had told me.

I arranged to meet with some Sudanese refugees in this country, and they confirmed that slavery was taking place and also that there was an ongoing genocide against the Christian and animist minority in southern Sudan. The present government in Khartoum was supported at its beginning by Osama bin Laden and established a radical Islamic state in Sudan. The government was paying marauders with the bounty they took to go through southern Sudan, burning villages, killing the men, raping and beating the women, and then taking the youngest and healthiest women and children as slaves.

I met with Akot Arec, a Sudanese man, in my home state. He had been one of the "Lost Boys" of Sudan. At one time this group of boys and young men, displaced by the ravages of war, ballooned to about forty thousand people. They wandered through southern Sudan for months, fleeing from marauders whose mission was to track them down and kill them. Eventually the boys were intercepted by government forces while they were trying to flee across the border into Ethiopia, and thousands of them were mowed down by machine gunners.

Akot tells the story of running across hundreds of dead bodies and through rivers of blood as he was escaping. Of the forty thousand who began that desperate journey, fewer than four hundred made it to safety. Eventually Akot was able to come to America where he started an organization called JumpStart Sudan, to get the word out about what's happening over there and to raise money for hospitals and food and shelter for displaced Sudanese refugees.

TAKING ACTION

That was my introduction to Sudan, which later led to my work in Darfur. I knew then that I needed to be involved. I led a delegation of Congressmen and staff and private citizens to see with our own eyes what was happening. We flew into Kenya and chartered a private plane to fly to the town of Yei, in southern Sudan, about thirty miles north of the border. Yei was the regional headquarters for the Sudan People's Liberation Army.

John Garang, the leader of the rebel forces in the south, met us in Nairobi, Kenya, before we went into Sudan. He was a giant of a man, both in spirit and in physical presence, and I developed a great admiration for him. We were led into Sudan by Daniel Eiffe, a former priest who was there as a representative of Norwegian People's Aid. He was a short, rotund, pugnacious Irishman, who reminded me of Spencer Tracy playing the role of Father Flanagan in the movie *Boy's Town*. Daniel was straight out of central casting.

He was one of the organizers for assistance to the south. This was one of the only trips I've made in an official capacity where the U.S. government didn't send any sort of military or diplomatic attaché to travel with us. Maybe, since our visit was unauthorized, they didn't want to risk it. They always sent at least one aide, but this time we were on our own.

We flew into Yei. I'll never forget our landing in that dusty town. It was a short, sandy runway, not far from a big hill. Our small plane stirred up the sand as we touched down. As soon as the pilot stopped and we left the plane, someone grabbed our bags from the cargo bay and handed them to us; then the bush pilot gave us a quick wave and taxied down the runway, heading back to his base in Kenya. This was such a rough area, the pilot didn't want his plane sitting on the runway where soldiers from the north could slip in and take potshots at it. And he didn't want it bombed from the air, either.

The government forces had old Russian cargo planes, and when they wanted to terrorize towns and villages in the south, and especially the rebel camps, they would fly over and shove bombs out the cargo doors. It was unsophisticated and imprecise, but the attacks were meant to strike fear into the hearts of the people, and they did that very well. It also kept many communities from reuniting and resuming their normal lives in the south.

THE LIGHT OF COMPASSION

One of our most striking meetings was in Yei. We were walking down the dirt road that was the main street of town. The bombers hadn't flown over for a couple of days, so the people were coming out of their homes and gathering in the streets, and quite a little crowd gathered when we arrived. One of the men who spoke a little English looked at me and said, "You must help us. What do you want us to do? Do you want us all to become Muslims?"

The look in his eyes was a mixture of fear, exasperation, and anger. He was obviously sick of what was happening to the people of that region, and since we were Westerners who had access to outside resources, this was his chance to make a loud, passionate plea for help. These desperate people were doing all they could to survive under terrible conditions and with endless attacks from the north. The government in Khartoum had been built in many ways by Osama bin Laden. His minions were intent on either destroying or enslaving any people who resisted their decrees and their interpretation of Islam, even if they were fellow Muslims!

Of course, we didn't want anybody to be forced into anything. Yet the people in Yei felt that the West wasn't doing enough to help. We saw something else in Yei that I will never forget. We were in the middle of a dusty desert town; we'd been dropped off by our pilot, and we didn't know when the next bombing raid would be coming.

The only way the people of Yei could escape the attacks by the cargo bombers was to crawl into old bomb craters and pits in the ground. When the bombs hit, they spread shrapnel in all directions. If the people hear the planes coming and crawl into one of those craters below ground level quickly enough, the shrapnel won't get them. Of course, if it was a direct hit, there was no escape. But usually they would be safe as long as they were below ground level.

As we were coming into the camp, I noticed a young, blonde-haired, blue-eyed woman working with a group of Sudanese women. She was moving through the camp without assistance or armed guards of any kind, trying to provide a little help and relief to the village. She worked for Catholic World Relief. It was astonishing to think that she was there, working selflessly and tirelessly, and loving these people who were in such incredible danger. Her faith was a beautiful testimony to the Sudanese, and to us as well.

This was something I had seen in other places. Whether it was World Vision or another nongovernmental organization or faith-based group, there were people in many places in Africa working tirelessly and selflessly to serve people who were struggling on the sheer edge of annihilation. Not all of them were there with religious organizations, but they were people who felt compassion for the suffering and wounded people of Africa, and they were doing whatever they could to help. I say, God bless them all.

When we returned to the United States, I knew we had to do something to stop the slave trade in Sudan. I told my family about what we had seen, and they were moved and disturbed by it. My daughter, Elizabeth, who was in the fourth grade at the time, told her friends at school about what she had learned. They raised about two hundred dollars to send to John Eibner at Christian Solidarity International, to help free the slaves.

A school in Aurora, Colorado, initiated a nationwide movement of kids raising money to buy the freedom of slaves. In Congress, the three of us who had taken that exploratory trip to Sudan, along with Congressman Wolf and others who had investigated this issue, worked together to pass the Sudan Peace Act. The legislation was an effort of carrots and sticks to push the Sudanese government to stop attacking that region of the country. It created a special emissary from the United States to Sudan, to try to negotiate peace between the north and the south and bring an end to the civil war that had been going on for more than twenty years.

The Value of Intervention

The entire issue captured me. It seemed impossible that something so ugly could still be going on in the world, but it was going on, and I wanted to do whatever I could to stop it. So I continued to read, learn, and speak to people with inside knowledge. The Sudan Peace Act was passed by Congress, signed into law by President Bush, and Senator John Danforth was named Special Envoy to Sudan in a ceremony in the White House Rose Garden on September 6, 2001.

The administration got behind this endeavor, and their efforts led to an agreement that is helping to reestablish communities in southern Sudan and is bringing peace. In addition, the region has been given the right of self-determination, and the new peace agreement brokered by the United States allows the people of the south to decide whether or not to secede from the government in Khartoum. That vote will take place in 2011, and most people anticipate that they will vote for independence, but much could change between now and then.

The good news is that the fighting has been reduced, and much of the slave trade has been ended in the south. There are still skirmishes here and there, and we still hear of incidents where people have been captured and traded, but it is nowhere near the scale of a few years ago. In the meantime, there are still many private relief organizations at work in the region, trying to restore order and render humanitarian aid. More help for reconstruction of the war-torn, ravaged south of Sudan is desperately needed.

Not long after my trip to the region, I attended an event at the National Prayer Breakfast hosted by syndicated columnist Cal Thomas. While I was there I was introduced to Martha Williamson, the producer of the *Touched by an Angel* television series. In a subsequent conversation with her, I pitched her the idea of doing an episode on the problems in Sudan to help bring greater awareness to the situation. And she did.

The series of connections, which led to a program on national television that in turn brought needed attention to this issue, emphasized to me once again our responsibility to help those in need. The program, first aired on September 26, 1999, and was about a U.S. senator who learned about the slavery in Africa. The people around her were saying, "Look, if you expect to get reelected, that's not the way to do it." So for a while she tries to focus on other issues, and she talks in the Senate about the need for higher wheat prices. But in the back of her mind she knows that slavery is still going on in Africa, and nobody's talking about it.

For a while she continues with business as usual. She tries to focus on what her aides and supporters are telling her. Her colleagues are saying, "You know, you're a rising star around here, and you can really go places if you stay on track." All the while, her conscience is eating away at her, until she finally realizes she has to say something about what's happening in Sudan. Even though it will upset an economic interest, importing goods from Sudan, she decides to speak up about the slavery and genocide, and she calls for government intervention.

At one point we see kids holding a carnival, raising money to free the slaves, and my daughter Elizabeth had a small part in that segment, which she enjoyed. At the end of the program, we see people released from captivity and returned to their villages. The program ends on a high note, but it leaves the viewer with the understanding that this is still a very real problem, and it's not over yet.

That was the premier episode of the 1999 season, and it created quite a stir, because quite a few people knew that the factual basis of the story was true. For the first time, many Americans understood that people were still being bought and sold in that part of the world and that it was up to us to speak out and do whatever we could to stop it.

A Constituency for Africa

The Sudan Peace Act was signed into law, there's been a peace agreement between the north and the south the past several years, and some communities are being reestablished in the south. Unfortunately, the same government in Khartoum has now moved the fighting to the Darfur region in the west, along the border with Chad. There are new initiatives in Congress and the Administration to address this problem.

The government in Khartoum is corrupt. They continue doing bad things, waging now a second genocide, this one in Darfur. This cannot be allowed to continue. My partner in the Senate on Darfur has been John Corzine, the Democratic senator from New Jersey, who left for the Senate to become governor of that state. Frank Wolf, the Republican congressman from Virginia who has spearheaded efforts in the House of Representatives, has been a key player from the start, along with Congressman Donald Payne of New Jersey. I'm happy to say this is another bipartisan effort with broad-based support on both sides of the aisle.

Senator Corzine was a former chairman of the global investment company, Goldman-Sachs. I know he had empathy for the suffering in that part of the world, and that's why he decided to take an active interest in stopping the genocide. It was not politically expedient, and there was no cachet in international humanitarian actions in Africa. Those of us who became involved in this issue did so because we cared deeply and personally about it.

Madeline Albright was secretary of state in the Clinton administration at that time, and I know she was tremendously moved by the genocide in Rwanda.

She was emotionally pulled to take some action to end that terrible tragedy, but ultimately the view that won out was that there was no constituency for Africa in this country. There simply weren't enough Americans, they believed, who knew or cared about the problems in sub-Saharan Africa to make it a policy initiative. I don't think the Clinton administration felt they could sell the idea to the public, so they left it alone. But that was a mistake.

I saw this firsthand in the town of Smith Center, Kansas, in the very middle of the United States. You can't get more "heart of America" than Smith Center, Kansas, which is about four miles from the precise geographic center of the bottom forty-eight states. I was holding a town hall meeting there, and I doubt if there were more than forty people in attendance. At one point a lady said, "Senator, I want to know what you're doing about Sudan."

When I first came into the Senate, I had been told that foreign-policy questions were a political death knell. You weren't supposed to talk about foreign policy, because constituents only wanted to hear about what was happening at home. But here was a woman in Smith Center, Kansas, who was asking me about Sudan, and I began seeing this more and more, particularly from Christians who were learning about the problems from Christian radio. This told me that there is a constituency for Africa.

MAKING IT PERSONAL

When Madeline Albright left office, she remained personally involved in these issues. Since that time we have met on several occasions to talk about helping others in tough situations around the world. We've recently been working on plans for a familiarization tour to Africa to introduce a group of civic and business leaders to the problems there. As principal of the Albright Group and chair of the National Democratic Institute for International Affairs, the former secretary of state is using her influence to bring about change in that troubled part of the world.

The battle that is taking place now in Darfur is being waged by the Janjiweed, a militia of nomadic Arabs who are attacking the mostly African Muslim farmers of that region. The Arabs are armed by the Islamic government in

Khartoum. They've been raiding villages and carrying out terrible atrocities.

The first briefing I had on this new outbreak of violence was shocking. It was early in the genocide in Darfur, and we met in a small, hard-to-find room in the Capitol. Once again, Frank Wolf had told me I needed to look into what was happening there, so I asked for a briefing, and State Department officials attended the briefing and showed satellite pictures. It was shocking to see village after village after village systematically burned and destroyed. The briefers told me that the raiders were moving through the region, burning the villages and destroying everything in their path.

Andrew Natsios, the head of the Agency for International Development (USAID), led the briefing. He told us that what we were seeing was mass systematic destruction on an almost unprecedented scale. It was clearly an organized burning and pillaging of hundreds of villages throughout the region.

After that meeting, Frank Wolf and I traveled to Darfur again to see for ourselves what could be done. Before we left I approached Tom Brokaw of *NBC News,* who served at that time on the board of the International Rescue Committee. I asked him if we were able to film what we saw, would he put it on the nightly news. This would be the first time, that we knew of, for film footage to be taken of the Darfur genocide. Brokaw didn't promise he would use our film on the news, but he did say that they would take a look at it. He also said that NBC would provide us with high-quality, lightweight equipment so we could get good footage. We saw tragedy after tragedy, and it was a gut-wrenching experience for every one of us. NBC did use a portion of that film on the network news.

They interviewed me, and during my interview they used clips of the Janjiweed and the burned-out villages. The name Janjiweed literally means "man on horseback with a gun." These men would come in on horses and camels, guns blazing. They were accompanied by government helicopters that would bomb the villages, killing or wounding people indiscriminately.

At that point, the helicopter pilots would land, and soldiers would run out and scoop up all the plunder they could find in the village and load it on the helicopters, or trucks, if they had them. If anyone was still alive in the village, they would often kill the men and rape the women. It was brutal. This went on for weeks on end in Darfur. Congressman Wolf and I photographed many villages, interviewed refugees, many of whom had been raped, and we were stunned by the inhumanity.

IMAGES OF DESPAIR

This is harsh country in the best of times. It's dry and very rough, and when the soldiers set fire to a village, it was absolutely certain that a lot of people were going to die—and they did. Frank and I visited the refugee camps. They were full of women and children. There were very few men left alive. The kids we saw were simply amazing—they were happy in spite of all the tragedy they had seen and lived through.

The children sang and danced, grabbed our hands, and wanted to hold on to us. There were hundreds of them, and when I looked at their smiling faces, I thought, *You don't realize how bad you've got it, do you?* They taught me to always rejoice, even in the face of great trials and trauma. I thought of the words of Jesus. He taught that we must come to Him as little children, hopeful and expectant, in order to be accepted into His kingdom. These beautiful children were joyful and hopeful in the moment, not worried about the future!

We also met women in the refugee camps who told us horrible stories of the rapes they had endured. Even while we were there, we could see some of the Janjiweed stalking the outside perimeters of the camps, just waiting for an opportunity to strike again. The women had to go outside the camps to gather wood to build a fire for the evening meal. Humanitarian aid workers from the United States and other places had given them food and oil, but they needed to cook it, and when you have forty thousand people in a small area, they go through firewood very quickly. The women had to walk miles to gather enough wood to cook the meal, and if the Janjiweed caught them out there alone, they would be raped. The men in the camps couldn't gather the wood, because they would have been killed if they went beyond the perimeters.

Those images have stayed with me. Many times when I went into my own backyard to gather branches fallen from our trees, I would think, *Those poor Sudanese women would give anything to be able to gather sticks like this.* You can't come back from a trip like that, regardless how much or how little you may have, without realizing how much we have relative to the suffering people in Africa.

Once you see it, you realize you've got to do something. This is why I encourage people to take impact trips to those places. You can take a cruise or ski trip, and a fleeting memory will remain with you. An impact trip to Kigali, Rwanda, will change your life forever. It will give you a profound sense of need and immediacy. You will also discover that you can do something to help. There are groups that help drill water wells. There are groups of doctors, nurses, and engineers who go as volunteers for a week or a month to heal wounds, perform surgery, and build buildings.

A HOPE FOR CHANGE

On the trip to Darfur, we chartered a plane with two South African pilots to fly us into the region. Congressman Wolf was going to stay a day longer, and I was going on ahead to the airport at Khartoum. When the plane landed, a group of about fifty local leaders had gathered to meet us. They formed a long reception line on the gravel runway. It was customary for visitors to walk down the line and greet each person.

When the door opened, a staff member from the USAID office stuck his head in the door and said, "If you're planning on leaving Darfur, you had better stay on the plane and leave now, because a *haboob* is coming in. You must leave now." I didn't know what a *haboob* was, but I was soon to find out more than I wanted to know.

We were able to greet some of the people on the ground, but then I got back in the plane and told the pilots, "If you guys don't think it's safe to fly, don't go. I don't have to get back to Khartoum today." I had flown in small planes all over Kansas, and I learned one thing: don't mess with the weather. If it doesn't look good, don't go. It's much better to wait.

The pilots looked at the sky and they said, "No, we think it's OK. We can fly." But I repeated to them, "I need to catch the plane in Khartoum, but if you don't think it's safe, don't go. We'll figure something out." No sooner had I said those words than the *haboob* hit. I discovered that a *haboob* is a sand and gravel storm, mixed with a thunderstorm, that hits you like a blow dryer on steroids.

When we got out of the plane, we could smell the rain in the air, but we were being pelted by sand and gravel. The energy of the raindrops hitting the ground lifts the sand and dust, and then the strong winds coming out of the storm blow the dirt and grit ahead of the storm. It can be quite dangerous.

The pilots thought we could wait it out, but the storm wasn't slowing. We entered the little three-story building that served as a control tower. The men inside checked the weather and said they thought it was going to remain stormy for several hours. I should explain that they were using equipment left behind by the British in the 1950s, which didn't seem to be much better than looking out the window and then calling another airport thirty miles away and asking, "How's the weather over there?"

We were convinced it wasn't going to get better right away, so we stayed the night. I was very grateful to sleep on a cot that evening. They told us this was a common occurrence in that part of the world. I saw a striking photograph not long ago of a *haboob* hitting one of the refugee camps. The photo showed an ominous black cloud hitting a camp that was little more than a collection of tiny huts made of cloth and sticks. It looked miserable.

And that was on top of everything else these poor people had to endure! Death by dysentery is common. Sanitation is nonexistent. The situation is still very bad, but people in America and other places are getting involved, and there's increasing pressure on the Sudanese government to change their deadly policies. There's at least a hope of meaningful change.

ARMED BARBARIANS

I've been to Africa four times over the last five years, to many different places. I was in Kenya, Congo, and Rwanda in 2005, traveling with Senator Dick Durbin of Illinois. At the time we cochaired the International Conservation Caucus, another bipartisan effort through which we're trying to get more conservation work going in Africa.

A local terrorist organization known as the Lord's Resistance Army (LRA) has been operating in northern Uganda for at least two decades. Uganda and Congo are right next to each other on the southern border of Sudan, and there's a lot of traffic between those countries. The Sudanese government didn't like the fact that Uganda had been supporting the Sudan People's Liberation Army (SPLA) with weapons and supplies in the south. So the government in Khartoum sponsored the LRA and sent them to terrorize the Ugandans.

This is not unusual for radical Islamic regimes. They fund terrorists to do what they want, and they've got deniability, so when they're challenged by America or the UN or some other group, they can say, "No, this isn't our militia. This is just a bunch of rebels." When there is a deadly militia like the LRA, headed by a cultish figure such as Joseph Kony, death, despair, and destruction occur on a massive scale.

The LRA has uprooted more than two million people in northern Uganda. One of their tactics is to raid homes and villages and steal the children. They make the girls into concubines and the boys into child soldiers. They force the boys to kill or be killed. If any child hesitates to carry out even the most savage order, they're shot or beaten or in some cases killed on the spot.

As a result, these children become brutal, ruthless killers without a conscience. And believe me, a twelve-year-old child with an AK-47 combat weapon is a very dangerous thing. There's very little rational thinking taking place at that age in that situation. They're highly volatile and reactionary, without a very clear concept of death or of the nature of pain. Their ability to inflict harm is terrifying.

Joseph Kony is a military leader who claims a dark spiritual mantle. He is feared for his military strength and his tactic of stealing children, but also for his reputation of legendary proportions as a darkly directed person. I've interviewed kids who his group has taken and have escaped, including one young man at a World Vision camp in Gulu, Uganda.

When I first saw this boy, he was wearing a University of North Carolina jersey. He had been captured at age ten, had somehow managed to escape a couple of years later, and was staying at the World Vision camp. When we talked, he wouldn't look me in the eyes because of the guilt and shame he felt for what he had been forced to do by the LRA. He said he had killed his own aunt as well as others. He was being rehabilitated by workers at the camp.

Hopefully, he will improve and be able to live a somewhat normal life but this boy will have a lot to overcome.

I left wondering what we could possibly do to help. The answer was to get the word out and let people know what's happening. I've learned that the American people are incredibly resourceful and inventive when presented with a problem. They always find ways to help. For example, there are nineteen- and twenty-year-old college students who have taken up the cause of the abduction of children in northern Uganda. They're raising money and awareness using the Internet.

A Practical Idealism

The challenge is formidable. One of Joseph Kony's tactics is to send gangs of raiders into rural homes at night to steal children. Many parents will send their children into a nearby town at sundown to sleep under a store awning where they will be safer. Groups of kids make this "night commute" of as many as five miles into town to spend the night and then return to their farms in the morning. This goes on night after night. It's a very harsh existence.

I'm pleased to report that there are people who care very much about the conditions these young people are living under. They want to do something about it. A beautiful expression of this is the work being done by a group of young Americans who became aware of the situation in northern Uganda. They saw what was happening, they knew it was wrong, and they decided to get involved and help draw attention to it. They set up their own relief effort and a Web site to get others involved.

First, they went to Uganda and filmed the night commute. They went with the kids when they left their homes before sundown, and they walked with them to a nearby town. They developed a deep affection for these young Africans, and when they arrived back home, the young Americans put together a compelling documentary called *The Invisible Children*. It was available for screening in schools and small groups and is now on the Internet. These young people are making a difference by simply caring for these abused children and drawing attention to what's going on.

The Invisible Children is a great documentary, and the response has led to a movement of young people all across the country who want to be a part of solving this problem for the children in northern Uganda. To help people understand what it's like to leave your home and walk for miles into town, and then spend the night on the ground, a "night commute" was organized in 159 cities all across America. People commuted to downtown areas and spent the night in parking garages, parks, and other places, to gain some personal understanding of what the children in Uganda suffer.

When students at Washburn University in Topeka organized one of these events, I joined them, walked the two miles in driving rain, and talked to some of the young people about why they were there. One young woman told me some friends had told her about the video. She watched it online, and she knew then that she had to do something. So she got involved.

These young people had never met anyone from northern Uganda, but they saw what was happening to the children and knew it was wrong. They knew it was unfair, and they wanted to do something to make it better. It was idealistic, but it was also practical. I see that a lot in this young generation. They're focusing on doing good things, and I'm convinced that will help to preserve and strengthen the goodness of this country.

Constructive Engagement

The college students who put together the documentary on the night commute wanted the world to know about the dangers the children in this part of the world are living with every day. The film immediately developed a following, and college students all over the country became interested in doing something to help. This is great, because it tells me that there's a level of compassion and activism on our high school and college campuses that we haven't seen for a long time. These young people want to do something real, even in places as remote and unforgiving as northern Uganda.

I applaud them for their willingness to get involved, and my hope is that we can harvest this moment and get more of our young people involved in these sorts of issues. I would love to see groups of students go in and work with the young people in northern Uganda. Yes, there's some danger involved, but the need is so great!

Too many young people have come to the conclusion that there's nothing much to believe in. Consequently, many young people are desperate for meaning in their lives. It is my prayer that more young people will get involved in these causes, helping people who are struggling in life-and-death situations. As I've said from the first, I'm bullish on this young generation. We have to be wise enough to help them find the right places to become engaged. Then, with God's help, they will change the world.

There are other people in Uganda who are trying to help in practical ways. I met a Dutch man with a small ministry in Gulu, for example, who bought a couple of acres near the town. He fenced it in and built a number of little sheds with concrete floors. Every night hundreds of kids who had made the night commute came there to sleep. The children were given water to drink and a burlap bag to sleep on, and some of the local adults read Bible stories to them before bedtime. They did this every night. These critical situations with such dramatic human needs require many creative solutions.

It sometimes feels as if we're in a swamp full of alligators, fighting our way out with a ball bat, just swinging as hard as we can all day long. I think it would serve us well to take some time each day to pause and lift our eyes up and think about what a blessed nation we have. What an incredible time this is in our nation's history! We have so much to be thankful for; we are a prosperous and successful nation. We have unlimited potential, but sometimes we just need to look up and recognize the incredible opportunity we have to make a real difference in the world for others.

12

CROSSING THE AISLE

The Democratic Republic of Congo is a neighbor of Sudan and another deeply troubled nation in that region of Africa. In 2005, Senator Dick Durbin and I took a trip into eastern Congo. It was a difficult trip. Along with North Korea and Darfur, Congo is probably one of the worst places to live on the face of the earth. Madeline Albright and I held a conference at Georgetown University, called "What You Can Do," encouraging students to make a difference in the world. During that event we came up with a list of the five worst places to wake up in the morning, and Congo was near the top of the list, well deserving of the distinction.

According to estimates I've seen, a thousand people die every day in the Congo from preventable diseases. There is no health care for most, and there's constant conflict between rival gangs. We flew into a refugee camp in eastern Congo, and we could see that the entire infrastructure had been blown apart. This despite the fact that the largest United Nations peacekeeping force in the world is operating in the region.

The peacekeepers are doing a good job of regaining some stability, but the place needs much more help. They need people to come in and help with the basics of food, water, health care, and education. Part of the problem is that there are other people who are profiting from the lack of stability in the country. There's an abundance of gold, copper, and other metals in the area, including coltan, which is a substance used in cell phones. Coltan is an abbreviated form of the name columbite-tantalite, an ore made up of niobium and tantalum. There are many coltan mines in the eastern regions of Congo. So there's no lack of natural resources, but there is terrible instability, and predators are everywhere.

There are a few serious mining operations, but there are also people who come in and mine these raw materials without paying the appropriate concessions to the government. The Chinese are especially complicit in this. I've heard stories that I have not been able to verify, of men coming out of the Congo with sacks of coltan ore on their backs. They take it to a central collection point where they receive a fee, and the ore is shipped to China.

INSTITUTIONAL CORRUPTION

On one of our travels in eastern Congo, we came to a camp where the authorities had recovered two gorillas taken by poachers. The Congo is an area where the mountain gorillas popularized by anthropologist Dian Fossey are found today. It's an endangered species, so the scientists at the encampment were careful about letting us get too close, because they didn't know what diseases we might carry and give to the gorillas. In this case they were able to stop the poachers and take back the animals, which were being transported to a private zoo in the Middle East. The poachers could fetch as much as fifty thousand dollars apiece for the gorillas.

Think of the provocation this sort of corruption offers for the poor people of that region. They can sell a gorilla to a trader for five thousand dollars, and that's a huge amount of money for them. Somebody on the other end is making forty-five thousand. Too much wildlife is being captured or killed, and the entire region is being robbed of its possessions.

The region needs our attention. It needs outside groups to come in and make the proper investments to stimulate legitimate commerce. They need at least rudimentary health care, water wells, schools, and the other essentials of life. Later on our trip, Senator Durbin and I met with Paul Kagame, the president of Rwanda, because we wanted to find out what it would take to restore stability in the region. At one point we asked him, "We've invested billions of dollars in Africa over the years. So why aren't things better than they are?"

We had seen the United Nations studies that showed things were no better and, in some nations, worse than they were twenty years ago in many parts of sub-Saharan Africa. Obviously one issue is the AIDS epidemic. Malaria is another problem. But there are also huge problems with incompetence and corruption. We asked the obvious question, "Where has all the money gone?"

President Kagame said, "Yes, that's an excellent question, and I would also like to know the answer to that. Many of the leaders of these countries would ask you the same thing. Where is all the money?"

The *New York Times* published a feature story around the same time about the money that had been poured into Malawi. Millions of dollars had been spent in Malawi, and the people were still in deep poverty and dependency. It reminded me of the welfare program in this country before Congress passed measures in 1996 to reform the system. We feel badly about a problem, we want to end suffering and hunger, so we throw money at it with a poorly designed program, and the problem only gets worse.

We did that in Africa. As a nation, the American people were horrified by the images of pain and suffering we saw on the evening news. For a time it seemed we couldn't turn around without seeing pictures of starving children and mothers with vacant eyes. People all across the continent of Africa were looking to the rich nations of the world for answers. We poured billions of dollars in aid into those countries—and nothing changed. The people were still desperate.

Here we are, decades later, and many Africans are in the same conditions or worse. When I left, I thought, *We've got to come up with a different model. The people of the United States are willing to help those in poverty in Africa. In the heart of America, people want to help. But what will we do?*

MEASURING PROGRESS

There was no doubt in my mind that we ought to help, but nobody wants to be throwing money down a rat hole or stuffing it into a dictator's pocket. We've done that, so our model has to be different. I thought, *Maybe we need to be looking at what people like Rick Warren are doing over there.* Warren, who wrote the best seller *The Purpose-Driven Life*, is raising and giving money to support faith-based groups and other nongovernmental organizations (NGOs) working in Africa, to help them pursue specific and measurable objectives.

Until now, government has apparently been content to supply cash to Third World countries with little accountability. This new model is much more targeted and has an accountability structure. I think this is a much better approach than the model that government has used in the past.

When we were in the Congo, our in-country hosts showed us the list of USAID projects. It was pages long, and it was soup-to-nuts and everything in between. I could imagine all the money being spent on those programs, knowing that little of it was going to alleviate the underlying problems. When we returned to Congress, I began working on a bill that said we would do four things with half of the American aid money to the region. We want to do them well. Those four things would include clean water, food and agriculture, medicine, and education. We would use half of our foreign-assistance money in Africa for these initiatives, but it would have to be used either for buying products or training the local people to do it. We can train local teachers or local well drillers, or we can supply them with low-cost water drilling equipment. We would require that anyone we supported in that way would have to pay us back in practical ways, such as drilling a specific number of wells at our request.

The idea was to make sure that these new programs were targeted, measurable, and that they would help develop the nation. This is what we did with the malaria program in Africa. According to the most recent estimates, more than a million children die from malaria each year—more than die from AIDS and cancer combined. Every thirty seconds an African child dies of malaria.[1] When we looked into how the money was being spent in the existing malaria programs, we found that 90 percent of the money was going for conferences and consultants. The African leaders I met told me, "We don't need any more conferences and consultants. We know what to do. What we need now is money for bed nets, drugs, and insecticides."

We heard that message loud and clear, so we're starting to get that one turned around.

THE CONGO PARADOX

The Congo is a perfect example of the problems faced in Africa. The Congo is one of the richest countries in the world in terms of natural resources; but greed, corruption, incompetence, and violence have reduced the people in that region to subsistence levels and below. When traveling in the Congo, it's impossible not to think of Joseph Conrad's *Heart of Darkness,* which was written about that place. The nonfiction book *King Leopold's Ghost* by Adam Hochschild, which came out in 1998, describes in painful detail the rape and pillage of the Congo by the Portuguese, French, Belgians, and other Westerners for more than two hundred years. It's a terrible legacy that has left the nation in desperate straits.

Having said that, and despite all the tragedy and hopelessness we've seen, I'm genuinely hopeful and optimistic about Africa. It's the Congo paradox. It's truly desperate, but I believe we're going to see amazing changes happening on the continent of Africa in the coming decade. We're seeing a new focus from the West that we haven't seen for a long time. We're also seeing the private sector engaging in this focus in a big and practical way, with people like Bono, the popular lead singer of U2, who is being very thoughtful and deliberate in the way he's going about getting involved; and the founder of Microsoft, Bill Gates, with his wife, Melinda.

In all the places I've traveled to in the world, where there's poverty, war, and unrest, there are groups from the West—many of them faith-based organizations —and they're working to make things better. More are coming, and many more small or new organizations would come if they could find the specific projects where their expertise is needed. That's why I'm encouraging USAID to help pinpoint the projects that NGOs and faith-based groups in this country can sponsor.

I've suggested that the government create a Web site detailing the various projects in Africa and other parts of the world where responsible organizations can get involved. They could say: Here's a list of 150 places and projects where we have contact with local participants. These are all programs that we've worked with and we think are valuable, and we would welcome your group's involvement to work directly with the people and help them help themselves.

I know from speaking all across the country that there are churches and other independent groups that would gladly sponsor projects in the Congo or

Sudan or Ethiopia, but they don't know which ones are legitimate and which ones aren't. But we have embassies all over the world. Our diplomats work with local organizations, and they know which ones can be trusted. So they could help link American groups with the people who are crying out for assistance. They could also maintain some oversight, to make sure that the relationship continues to be safe and beneficial for all parties.

CARING AND COMPASSION

The dividends in terms of help to people who are in distress would be tremendous. But there's an even greater reward, caring for people in this way would help our own souls. If we will engage Africa, they will grow our souls. It's the biblical story of Lazarus and the rich man. At the Georgetown conference Madeline Albright and I did, I told that story. I didn't say that it was a parable from the Bible, but I told about the rich man who lived in luxury every day, while poor Lazarus was lying at his doorstep, begging for the crumbs from the rich man's table. Lazarus was so poor and sick that the dogs licked his sores.

I read the passage aloud to the conference participants. I suggested to them that this is really the story of Africa and the West. We're the rich man, well dressed and prosperous, and poor Lazarus, sick and starving and lying there in distress, represents many people in Africa today. At the end of that story, the rich man goes to hell because of the hardness of his heart. The point of the parable is that if we will reach out to Lazarus, he'll help show us the way. Our compassion for "the least of these" can restore our souls.

We're seeing a lot of people who understand the message in their hearts. Bill Gates, founder of the Microsoft computer empire, is often described as the richest man in the world. I understand he took an animal safari to Madagascar, a depressed island nation just off the east coast of Africa. He saw how badly the people were living, and it touched his heart. At that point he said, "I can do something to help." He has funded several global health initiatives that are having major positive impacts.

We need to encourage more people to visit Africa, because if they see what it's like, they'll want to do something. All of us can do something. Rick Warren didn't know very much about Africa when he wrote *The Purpose-Driven Life*, but the success of that book allowed him to travel there and discover places where he could help. His work began with AIDS relief, but now he's also working for economic development, working through a network of churches to provide medicines and other things that are desperately needed.

Something we have in this country that's truly unique is a church on almost every street corner, and sometimes more than one. Rick Warren said the biblical model for maintaining the well-being of a community is to visit that community and find "an honorable man." He may be a Christian or may be of a different faith, but you find that man or woman who is honored and respected in the community, and you do your work through that individual.

Rick Warren and Ted Turner were guests on a program sponsored by *Time* magazine in New York City dealing with health care for the Third World poor. They were there in the morning, and Madeline Albright and I were invited for the evening program. This is one more example of Left-Right cooperation that is so encouraging. I was glad that Secretary Albright and I could be part of an event like that, drawing attention to the needs in a part of the world that we both feel so strongly about.

If this sort of focus can broaden, and if we can see people from all walks of life getting involved, then I think we're going to see the most amazing things happening in Africa. And it's going to affect our souls in the process.

LEARNING TO COOPERATE

Working successfully in these areas generally demands that we must be able to work with individuals and groups who may not be our natural partners. It means that we have to work with some who may be on the other side of certain issues or, as in Congress, with individuals who may be on the other side of the aisle politically. Over the years I've worked with a wide range of groups and with individuals like the late Senator Paul Wellstone, with whom I disagreed on a number of policy issues but who, in some circumstances, could be a very effective partner on bipartisan measures.

When I need to work with folks on the other side of the political aisle, I generally go directly to the person whose input and assistance I need, and we compare notes on the issue and where we may be able to agree. That happened on the African American Museum project when I spoke with Representative John Lewis. It also happened with legislation that cosponsored with Senator Kennedy to help save Down syndrome children in the womb.

To work with someone on the other side of the aisle, the first thing I have to do is to stop judging that person. I can remember presiding in the Senate and seeing someone coming into the room with whom I'd debated on key issues. As I watched that person, I would make an instantaneous judgment: *lefty, liberal—on the wrong side of every important issue.* Mentally I shoved that individual aside.

As soon as I have those thoughts, my spirit reacts, and I immediately go through this sort of mental dialogue: *Now look what you've done! You've judged this person.* And in my own defense I'll think, *Yes, but it was just a thought, and I didn't say anything!* And then I think, *Yes, but as long as you feel that way, your reaction to that person will be one of judgment, and he will feel your judgment.*

I have to confess my judgmental attitude and ask for grace to be able to see my political adversaries on the other side of the aisle the way that God sees them. That has been a big step for me, but one that I needed to take. I understand, of course, that I'm not the only one who's being judgmental—it exists on both sides of the aisle. I can't do anything about what that other person may be thinking; I can only deal with my own thoughts and actions. I'm confident that this is the right thing for me to do.

Step two in the process is to make an effort to find someone on the other side who may be willing to cooperate on an important piece of legislation. When I was working on the Down syndrome bill—designed to get more parents to keep their Down syndrome children or be willing to put them up for adoption—I knew that Senator Kennedy cared a great deal about people with disabilities, so I approached him.

It took some convincing to get the disability advocacy community to come along, because they feared that partnering with us would divide their group. But when I pointed out that 80 percent of Down syndrome children are being killed in the womb, they agreed and helped approach Senator Kennedy with the bill. That's how the partnership came about and how we were able to take a bipartisan bill to the Senate floor. All we were asking was for parents to be fully informed of their options. We didn't set out to restrict abortions but to make sure that parents in that situation would be given all of the information currently available. Beyond the issue in that bill, that sort of bipartisan partnership is a good model for the kinds of cooperation we need in dealing with problems.

THE MORAL DEBATE

Not all the disagreements in Congress are cross-the-aisle debates. Sometimes they're within our own party, and there are a couple of situations that come to mind in that regard. The first involves my debates with Senator Arlen Specter, a fellow Republican who has been one of the primary sponsors of legislation on the other side of the issue regarding destroying human embryos for stem cells. I like Arlen, and we get along very well. We serve together on the Senate Judiciary Committee. Arlen knows how to get things done. But we're generally on opposite sides of the life debates.

Our debate on CBS's Sunday morning program *Face the Nation* in 2005 is one example. The topic that day was human embryonic stem cell research, and Arlen had been diagnosed with cancer. He was going through chemotherapy at the time and he'd lost most of his hair and yet continued to work dilligently every day as a public servant. I am against research that destroys human life. Arlen, on the other hand, was for funding research that destroyed human embryos if it might help other people. He was arguing that human embryonic stem cell research is a source of hope. I was cast as the young man who was trying to stop it.

He made a point that probably captured the whole debate. To a vast majority of the people in this country, the embryo in the womb is a human life at its earliest stage. At one point I looked at him and asked, "Arlen, when did your life begin?" It was a point of debate he had heard me use many times in Senate hearings, so he wasn't surprised by it. This was my left hook. My point was that we each began as a human embryo. If the obstetrician had killed him when he was an embryo, Arlen wouldn't be here today.

I was also prepared to ask him on camera if he was a person or a piece of property to be manipulated and disposed of at will, but he wouldn't answer the first question. Instead, he said, "Right now I'm not concerned about when my life began. I'm concerned about when it ends." Then he said that he believed there was at least a chance that embryonic stem cell research could lead to cures that would help extend life.

It was a good retort. Furthermore, his statement made it perfectly clear what the debate was all about: using one human life for the benefit of another. We all want cures, but at what price? Some are willing to sacrifice a weaker human for the benefit of a stronger, but I am not. Furthermore, it's a false choice, particularly when there are other, more promising options. Obviously, there is still widespread disagreement on this topic, as I've already illustrated in Chapter 5. Senator Specter and I work together on many issues, and while we haven't reached common ground on this one, we will continue to work together in the coming years. What I've tried to emphasize in my own comments on the stem cell issue is the fact that human embryos are young human beings. Some people have made the argument that they're just spare parts. They've been created in the laboratory from the sperm and egg of two people and then frozen in such a way that they can be retrieved later and implanted in the womb of a woman who will carry the child to term. It's true, they're frozen. But they're not spare human lives. There is no such thing as a "spare human." They're not extraneous humans who can be used or killed at random.

For democracy to work as it was designed to work, we need to be engaged in the battle of ideas, and we need to find our way through dialogue and debate to the best and most justifiable political solutions. The Republican Party has a long history of defending life and following a moral position on policy issues. America would be much better off if both sides could take the high road when it comes to the sanctity of life.

13

IMMIGRATION REFORM

Immigration reform is a complex and passionate issue, which at the writing of this book is yet to be resolved. There are dozens of measures before Congress, coming from every direction, and the White House has come at the issue as well. It's obvious that we need to take steps to safeguard our borders and stop illegal immigration, but we also need to have compassion. It is a complex issue involving real people and real problems.

The immigration debate had an odd start for me. I was Kansas's secretary of agriculture during the late 1980s, and one of the problems we were wrestling with at that time, and still are, was a serious shortage of medical doctors in the rural parts of our state. It was hard to recruit doctors to come in and set up a practice. When we did find doctors who were willing to come, many times their spouses weren't willing.

We decided to participate in a program to bring in foreign-born physicians to serve in rural areas. We estimated that 20 percent of the state of Kansas would have been medically underserved if it weren't for foreign-born physicians. A sign of the change that took place could be seen in a meeting I attended in Ulysses, Kansas, in the southwest part of the state, at which all the doctors in the community participated. There were five physicians, and it was like a UN meeting. One was from Ghana, one was from Pakistan, one was from Trinidad, and two were from Canada.

That made the point to me: if we had been only recruiting U.S.-born physicians, that community (like many others in our state) would not have had any medical care at all. There are scholarship programs now that are designed to attract U.S. students to work in these medically underserved areas, and some do. But it's becoming more and more difficult to attract them.

During my term as agriculture secretary, the Soviet Union was still in existence, and the USA had been pushing the government in Moscow to ease restrictions on Russian Jews, who were living under very difficult circumstances in that country. This was the era of the Jackson-Vanik amendment, contained in Title IV of the 1974 Trade Act, which made improved trade relations between the USA and Russia subject to the loosening of restrictions on Jews who wished to emigrate to Israel or the United States.

I began meeting with immigrant aid groups and some of the officials in the first Bush administration who dealt with such things. I began putting together a plan to get Jewish physicians from the Soviet Union who could be trained to U.S. specifications and licensed in this country to come and practice in Kansas. I worked with the Kansas Medical Society and others to help put the plan together. We needed doctors; they needed some transitional training to get up to U.S. standards. We were willing to work with them through the medical community and other agencies to secure the funding.

We were able to get an initial promise of a grant from the Bush administration for this purpose, but, sadly, it all fell apart. We weren't able to put the pieces together and make it happen. I learned some important lessons along the way, and that started my interest in immigration policy. I could see that this was one way to meet specific needs in this country, and there was a variety of needs to be met if we could come up with innovative solutions.

REAGAN'S SHINING CITY

I have continued to be interested in immigration. There's a lot more passion on this issue now than there was when I was secretary of agriculture, but the immigration debate has always been characterized by strong opinions. It's always changing the face of the country, and it always seems to be that the current group seeking to get in isn't good enough for the people already who are here.

At one time it was the Chinese who weren't good enough, then the Italians, and then the Irish and East Europeans, even though we're a nation of immigrants.

I believe in the Reagan philosophy that America is "a shining city on a hill." I remember President Reagan's famous statement in his Farewell Address in 1989. He said:

> I've spoken of the shining city all my political life, but I don't know if I ever quite communicated what I saw when I said it. But in my mind it was a tall, proud city, built on rocks stronger than oceans. Windswept, God-blessed, and teeming with people of all kinds living in harmony and peace. A city with free ports that hummed with commerce and creativity, and if there had to be city walls, the walls had doors, and the doors were open to anyone with the will and the heart to get here.

Ronald Reagan was the president who signed the 1986 immigration bill that has been roundly attacked in recent years. I believe he always intended for us to be open and hospitable to men and women who want to come here legally for a better life, and that's something I have supported from the beginning.

The current debate is a tough debate, but it's also a critical debate for the future of the country. It's as much about the future of the country as anything else we deal with in Congress. We're at a high level of foreign-born entrants at this time. Nearly 12 percent of the current U.S. population is foreign-born, which is one of the highest levels in the history of America. But this is also a global issue. After the fall of the Berlin Wall, people began moving all over the world. It happened in Europe, the United States, and many other places, as people saw opportunities to make their lives better. Some of this movement was legal and some was illegal, but they're coming from everywhere and going everywhere. It's not just our own borders that are being tested.

ON THE BORDER

I visited the border between Texas and Mexico with then Attorney General John Ashcroft on an exploratory trip. I have since been back to the border in

Arizona with Secretary of the Department of Homeland Security Michael Chertoff. We were examining border enforcement, and had visited the detention facility in El Paso. As I looked around at the people who were incarcerated there, I saw Asians, Europeans, Latinos, and Africans. I asked the warden how many different countries were represented in the facility. He told me there were people from forty-nine different countries. That was a real eye-opener.

El Paso is not normally the crossroads of the world, but the world was apparently coming there to enter this country. Most of them had come through South and Central America into Mexico, and somehow they were able to find a way to cross over into the United States. This is a major problem for the world.

It seemed to me that some of our basic principles were at cross-purposes with our immigration problem. One principle is that we are a nation of laws. We believe that laws are meant to be obeyed, and if you violate the law, there should be judgment and suitable punishment. That's a key principle of American democracy.

On the other hand, we're also a compassionate society. We want to try to help those who are less fortunate than we are as much as we possibly can. And this is where these two principles come into conflict. We have people crossing our borders illegally, breaking our laws, and circumventing the system established by law for entry into the country. They've broken the law, but in many cases they're escaping from hard lives in countries where there's little hope of improving their lives. So what do we do?

As I read the Old Testament, I kept coming across key categories of individuals whose needs God holds in high regard. We all know about the admonition to care for the widow and the orphan, and there's nothing we wouldn't do for widows and orphans. In the last book of the Old Testament, God declares, "I will come near you for judgment; I will be a swift witness against sorcerers, against adulterers, against perjurers, against those who exploit wage earners and widows and orphans, and against those who turn away an alien" (Malachi 3:5 NKJV).

The New Testament says that this is a test of true religion. "Pure and undefiled religion before God and the Father is this," according to the apostle James, "to visit orphans and widows in their trouble " (James 1:27 NKJV). This passage, along with a number of others, mentions the ways in which true faith may be observed, and one of them is the clear admonition not to mistreat or deny aid to the strangers in our midst. From beginning to end, Scripture speaks about caring for the foreigner in our midst and the sojourner among us and the one in difficulty.

Whether it's these passages, or the passage in Matthew 25 where Jesus speaks of the importance of caring for "the least of these, my brothers," it's clear that this is something that's very important to God. Yes, many of the immigrants in our cities today have broken the law by coming here without proper documentation. But the Bible says we are measured by the level of compassion we extend to those who are clearly in need.

Thinking about this helped me frame my position on this critical policy issue. There need to be consequences for any individual who comes here illegally, and the punishment should fit the crime. As much as we can, we also should be as compassionate as possible in helping people in difficult circumstances.

The Impact on Industry

I was in Wichita, Kansas, in early 2006, talking with people in the meatpacking industry when the big protest marches were taking place in Los Angeles, New York, and elsewhere. The packing plants, by and large, were all shut down during the protests, because this is an industry that historically employed first-generation immigrants. This had an impact on the state and the region because meatpacking is big business in Kansas. The managers of one of these companies invited me to come to Dodge City and meet with some of the people in his plant, so I went.

First I heard from the corporate leaders about how their business would be affected if the government decided to enact harsh policies reducing the number of immigrants. Then I talked to some of the men working in the plant, to hear their stories and how all this was affecting them. In one case, a man told me about someone he knew who had crossed the border illegally and made his way as far north as Kansas. He came from a poor village and was an unskilled laborer, so there was no way he would ever qualify for legal admission.

If he tried to come here as an agriculture worker, he would have to provide convincing evidence that he intended to return to his home country. More than likely the U.S. embassy staff in Mexico would say that it's doubtful this guy would ever return. So he came to Kansas illegally, purchased falsified documents, and a short time later learned that his mother was sick and dying in Mexico. He wanted to go home to see his family, but he could not.

On a later trip to the Arizona border, I did interview Mexican nationals who had been caught trying to enter America illegally. Most just wanted a job, but as many as 10 to 15 percent have a criminal record.

In December 2006, federal agents of the Department of Immigration and Customs Enforcement carried out a series of raids on Swift & Company packing plants in Cactus, Texas; Grand Island, Nebraska; Greeley, Colorado; Hyrum, Utah; Marshalltown, Iowa; and Worthington, Minnesota. The purpose of the raids, I was told, was to apprehend immigrants who had used falsified papers to enter the country and gain employment. In some cases these individuals were using forged identification or the Social Security numbers of actual persons. The Department of Homeland Security continues to prosecute these cases.

MACRO AND MICRO VIEWS

In the macro, everybody believes we need to tighten restrictions and enforce the borders. But in the micro, the immigration situation often flips. While people's visceral reaction on the macro is to kick people out, on the micro they fight for them to stay. And I've seen this time after time. We have a community in western Kansas where a family lives who immigrated from Romania. They came here as refugees to a community of about a thousand people, but they were going to be sent back to Eastern Europe because the threat of physical danger that brought them here no longer existed in that part of the world. It's true they had been in great danger under the Ceausescu regime, but communism had collapsed, the government had changed, and now the situation was much better. So the Immigration and Naturalization Service was sending them back.

The people in the town were shocked. They said, "Wait a minute! These people have been here for a decade, and they're good, hard-working people. You can't just send them back!" And that's true. I've met the family on a couple of occasions, and they're delightful people. The father works as a carpenter, the mother works in the community, and one of the daughters recently graduated from pharmacy school at the University of Kansas. The good news is, they had proven their value to the community well enough that we were able to get a bill passed through Congress so they could stay, but it wasn't easy. When we gave them the news that the bill had passed and been signed, the entire town turned out to celebrate the occasion.

This sort of thing only reinforces what I've said about the difference between the macro and the micro views of these cases. In the macro, people want to throw them out, but in the micro, when they see the human emotions and the human soul, they'll fight to keep them. That's another case where our basic principles seem to be at cross-purposes. People do want to help the foreigner in their midst—when they know him. I'm not naive about this issue. This will continue to be one of our most difficult problems. Immigrants are a great gift to this country. I believe that the vast majority are people who want to come here and find jobs, earn a living, pay their taxes, raise their families, and become contributing members of society. But we need a legal system that works, not an illegal one.

A significant percentage crossing the border have a criminal record, are smugglers, or are carrying drugs. Some even have terrorist intent. They must be caught! This is a huge issue and one we simply have to resolve. We will have to resolve it in a comprehensive fashion. But I also hope our conservative movement can embrace people who want to come to work and live in this country, because if we fail to do that, I fear we're going to lose support from the immigrant community that should be a natural group to support conservative principles.

By all rights this group should be a base of support for the conservative cause. They generally have come to work. They're finding jobs and making a contribution. They mostly are religiously oriented and committed to strong families.

THE NEED FOR ASSIMILATION

We must make sure that those coming to America assimilate and become Americans. One of the biggest concerns is language. For generations people have immigrated to this country speaking their native languages. In many cases, those in the first generation will have limited English language; the second generation will have fluent English and only modest knowledge of the other language. The same happens with culture and often with national identity. That's the way assimilation often works.

But with such a large wave of immigration right now, we need to work harder on this aspect. We need to help more people learn English. For generations we've required people who apply for citizenship to have a basic grasp of our language, our history, and how our democratic form of government works. They take special courses in civics and customs, and when they swear allegiance to the flag of the United States of America, they renounce allegiance to any other flag, nation, or ideology. We must be sure these kinds of requirements are implemented all across the country.

Immigrants who never learn English will be handicapped in everything they do. There are communities in which they can survive with limited English, but we need to help these people learn the language so they can truly participate in the advantages of our society. I believe that is a priority.

Another area of concern is our history and the principles around which America is organized and holds together. Some in America already seem more than willing to reinterpret our history and values and not require new Americans to learn them, which would look to most of us like a total surrender of American values.

The late scholar and lecturer Russell Kirk said that a nation is its culture. The history we've established over four hundred years is who we are, and no society that simply throws that away or reinterprets it for current purposes can hope to survive. Many are rightly concerned that we can't allow the disrespect for traditional American values to diminish the importance of the American culture. A number of books have been written in the last couple of years on what some perceive as a systematic dismantling of our culture. Some of those authors blame it on the Bush administration. Others blame it on the Left or some long-term conspiracy. In my opinion, most of the arguments are over the top, because our loyalty to this nation and the level of respect we have for our traditions and customs are simply too deep for any one group to undermine the nation in that way.

I will say, we have a lot of work to do. We need to address the pressing problems of the day, including the unrestricted flow of aliens across our borders, and we need to require that people who come to the United States learn to speak English as quickly as possible. We need them to do it for our purposes as a nation, but we also want them to do it because it's going to be good for them. It's important for the country to have a common language. Language is an important factor.

Senator Lamar Alexander put forth a bill that would require schools to teach more civics and give our students a better understanding of what it means to be a citizen of the United States of America. I think we need to do that. Not everyone has the same heritage or background in our culture, so we need to be more purposeful about informing them concerning our values and traditions.

SECURING SOCIAL SECURITY

The biggest key to border security may well be the Social Security number. People who come here believe without question that they will be able to get a job. We need to tell people before they try to come here illegally that if they show up at a work site without a valid Social Security number or other legal documentation, they won't be able to get a job.

The federal government has a lot of work to do to make that a reality, because our current Social Security system is not doing a very good job at the moment. We have more than five hundred billion dollars in the Social Security system from bad numbers or unclaimed accounts. Some of it is from people who didn't claim their benefits, but a lot of it is from people who have earned wages and paid their Social Security taxes with false numbers.

We need to set our system up so that when somebody shows up at a job site with a name, date of birth, and Social Security number, that information can immediately be sent to the Social Security Administration over the Internet by secure transaction. And then it immediately responds back to the potential employer with a red light or a green light. Green light means no problem—go ahead and hire the person. Red light means you cannot hire this person, and if you do, there will be serious consequences for both the employer and the individual concerned.

There's no reason the government can't do that, and I think it's key. If we don't have some type of enforcement that makes it unprofitable for people to come here illegally, then there's almost no way of keeping them out. People are pretty ingenious, and they'll find ways to get in.

The other side, however, is that much of our economy could not run without the immigrant workforce that's coming in. We need a willing workforce, but the fact of the matter is that it needs to be a legal work force and not an illegal one. There's a lot more work to be done on the immigration front during the next few years. This is one problem that's far from being solved.

✷ 14 ✷

A CRISIS IN THE EAST

I've dealt with hundreds of issues in Congress during the past twelve years, and in addition to many successes on the domestic front, I would say that some of my best legislative successes have been in the area of foreign relations. A measure I put forth for lifting the sanctions on India and Pakistan allowed the United States to forge stronger ties with those countries, and we're already seeing the dividends. Pakistan has many factions, including some that are hostile to our interests, but the government has been very helpful to us in the war on terrorism. By the same token, India has become a good friend of this country and an important developing ally in that region of the world. I believe it was our improved political and diplomatic relationships that made these things possible.

The North Korean Human Rights Act, which I sponsored in the Senate, has been an important part of our effort to confront the despotism of North Korea and to address the terrible deprivations that exist in that country. Along with these initiatives, the Silk Road Strategy Act and the sex trafficking bill I helped author all contain major foreign policy initiatives.

The Silk Road Strategy Act was one of the first major legislative accomplishments I steered through Congress. It was aimed at the countries in the southern regions of the old Soviet Union. This region had been known as the "silk road" as far back as the time of Marco Polo and the trading caravans that traveled through those regions in the fourteenth and fifteenth centuries—Kazakhstan, Tajikistan, Uzbekistan, Kyrgyzstan, Armenia, Azerbaijan, Georgia, and others. Our objective was to bring these nations into regular commercial and diplomatic relationships with the West, rather than forfeiting them to slide back into the Russian sphere or to become part of the Islamic world.

I have traveled in most of those countries several times, meeting with the leaders, forming the Silk Road Caucus, and building strategies for ongoing relationships. I could see that these countries were going to be making a choice. The Russians were trying to pull them back into their sphere, and the Iranians and Saudis were trying to pull them into the Islamic world.

The leaders of the countries were old communists, and they didn't want to be controlled by radical Islam; but at the same time, they didn't want to be controlled by Russia. I built a solid portfolio in this area. After that we were able to get the sanctions lifted on India and Pakistan, based upon the realization that India would become a great friend of the United States after the fall of the Soviet Union. And that has, in fact, become the case.

MULTIPLYING THE EFFORT

To make these programs work, we also tried to reach out to individuals who share our concern for reform in these parts of the world. For example, I met with Bono in early 2006 to compare notes on what he was doing in Africa. Bono, beyond being a rock star, is also known as a supporter of the relief efforts in Africa. When he spoke at the National Prayer Breakfast in February of 2006, he told a story that really hit home with me.

He said he had been traveling the world for years, asking people to pray for him and to ask God to bless his work. One day someone asked, "Instead of asking God to bless your work, have you ever thought of just joining Him in His work?" He said that question opened his eyes and changed his thinking on how to organize his efforts. As soon as he said that, I began thinking about my work in places like North Korea.

It's not something I started, but when I spoke to a group of North Korean activists connected about North Korea and heard the stories of the challenges in that part of the world, I felt that God must really be concerned for these poor, downtrodden people. I jumped on the topic and began doing research and study. Not much had been done in Washington to support North Korea in more than fifty years. Some things are happening now.

I took a trip to Thailand to familiarize myself with what's happening in that part of the world, particularly with regard to the sexual exploitation of children and sex trafficking. As I said in chapter 10, it's tragic what's going on globally in human trafficking. The governments in some countries have a history of turning a blind eye to the problems.

A great struggle of our age is the contest between human rights and totalitarianism. This is an ongoing struggle, but nowhere is the contest more visible than in North Korea. I met a lady named Soon Ok Lee in my office in Washington, DC, early in my research into what's taking place in North Korea. Soon Ok Lee is the author of a book called *Eyes of the Tailless Animals*, which is a powerful story about her imprisonment and torture for six long years in a North Korean gulag and how the resolute courage of the Christian prisoners she met changed her life. It's a heartrending story.

When she managed to escape from North Korea, Soon Ok eventually made her way to North America, where she was hosted by Susan Dysart of the Korean Defense Forum. Susan is a lady of faith who has a huge heart for North Koreans. When they came to my office, Soon Ok sat on the couch and told her story.

She wasn't a Christian at the time of her imprisonment, but she noticed that Christians always received the worst treatment in the gulag. They had the toughest jobs and the harshest living conditions. One day the guards lined up eight Christians in front of the other prisoners. The guards told the Christian prisoners they had two choices: they could renounce their faith and be set free from prison, or if they refused, they would be killed. The guards demanded that the prisoners renounce their Christian beliefs, but none of them would do it. There was a foundry in the gulag, and at that point, Soon Ok said, the other prisoners watched in horror as red-hot-molten iron was poured on their heads, killing all eight of them.

Soon Ok said she had seen Christian prisoners harassed and tortured many times during her imprisonment, but never saw any of them renounce their faith. She didn't understand that. Why wouldn't they just say what the guards wanted to hear and go free? Obviously there was more to their beliefs than she understood. She would later discover what it was that gave them such courage.

That was my introduction to Kim Jong Il's North Korean gulags and his treatment of his own people. North Korea has been called the Hermit Kingdom for many years. Not much information has come out of North Korea in a long time, but that began changing when news of massive starvation began reaching the West. Probably three million men, women, and children have died of starvation and deprivation in North Korea during the last fifteen years.

After the fall of the Soviet Union, the North Koreans could no longer count on support from that regime, and the Chinese weren't helping much either. Consequently, up to 10 percent of the North Korean population has died of starvation since the mid-1990s. To make matters worse, the North Korea dictator now seems intent on provoking a nuclear standoff with the West, by testing nuclear weapons and possibly selling technology to Iran and other rogue regimes.

SHINING A LIGHT IN DARKNESS

In the rotunda of the Russell Senate office building, members of Congress are allowed to set up displays of various kinds. When I hosted a gathering of North Korean refugees who had escaped into South Korea, I made arrangements to display some of their drawings showing what these people had witnessed and lived through in that country. They were some of the most powerful and soul-stirring drawings I have ever seen.

One of them showed a mother feeding rat poison to her children because she didn't want to watch them starve to death. Another showed a group of children pleading with their mother, who was standing on the railing of a bridge, begging her not to jump to her death. She was planning to jump because she and the children were starving to death, and she didn't want to watch her children die. These and many other equally graphic pictures were drawn by these eyewitnesses of the mass atrocity. We displayed a number of them to help our colleagues better understand the scope of what was happening in North Korea.

Everyone who passed through the rotunda and saw those pictures had to be deeply moved by the images. Because of the information coming out of North Korea today, many Americans now know that it is a brutal, totalitarian state that is killing its own people and shows no respect for even the most basic human rights.

Since that time I've had the opportunity to work with the Korean Church Coalition, a dynamic group of people. Most Korean Americans have come to this country, worked hard, and minded their own business. They haven't become involved in politics particularly. The church is very important to them. They focus their energies on their businesses and their families, and that's been more than enough for most of them. But what's drawing them into politics has been the situation in North Korea and the lack of human rights.

Recently they've become very involved and very aggressive in the confrontation with North Korea. They're also funding various underground railroads that exist along the China–North Korea border. In 2001, I traveled to the region to see for myself some of the things going on at this border. I didn't expect to see much, since the presence of Chinese authorities would no doubt drive the refugees away, and I didn't want to get anybody hurt.

I planned to visit Beijing at some point and ask the Chinese government to live by their international obligations, contained in the United Nations Treaty on Human Rights. This treaty required the Chinese not to send North Korean refugees captured in China back to North Korea. It's called "refoulment," sending them back into hostile territory and the possibility of torture or death. They know the North Koreans would be going back to punishment, at the very least, and we were pleading with the Chinese government not to do that.

THE ROAD TO FREEDOM

When I visited the border region, I could see a few guard towers here and there, but basically it was an unguarded border. What a stark contrast with the border between North and South Korea, which is one of the most intensely guarded borders in the world. There is great hostility between the North and the South. The northern border, however, is a different story, in large part because the Chinese were allies with the North Koreans in the 1950s during the Korean War and continue to be an ally today.

The Tumen River separates North Korea and China. It's not fenced, and I didn't see a border compound or a heavy concentration of guards on either side. It's a fairly shallow river, and apparently refugees could come across the river at that point easily. There may have been a couple of sleepy Chinese guards every twenty or thirty miles along the river but no obvious border patrols. There was seemingly no concerted effort to keep the North Koreans out.

We estimate that around four hundred thousand North Koreans are living illegally in China today, just living off the land. When I spoke to some of the local officials, they looked at the North Koreans as their way of helping the poor, so the local Chinese population allows a certain number of refugees to live there at a subsistence level. We would see them at the local marketplace; they were easy to spot. They call the Korean children "swallows" because they dart in and out. And anyone can tell by their shabby clothes that they're in desperate need.

The local Chinese citizens don't have a problem with the North Koreans being there, because they realize how difficult life is for them in North Korea. They tolerate a certain number of them, pretty much the way any society would tolerate gleaners who follow along behind the grain harvesters, picking up the scraps. And if they get a little of the food the Chinese throw away, that's fine. That's their way of helping out.

Several people I've spoken to about conditions for refugees told me that it's relatively easy for them to escape into China, but it's much harder to go from there to a third country. Because of the way the Chinese guard their borders with other countries, they don't want to allow these North Korean refugees to pass through.

The number of North Koreans who have successfully escaped into South Korea has skyrocketed during the last ten years. More North Koreans have managed to escape to the south in the last decade than made it in the previous fifty years combined. We've now accepted our first refugees from North Korea into the United States.

According to the testimony of the women I've spoken to, all of the North Korean women who are captured after they manage to escape across the border into China, are abused and/or sold into slavery. The women told me they're priced and sold like cattle based on their age and their looks. One of the highest trafficked areas in the world at the present time must be the Chinese-Korean border. This is partially due, I believe, to China's one-child policy, because there's a shortage of women of marriageable age. The male-to-female ratio in China now is 55/45, men to women, and that's a dangerous and unhealthy imbalance.

EXPOSING OFFICIAL TREACHERY

Obviously, something has to be done. My conversations with Korean refugees and members of the Korean Church Coalition eventually led to the introduction of the North Korean Human Rights Act of 2004 in both houses of Congress. The bill was signed into law on October 18, 2004, by President Bush, and it established the office of Special Envoy for Human Rights in North Korea. Jay Lefkowitz, who formerly served as General Counsel of the Office of Management and Budget, was named to the post by the president, and his job is to monitor relations with North Korea and to negotiate with them for progress in human rights.

Under prior law, the United States could not accept refugees from North Korea because the constitution of our allies in South Korea declares North Koreans to be members of a united Korean republic. So any North Korean who flees into South Korea is automatically accepted as a citizen of South Korea. By our refugee laws, we could not accept a citizen who has a right to go somewhere else. One of the reasons I wanted to change the law was so that Americans could start hearing what's happening in North Korea. The best way to do that is to hear from the people who have lived under that totalitarian system.

The other aspect of this is that we've focused so much on the missiles coming out of Korea and the threats associated with their nuclear technology development, that we haven't spent a comparable amount of time on the human rights issues. The former Soviet dissident, Natan Sharansky, who was a refusenik under the Soviets and is now a friend and ally of mine, tells me that one of the keys to the fall of the Soviet Union was not just confronting their nuclear and missile technology, but confronting what the government was doing to their people. The Soviet Union was a heartless totalitarian state. A big part of our victory in the Cold War was making known to the world how the people of Russia and the Soviet satellite countries were being treated by their leaders.

When President Reagan dared to speak out about the lack of human rights under that repressive regime, he undermined the authority of the Soviet state. If all he had done was to attack the build-up of Soviet nuclear missile technology, the Soviet government could have used his remarks to provoke nationalist sentiment in the people, much as Kim Jong Il is attempting to do today. But when the president questioned the lack of human rights and the mistreatment of the Soviet people, that undermined the regime, and it contributed in a big way to the eventual collapse of the Soviet empire.

I believe this can happen in North Korea as well. If we can get more information out about what they're doing to their own people, that can be valuable in hastening the collapse of that evil regime. We must, however, continue to aggressively confront them about their nuclear missile program. This, in turn, will have a direct impact on Iran, since North Korea is a supplier of missile technology to Iran, and those two members of the Axis of Evil work together.

I think it goes without saying that focusing on human rights violations can also be used effectively against tyranny in the Islamic world. We don't want to stop talking about the technology issues, but when we add the human rights component, it can be a powerful one-two punch, because it helps people understand the sheer barbarity of the regime.

Until recently, we didn't know much about what went on inside North Korea. Now that refugees are coming out of North Korea, we're discovering how repressive the government of that country truly is. The "beloved leader" is killing his own people. One of the most striking images I've seen is the night map of the Korean Peninsula taken by satellite. That tells the whole story. On the upper portion you can see the lights of China; on the bottom portion you can see the lights of South Korea. But in the middle, where North Korea is located, there is only darkness. The nation is so impoverished that the people have virtually no electricity for lights at night.

This tells me that systems matter. The people of North and South Korea are the same people, ethnically and racially. They have the same blood. Yet, in South Korea you see a prosperous nation with the eleventh largest economy in the world; and in North Korea you see a failed state, ruled by a feudal system of systematic abuse and repression of the people. The people of North Korea are starving to death, not only physically but also emotionally, spiritually, and intellectually. Their leader is doing this to them.

So systems matter, and freedom matters. What the country allows and what the people accept as the dominant economic and political system determines how well and even how long they can survive. Ironically, the capital of North Korea, Pyongyang, was once known as "The Jerusalem of Asia." Before the Communists took over in 1945, that area of Korea had a large and dynamic Christian population and even sent missionaries throughout Asia and the world. But today, all forms of religion are repressed, and none more so than Christianity.

DARKNESS AND LIGHT

Terror is a tool of darkness, bitterness, and hatred. It's an evil tactic that must be confronted and renounced by all civilized nations. When I was in Jerusalem, I issued an appeal to the leaders of Syria and Iran to renounce the evil tactic of terrorism and embrace the nobility of their heritage. At the same time I thanked the nation of Libya for renouncing weapons of mass destruction and for agreeing to open a corridor for humanitarian assistance to the people of Darfur. I also said that we need similar evidence of cooperation from countries like North Korea, who continue to defy international conventions and abuse the most basic human rights.

When I addressed the Israeli Knesset in July 2004, I told them how much the American people care for their country. Israel is a promised land, a thriving democratic, free-market nation. We are close allies due to shared values. They have fought terrorism longer than we have and know its lethality and pain. Terrorism is evil and must be rejected by all civilized people. Terrorism has been waged against innocent and vulnerable people in Israel, America, Britain, Spain, France, and many other countries because we're free, and we reject the terrorists' evil beliefs.

People everywhere long for freedom. This is the first principle of America's war on terrorism and the cornerstone of our efforts to reach out to newly emerging democracies. We want to encourage all nations to honor the longings of their citizens for freedom and give them the right to select their leaders. What a difference it makes when people are given a choice. When people are given the freedom to vote their conscience, they choose systems that maximize liberty and minimize the dehumanizing programs of tyrants and dictators.

Democracy isn't perfect, but it's certainly preferable to tyranny. Winston Churchill offered a compelling assessment of the strengths and weaknesses of democracy in an address before the British House of Commons. He said:

> Many forms of Government have been tried, and will be tried in this world of sin and woe. No one pretends that democracy is perfect or all-wise. Indeed, it has been said that democracy is the worst form of government except all those other forms that have been tried from time to time.

I think that's a fair assessment, and democracy is definitely where the world is going today. But we can't afford to wait for democracy to emerge while millions are being subjected to starvation, abuse, and brutal repression. This is happening in too many places in the world today. America's voice needs to be heard in those places.

There are forty-five nondemocratic countries in the world today. The number is shrinking, thanks to reforms taking place in every region. For a nation to grow and thrive, the people must be free. They need the ability to select their own leaders, and they need to be heard on issues of consequence. Free, democratic nations can do amazing things, and to limit that power and resourcefulness by restricting and controlling the voice of the people is to limit the opportunity of those men and women to thrive.

When President Bush referred to the tyrannies of Iraq, Iran, and North Korea in 2002 as the Axis of Evil, he was identifying the ideology that tramples on human dignity and subjects men, women, and children to slavery and subjugation. He was telling the world that the United States is opposed to tyranny, and that this nation will continue to resist totalitarian regimes that sponsor evil and trample on human dignity wherever they may be.

Terrorism, tyranny, slavery, and despotism—these are evils of our time, but evil can't stand the light of truth. Lies, no matter how clever and nuanced, cannot prosper when people choose to live by the truth. Truth always wins in the end. The task of building a free and independent nation is not an easy one. It requires patience, and many times it means suffering through conflict, loss, and indignities along the way. The founders of this country certainly proved that to be true. But it's worth the price, and those who fight for truth and resist evil will triumph in the end. That's a truth we can share with the world.

☆ 15 ☆

SHOWDOWN IN THE MIDDLE EAST

On my first trip to Israel, I was struck by how small that country is. The fact that this nation—in a land that has been at the center of so much history for such a long period of time—is so very small was really surprising to me. It made me think of the story of David and Goliath. Israel is truly the David in the region.

I'm from the Midwest. I'm used to a relatively big geographic state, and my state is a large state in a much larger country. Israel, on the other hand, is a small nation, with a total area of about 9,000 square miles, and a total population of less than six and a half million people. Israel is surrounded by Arab countries occupying some 6.5 million square miles of territory in the Middle East (more than 600 times the landmass of Israel) and with a predominantly Muslim population of 400 million people. You can drive across Israel at its widest point in less than two hours, or take a helicopter from the Jordan River to the Mediterranean seacoast in half an hour. Less than fifty miles across—that's how small it is.

The names of the places I visited were gigantic in my mind, having read the stories in the Bible about Jericho, Jerusalem, Bethlehem, and Nazareth, and the regions of Judea and Samaria. I remember being at the spot on the Jordanian side of the Jordan River where they believe Jesus was baptized by John the Baptist. My guide said, "I want you to look up from where you're standing. To your right is Mount Nebo, where Moses looked into the Promised Land. To your left is Jericho, which you can clearly see. And where you're standing now is the place where Jesus was baptized. Can you believe it?"

It was hard to believe that I was standing in such a place. The trip occurred during a period when there was a heightened terrorist alert in the country. My tour guide and I were alone. But I was in awe. It was staggering to think about all the history and all the influence that had come from there. The entire Jewish and Christian world, Western civilization, and the beliefs and values that have shaped the world for thousands of years all began in that place.

THE DREAM REBORN

I also remember my reactions on another trip to Jerusalem, when I was staying in a hotel just outside the old city. Looking out my hotel window and seeing the Star of David flying over the ancient ramparts, the thought hit me that God does keep His promises. That flag hadn't flown over the city of Jerusalem for nearly two thousand years. From AD 70 , when the Roman emperor Titus laid siege to the city and wiped Jerusalem off the map, until the 1967 War, when Israeli forces recaptured the capital, the Jewish people had been evicted from the land, and their flag was gone.

With virtually every other group of people, after they've been dispossessed from their land they cease to exist as a people within a hundred years. Their name may continue for some time, but as a cohesive people they've ceased to exist. The Jewish people had been dispossessed of their land for almost 1,900 years, but God's promise was faithful. He had given the land to Abraham and his descendants, and today that ancient nation is back.

When I told Brent Scowcroft and Jim Dobson a few years ago about my reaction to seeing the Star of David over the old city, they both told me similar stories that happened to them as children. They both still remembered the day the modern nation of Israel was reborn. Their mothers took them aside and said, "Something very important has happened today. The nation of Israel has been reborn, and this is something we've waited for, for a long time." That happened in 1948, but they both still remembered that day and the importance it had for their mothers and them, and for Jews and Christians everywhere.

Today Israel faces an existential threat from radical, militant Islam to its very survival as a nation. This is not hyperbole or a hypothesis; it's a fact. It's based on numerous declarations like the proclamation by the Grand Ayatollah Ruhollah Khomeini that established the current government of Iran and called for the utter destruction of Israel. This doctrine is now being proclaimed by the current president of Iran, Mahmoud Ahmadinejad, who has called for Israel either to be moved to the West or wiped off the map. And, simultaneously, he is also calling for the destruction of America.[1]

Israel has faced threats from radical Islam, with daily terrorist threats by people seeking to kill innocent civilians in Israel, but the people carry on courageously. America needs to support them, and we need to stand with them. We must confront those who want to destroy us and our allies, such as Israel. We're not going to be intimidated by their threats.

But the second part is that we need to engage those countries that will work with us, particularly those in the Muslim world, and their citizens in the global economy. We should tell them that while we will confront those who seek to destroy us, we want to engage those who are willing to engage with us on a peaceful basis.

It's also my hope that, increasingly, we would see the Islamic region of the world grow economically. We want people to have opportunities for education. We want people everywhere to be able to take care of their families. But we will not be blackmailed by those nations and their leaders who hate us and who mean to do us harm.

With regard to the situation in the Middle East, there are a number of issues that need to be considered. One of them is that the city of Jerusalem ought to be declared the undivided capital of the state of Israel. Many people are saying that the region needs a two-state solution. In the long term, there are people who think it would be a good idea to have a Palestinian state. There are real questions about how this would work, however, and how such a state would be governed. The early results of the Palestinian Authority are not promising.

My own position is that we need to insist that Jerusalem be the undivided capital of Israel. I have a bill in Congress that would affirm that position. Israel is the only nation of which Jerusalem has been the capital, and its importance to the Jewish people and the Jewish faith is undeniable. Jerusalem is mentioned more than seven hundred times in the Old Testament. It is central, and while there's a discussion taking place about a Palestinian state, there ought to be an equally adamant conversation taking place about the final status of Jerusalem. Jerusalem has been the capital of the Jewish people for three thousand years, and is the seat of the state of Israel's government, parliament, and supreme court. Yet, Israel remains the only country in which the USA does not place its embassy in, nor does it recognize, the city designated as the capital by the host country. The time has come to fix this long-standing inconsistency. We must resolve this issue before any final peace settlement between Israel and the Palestinians.

RADICAL ISLAM

The confrontation with radical Islam is as serious an issue as we've ever faced, and it's well past time for us to be clear about what's really involved in this debate. I think we've probably been ill served by calling it a "war on terror." Terror is a tactic, a tool. It's like saying, I suppose, we'll have a war on land mines. It doesn't make clear who we're fighting.

The people we're fighting are Islamic fascists who subscribe to a radical ideology of world domination against us, Israel, even against other Muslims who do not agree with their extremist views. It's a movement that aims to establish an Islamic caliphate, a dictatorship in that region of the world, with a leader who is simultaneously the leader of the government and the religion. They have been focused on this objective for years. They've been going about it in two principal ways. The first step is to get the United States out of the Middle East. The second step is to depose the current regimes in the region and establish the caliphate.

This is why countries like Saudi Arabia, Egypt, Jordan, and Pakistan have been willing to work with the United States. The leaders in those countries know that this group of radicals, often funded by Al Qaeda or the government of Iran, are dedicated to the destruction of the governments in their countries. This is serious business.

We must have a clear mind and clear language about this threat. The aim of these radicals is not merely to destroy the United States but to destroy the entire

West, including all of Europe. This is why we're seeing attacks by Islamic radicals in Europe and Israel. They've said that Israel is the "little Satan" and America is the "great Satan," and they see Israel as an outpost of the West in their part of the world. There can be no compromise with this evil ideology. We have to confront it and defeat it. We have to confront it aggressively and by every means necessary, and we have to engage the rest of the Islamic world in as many ways as possible—culturally, economically, and educationally—in order to build relationships and solidify ties with those who will constructively engage us.

George Will had a great analogy for this in a column he wrote in the days following 9/11. He was writing about the struggle between radical Islam and the West, and he said that what the terrorists did was the equivalent of jamming a dagger in the back of a computer. On one hand you have one of the most ancient of weapons, a dagger, and on the other you have the consummate tool of modern technology, the personal computer. It's an incongruous matchup, but jamming a dagger into a computer can be a very effective way of shutting it down.

I have to say that there are days when I'd like nothing better than to do that myself! Computers can drive you crazy. But the point is that even an ancient weapon can stop a technological marvel if it's done in a certain way. It's an effective way of shutting down the Western economy and bringing a stop to many of the systems we take for granted. But such primitive tactics can only succeed if we don't take steps to engage the responsible members of that society and invite them into the modern global community.

THE PROSPERITY PRINCIPLE

If more people in the Islamic region felt they had a share in the global economy, in the world educational system, and in international society, then they would be more likely to engage the West rather than to attack it. It's my hope that we can expand the global sphere of prosperity in such a way that these nations and most of their people will disavow violence as a means of changing policy and look instead to constructive dialogue, economic interaction, and political engagement.

I've seen a map drawn by a defense expert that shows where terrorists predominantly come from, and it also shows where the global economy is most active. It should come as no surprise that terrorism tends to come from places where there is a mix of poor economic conditions and radical ideologies. There the people feel both kept down and as if they have nothing to lose. It's easy for them to buy into the concept that radical, fascist Islam is the way when nothing else seems to be going their way.

If terrorist ideologies were not tolerated and they could economically take better care of their families and have some expectation that there would be opportunity and hope for the future, I believe they would be much less likely to become terrorists. We have, of course, seen homegrown terrorists who've grown up in the West, and they've carried out attacks despite the fact that they've had ample opportunities for personal fulfillment. Still, the majority, by far, of those willing to commit acts of terrorism come from areas where the potent brew of extremist Muslim ideology is tolerated and poverty is prevalent.

FIRSTHAND ENCOUNTERS

I saw militant Islam being planted and spread when I was traveling in Central Asia, working on the Silk Road Strategy Act. As I indicated earlier, we were trying to unite the countries on the southern tier of the former Soviet Union, to bring them into an economic alliance and orient them toward free markets and open societies. On my trips to the region, I have made it a point to meet with the security people as well as the leaders. When I asked them about their most pressing problems, they invariably told me that the most serious threat was the invasion of radical Islam being funded from Iran and Saudi Arabia.

I heard this everywhere I went. The Muslim radicals would come in and build a community center and then a mosque, which was fine with the local leaders. But then there would emerge some localized radical group that was ready to make problems. The Iranians and the supporters of Wahhabism in Saudi Arabia were sponsoring this throughout the region. This was the most significant destabilizer in Central Asia.

Part of what we were trying to do in the Silk Road Strategy Act was to keep the Central Asian region from going back into the Russian sphere or being pulled into the sphere of radical Islam. These governments had been satellite regimes for decades. They were new at governing themselves, and they had never known anything but authoritarian leadership up to that time, so that was their natural inclination. But we believed things could change for the better.

Many of their leaders were brought up as communists, but we wanted them to come together on an East-West alignment instead of the more familiar North-South alignment. They were being probed by other interests as well.

All this is to say that the interface between the West and the Islamic world will continue to be one of the key foreign policy initiatives of our time. Consequently, we will need to weave our way through this without making an enemy of Islam, but nevertheless we must be ready to confront those who seek to do us harm. That's a very difficult challenge, but it's important that we face it. The end results will be the expansion of liberty around the world.

There is always the pressure and tendency to appease dictators in exchange for stability in a region. When we let exigencies get in the way of principles, we always pay a price. During the 1970s we supported a number of dictators in Central America who stood in the way of the expansion of freedom and democracy. They were tyrannical, but they were against the communists, and that was good enough for us.

Eventually the people in Central America began to question our motives and beliefs. They would say, "If America believes in freedom, then why are they propping up dictators?" So our willingness to support bad guys in order to maintain stability in the area spawned a great deal of ill will against the United States. We've seen the same thing happen in other regions.

We must constantly push for liberty and democracy. Perhaps at different speeds in different circumstances, but it must always be central to the American foreign policy agenda everywhere.

A PERSONAL COMMITMENT

After 9/11 we saw people in Egypt, which is supposedly a friendly nation, cheering the fact that Islamic terrorists had flown planes into the World Trade Center and the Pentagon, killing nearly three thousand Americans. At the same time we saw people living under the thumb of the ayatollahs in Iran, mourning for the United States and holding vigils with lighted candles. How do we make sense of that picture?

We've been supporting the dictator in Egypt for a long time, and the people of that country have been questioning our motives and our judgment. In Iran, we've been confronting a dictator and the ruling mullahs in that country. This, of course, is not the only factor, but as we think about what kind of policy decisions we will make in this difficult era, we need to remember that we're asking for trouble, sooner or later, when we violate our basic principles and beliefs.

The fact is, we have to work with people of all sorts in many places. We don't force them to adopt our beliefs or standards. But having said that, we have to stand by our principles in easy times and hard ones. We have to conduct our affairs in ways that will benefit our own people. Diplomacy should never mean sacrificing our own vital interests to buy the goodwill of others.

I've been working in this area for most of the last decade, since my first days on the Foreign Relations Committee in the House, so I'm interested in how foreign policy decisions are made. These are also matters that I care about personally, and I've made a commitment to be a part of this discussion. For as long as I'm in government, I will do everything I can to see that we make decisions that are logical and productive, and that we can live with for the long run. I will never be satisfied with anything less.

It's a given these days that the United States has become too dependent on oil from places that are politically unstable and, in many cases, from countries that are actually hostile to the United States. That would include countries such as Venezuela, Russia, Central Asia, and perhaps some Middle Eastern nations that have been unreliable allies. Oil has become not only an issue in the economy and at the gas pump, but it has also become a major security issue, and it's past time for us to start dealing with it.

Because of my background in agriculture, I'm enthusiastic about the opportunity this situation could pose for farmers in the heartland of America. Farmers have had difficult economic challenges for decades now, producing more and more for cheaper and cheaper prices. Farmers in the Midwest have been forced into the position of the least cost producer. They're constantly challenged not only by changing weather, but also by changing markets.

I recently heard about a white wheat test plot in Kansas that produced more than a hundred bushels of wheat to the acre; I've never heard of that kind of yield before. Our capacity to produce continues to grow, and we're getting better at the genetics—crossing genetics from outside the species to produce heartier, healthier, higher-yielding crops. For decades now agriculture in this country has been sailing against the wind, but for the first time in my lifetime I think our farmers may have a chance to turn it around and go with the wind, based on both energy and the environment.

ALTERNATIVE FUELS

My interest in ethanol goes back to when I was a cub reporter for a radio station in Manhattan, Kansas. KSAC was the public radio station, and we were in the farm crisis of the late 1970s and early 1980s. It was a time when farmers were going bankrupt in large numbers. I attended a rally at the beginning of the American Agriculture Movement, popularly known as the AAM. The movement was a cry of desperation. Farmers were being hammered by low market prices, rising costs, and skyrocketing interest rates. There was a lot of anger and resentment, and the AAM was the result.

When I went to investigate what was happening, there was a huge crowd of farmers gathered on the Kansas State University campus in Manhattan, and they were fired up. This was the era of the tractorcades on Washington, DC, and these were my friends and their families. I had been state president of the Future Farmers of America and had traveled to meet farmers all across Kansas. Farmers are hardworking people, and I knew they were going broke. Things were just not working, and they were understandably angry.

One of the big things that came out of this era was ethanol. That's how they were going to fix this marketplace, by turning grain into alcohol and expanding the industry from food and fiber to include fuels. There was a speaker at the rally talking about on-farm distilleries. In other times this had been done for other purposes—for human consumption. But these were going to be farm-scale ethanol operations, and the farmers would turn their grain into alcohol to burn as fuel for combustion engines. That was going to be a key part of the solution to our farm economic woes.

Of course, a number of economists were saying it wouldn't work, and I was skeptical as well. People in the automobile industry were saying that ethanol would destroy rubber hoses and other engine components. But the farmers' enthusiasm was undaunted, and several of these men built farm-scale distilleries. I went to see one of them in eastern Colorado. It was built by one of the AAM leaders. I interviewed him and looked at his operation with some agriculture engineers.

When I looked at the numbers, it didn't seem to work economically or energy-wise then. But you could see that the passion and the possibility was there to make it happen someday. And that's what has happened. Through the years they were able to overcome automobile industry concerns and get them to adopt a 10 percent ethanol standard. At one time the industry warned against a 10 percent mixture; then they endorsed it, and now General Motors is marketing it. They coined the phrase "Yellow is Green!" meaning that using ethanol made from farm products is not only acceptable but environmentally sound as well.

Midwest vs. Middle East

I recently spoke to a car dealer in my state who is putting in a biofuels service station next to his dealership. It will sell E-85 ethanol fuel, which is 85 percent ethanol and 15 percent gas. We now also have biodiesel, which is diesel fuel made most often from soybean oil. At a time when we need to reduce our reliance on foreign oil, we now have part of a homegrown solution that is safer, cleaner, and cost-effective. We can eventually meet 10 percent of our fuel needs with grain ethanol and another 35 percent of our needs with ethanol made from cellulose—which has been referred to as "gas made from grass."

The first cellulose plant is soon to be built in Idaho, and one is going up in Kansas as well. There are more and more ethanol plants popping up across the countryside, producing grain-based ethanol, all of which means we can be more dependent on the Midwest and less dependent on the Middle East. If we can get to the point that 45 percent of the fuel we need is from ethanol instead of importing fossil fuels from highly unstable, hostile, and war-torn parts of the world, then we will have more security and more reliable sources of fuel for America's future needs.

The new generation of flex-fuel cars can burn either gasoline or ethanol, and the hybrid cars being produced now in this country and abroad can run on both fuel and electricity. These things, in various combinations, provide us with a whole new array of options. One of my family cars is a hybrid, and we get upward of forty-one miles per gallon in town. My teenage daughter, I might say, gets about twenty-seven miles per gallon in the same car, so it does matter how you drive! But I'm excited about the opportunities and improvements these energy alternatives can bring us, and I'm strongly supporting this technology.

When I served as Kansas's agriculture secretary, we showcased biodiesel fuels by using animal fat made into biodiesel in the city buses in Topeka. We got together with the officers and managers of the Topeka Transit Authority, and their engineers agreed to burn a fat-based biodiesel fuel for a period of time. At our request, a local manufacturer processed inedible tallow from the meatpacking industry, and this was made into the biodiesel fuel we tested.

It was very interesting. Many people were concerned that it would gum up the engines, and it's true that this fuel would tend to coagulate in the winter if the temperature dropped too low. And in the summertime, the exhaust from our buses tended to smell like french fries. But that smell was highly preferred, even if it made you hungry for McDonald's, over the normal exhaust of a diesel bus coming into your car.

It was a modest beginning, but now we're seeing biodiesel coming into the marketplace in a big way. I was in a Kansas salt cavern a few months ago, and they were burning 40 percent biodiesel in some of their mining equipment. They were using a soybean-based product, because it burns much cleaner than regular diesel. The biodiesel fuels are market competitive now with today's oil prices, and I think we're going to see this become a bigger part of the picture in our search for energy answers.

A Revitalized Economy

Since the 1930s, farmers in this country have been paid subsidies by the federal government not to grow certain crops. In the beginning they received subsidies to supplement their income so that America's farm families could remain on their farms rather than sell out and move to the cities. Later, however, they were paid to limit their production in order to hopefully maintain more stable prices for farm products. It would be my hope that we can have farmers receive reasonable income producing for the market instead of for the government. And that's the farmers' desire as well. Producing crops as energy alternatives could be a key way of making that happen. We need farmers to get a piece of the energy pie.

A lot of land in our country is in the Conservation Reserve Program. There are about forty million acres in long-term grass set aside. This includes land that serves as buffer zones next to rivers, and some of it erodes fairly easily if not properly cared for. My hope is that in the future we could harvest that grass for ethanol production. We could then leave the land in grass, and it would be serving a dual purpose—soil retention and the manufacture of cellulose-based fuels.

This is part of the energy and environment equation that can provide answers for the future of agriculture in this country. Using farm products in this way helps with our energy needs and our environmental concerns. Agriculture provides a carbon cycle that is essential to soil enrichment. As you release carbon dioxide (CO_2) by burning ethanol, you're fixing CO_2 by growing corn and grasses. You're creating a carbon cycle that is beneficial for the environment.

Something else that can happen is exciting to me, which is the idea of creating niche markets for agriculture by finding new substitutes for petroleum-based products. For example, you can make plastics from oil, but you can also make plastics from starch that comes from corn. There's a shirt in a museum in Iowa, I'm told, that's made out of soybeans. It was made in the 1930s to show people the versatility of soybeans and how fibers from agricultural products could be used for a multitude of nontraditional applications.

The legend is that when the shirt gets wet, it smells like soybeans, so you might not want to wear it in warm weather or when it's raining. The remarkable thing, however, is that they could do it at all—make cloth from a food product—with 1930's technology. Recently I've seen cloth made of corn and wool, and carpet made completely of corn. I think we're at the front edge of this, and we're at a moment in both history and international diplomacy when we can foresee a lot of products that have been made from oil imported from the Middle East being made now from soybeans, corn, milo, or wheat grown in the United States. That could be good news for farmers and diplomats alike. A golden era for U.S. agriculture, a helping hand to the environment, and breaking our dependence on Middle East oil.

16

LONGER, HEALTHIER,
BETTER LIVES

The leading cause of fear in the United States today is not terrorism, traffic accidents, or what may happen to your children, although those are all very important areas of concern. According to polling data, the leading cause of fear among Americans is the fear of cancer. And for good reason. One out of two men and one out of three women at some time in their lives will have cancer.

The reason for the high cancer rate among men is that men typically have more varied types of the disease, as well as a higher ratio of smokers than women. Men's jobs can put them at higher risk; and the fact that men are generally not as careful about diet and nutrition as women is also a factor. Prostate cancer is a concern that's unique to men, and I remember the words of one physician who told me, "If you live long enough, you're going to have prostate cancer." I'm not sure there's any empirical proof of that statement, but it tells us nevertheless how widespread the problem has become.

Yet, despite the high level of concern, deaths from cancer have actually gone down in this country over the last two years. The mortality rate varies considerably depending on the specific form of the disease, but in general the number of deaths from cancer in this country has dropped as diagnosis, therapy, and prevention have improved. According to the American Cancer Society, about 560,000 Americans died from cancer in 2006, and the number is declining slowly but steadily.[1] This is great news. But there's reason to believe we can do even better.

Ninety-two senators signed a letter that Diane Feinstein and I circulated that called on the administration to set up a focused program to eliminate deaths by cancer by the year 2015. Considering the state of medical technology today, this is not an unrealistic expectation. I've met with a number of cancer experts who believe that, with aggressive pursuit of all the scientific opportunities and options, we can realistically expect to stop deaths by cancer in this country in the next ten to twenty years. This is not to say that people won't get cancer, because they will. But with suitable treatment they won't die of the disease.

Eliminating death by cancer is one of my favorite things to talk about, because so much is being done in this area. I remember the first few times I spoke on the topic. I wasn't sure what to expect from the audiences I addressed, but I soon discovered that most people want to know more about what they can do to help bring this threat to an end. I cochair the Cancer Caucus in the Senate with Senator Feinstein, and we've worked on cancer issues for a period of time. I had melanoma, and my father had colon cancer. We're like most families in this country, where cancer is a familiar topic and a dreaded word.

In some of my speeches on this subject, I've said that I think those of us in Washington, and those in my own party, need to get some new plays in our playbooks. One of those plays is a plan to end deaths by cancer in ten years. When I say that, a hush comes over the audience, and some people look at me like, *OK, Sam has gone over the edge this time!* But then the look on their faces changes, as if they're thinking, *But could that really happen?*

They had never heard it expressed that way, but they wanted to believe that this might be a real possibility. There are a lot of things we could give the world, but if the number-one fear is death from cancer, then giving them back the gift of life would be a wonderful gift. Invariably the crowd falls silent as they consider the importance of what I'm saying.

A Lifesaving Gift

It would be a gift that only this country could give the world. With the technology, the medical knowledge and research capacity, the amount of investment needed, and the abilities we have concentrated here in this country, we have everything needed to make this a priority, and we're really the only nation that could make such a significant contribution.

We've already doubled the funding of the National Institutes of Health during the last ten years, although recent funding hasn't kept pace. We've doubled the effort in the biological sciences. We've sponsored the Human Genome Project and mapped large areas of human DNA. We've put more money by far than any other country into the development of pharmaceutical products, and we have the most advanced programs for early detection techniques.

It's doable, but it's going to take a combination of things to make it happen. One will be a change in lifestyle. There are personal responsibilities in this, as in everything in society. But for our part, we need to be pushing for more and better detection techniques. We need to be pushing for more treatment options in the system, and we need to be able to support these options publicly for individuals who can't afford them.

One bill that I've put forward on this topic involves getting more cancer drugs field-tested more quickly. In the early days of the AIDS crisis, we didn't know at first what we were dealing with, and we didn't know how to treat it. For a lot of people who had AIDS, we didn't have any kind of standardized treatment regimen. Regulations were loosened in the system on drug treatment, and this allowed doctors to try new regimes with patients who had no hope.

By their own doctors' judgment, these patients were in a terminal situation and they were going to die. So we let the doctors try drugs and treatments, with their patients' consent, that had not gone through the normal process of government-sponsored trials, and we let them experiment with them in combinations. As a result, they came up with what we now call "AIDS cocktails" using a wide array of drugs, and it worked. Quality of life was improved, suffering was reduced, and life was prolonged.

I believe we need to allow that same system to be implemented with cancer patients who have no hope. They've been told by their physicians that there are no further treatment options available, and life expectancy is short. We should allow those patients access to treatments in earlier phases of clinical trials and allow their doctors to use various drugs in combination as potential therapies.

We found in the AIDS research that it wasn't any one drug that did the trick: it was a cocktail of drugs. Perhaps in cancer treatments we may find that one drug might produce a 10 percent reduction in the size of the tumor, and another drug would produce a 20 percent reduction. But in combination, they produced a 90 percent reduction.

This has been an issue that has been editorialized extensively by the *Wall Street Journal*, and it has been discussed at length with regard to the court case of a woman who recently sued the federal government for being denied Phase One treatment trials, which is the earliest phase of treatment. I believe that if we could allow this to go forth robustly, we could find treatments and cures much more rapidly.

A MATTER OF FOCUS

In 2004 there were only six new drugs approved for cancer treatment. We need more treatment options. This is particularly true for those who have no other recourse and have run out of options. They know that what they will be trying is unproven, and there will, of course, be failures along the way, and possibly even false hope. But undoubtedly something can be learned that will improve cancer treatment. I think this is one of the great contributions that can be made to improve society.

There have been some recent announcements about the new drugs that reduce the side effects of chemotherapy so that patients will be better able to continue those treatments. In some cases, chemo is so painful that many people simply refuse to take a second or third round. But these drugs alleviate the objectionable symptoms and allow cancer patients to go ahead with these treatments. This means that there is a much better chance the treatment may work .

I spoke to some individuals in the oncology community in Wichita, Kansas, who told me that there's a significant number of people who are diagnosed with cancer and given an appointment time to come back and begin treatment who never show up. They don't want to face the disease or the treatments, so they just go home and wait it out. Drugs that would relieve the stress, the side effects, and the immediate symptoms are a marvelous way to improve the chances of a cure for all.

There's another change that I'm pushing with the FDA. The Food and Drug Administration is one of the most powerful agencies in the government for its impact on life, and their ability to approve or reject pharmaceuticals determines which products and treatments make it out of the laboratories. My goal has been to get more treatments out there for neglected diseases. This initiative has a bit of a history, but I think it's an important area.

The fact is, 10 percent of the diseases in the world will receive 90 percent of the pharmaceutical research. They're the 10 percent of diseases that Americans commonly suffer from, such as heart disease, cancer, Alzheimer's, and other diseases that are common in an affluent society. Ninety percent of the diseases that people get in the world at large, however, receive only 10 percent of the funding. These diseases tend to be most common in parts of the world that don't have substantial funding or market structure. Drug development is based largely on market structure, meaning that it's costly and demands a high return on investment.

Pharmaceutical research is cost intensive, and hundreds of millions of dollars go into the development of a single drug. The financial analysts will ask, "Can we make money with this product?" If the answer is, "Yes, we can make money," then the research more likely will be funded. But if the need happens to be in the Congo or Rwanda, there's no market and not much way to make money, so more than likely that research won't happen.

NEW RULES FOR RESEARCH

I looked into this situation as I was getting ready for a trip to Sri Lanka after the tsunami of December 26, 2004. A group in Kansas had organized a medical aid effort to ship food and supplies to that devastated region. We held a press conference in New York to let people know what this group was doing. Before I left New York, I had a meeting with the CEO of Pfizer, one of the largest drug manufacturers in the world. I wanted to thank them for their contribution to the tsunami relief effort. I also wanted to talk to them about this issue of neglected diseases.

When I met with the CEO of Pfizer, I told him how much I appreciated his help, but toward the end of the meeting I said, "You know, we need to do more to help those affected by disease in the Third World. I don't want to face my Maker knowing that 90 percent of the diseases in the world are not being properly treated because the best medical researchers in the world were too busy making drugs like Viagra."

I said, "I know there are a lot of people out there dying of very basic diseases like tuberculosis, malaria, and dysentery. I also know that many problems stem from the fact that these people live in poor nations without a lot of money to invest in better sanitation, mosquito control, and the like. But it seems morally wrong to me, knowing the suffering that exists in the world today, not to be doing all we can do to help the people overcome these diseases and regain some measure of dignity in their lives."

He understood what I was saying. I am sure he'd heard the argument before, and almost immediately said, "Yes, I agree with you, and I have a solution to propose. Let's agree on a list of the most urgent priorities—the diseases like tuberculosis, malaria, and HIV that are devastating poor nations. We will invest more in researching medicines for these diseases. And for every successful treatment we discover, develop, and prove safe and effective, Congress will allow us to extend the patent on another product we already market for another five years.

"We do try to help as much as we can," he said, "but we're not a charity. We're not the government, and we don't have unlimited resources.

"This is a marketplace signal," he said and explained that Pfizer responds to the marketplace.

It was an intriguing idea—giving pharmaceutical manufacturers five years of additional patent protection sounded a bit rich—that could be worth billions in lost revenues. But if we could come up with a bill in Congress that allowed up to a two-year patent extension on another medicine, then that would be a solid incentive for these companies to fund research and development of treatments for the diseases of the developing world. And that made a lot of sense to me.

When word of this got back to Washington, however, I started getting push-back from lobbyists who were concerned that this would raise the price of health care. They provide a lot of medicines, such as Lipitor and Viagra, under their benefits programs, and extending the patents on those medicines would mean that they would be paying prescription prices instead of generic prices. But I'm still optimistic about this idea, because it's a way for us to use the dynamics of the marketplace to come up with treatments for pernicious diseases in other parts of the world.

If a program like this were to be approved, the pharmaceutical companies' response would be to fund a lot more in the way of research themselves, or through smaller companies, to discover possible treatments and cures for neg-lected diseases. We get research on ancient diseases affecting hundreds of mil-lions of people globally. They get short patent extensions. That sounds like a winning, market-based solution to a tough, global problem.

A System That Works

Another area of study and legislative research in the health-care field is the need to have personal, electronic medical records. I have presented a bill to create independent medical records banks, so that anywhere you go as a patient, you can take your full medical record with you. At this point medical records are often huge files of medical documents that are unwieldy and not at all user-friendly. The new records I'm proposing would be digitized, and they would belong to you, not the medical facility.

I realized during the aftermath of Hurricane Katrina that if there's a disaster of the magnitude that destroys the documents kept by the physician or the hos-pital, then your entire medical history can be lost. This happened to thousands of people in New Orleans. In addition, there are too many medical mistakes taking place because of the way medical records are kept. One doctor orders a test that another doctor doesn't know about, or one doctor orders a drug that another doesn't know about, and sometimes this can be a fatal oversight. We need a better system for keeping records, and we need to make sure that the patient—and his or her family—is in charge.

It always seemed odd that when I would go to the doctor's office, they would pull out big, bulky files with my medical records. If I visited a specialist or a new doctor, they would have no idea what was in that record. And it's more and more common that people live in one place and work in another, as I do. My home is in Kansas, but my job is in Washington, DC, and I occasionally meet with doctors in both places. If I could take those medical records with me, however, my entire medical history would be up-to-date and instantly available.

There are many good examples of how personal records could be stored so that the individual and the concerned organizations could have instant access to them, yet the record would remain secure. Banks and investment companies do this, of course. Online banking has been doing it for years. What we're proposing is to allow independent groups to create medical records banks, like a credit union, where all of your medical records could be digitized and stored.

You would have access to this information. And if you choose, you could have the information on a magnetic strip on a card. When you go to your doctor, you could take your medical record with you. It could be read on a digital reader by a physician and updated each time a particular treatment is administered.

This could be done by nonprofit entities or by for-profit "health records banks." If you were willing to allow your records to be used anonymously for the purposes of medical research, your account would generate revenue. In this case the record bank could pay you for the use of your record data or use this money to reduce the cost to you of maintaining the system. This would be entirely up to you!

This could be helpful to medical researchers who would have access to blinded information in your records. The documents would not include your name or personal data, but it would help research scientists to better understand certain conditions, treatments, and outcomes. Again, this would be a voluntary program, of course, and the patient would have the first and last say on what is done with his or her records. And we would need iron-clad safeguards in place to protect the patient.

I believe we will see this happening in the near future, and it will improve quality and reduce the cost of medical care. With this system, there wouldn't be nearly as much confusion, misdiagnosis, and duplication of services taking place. Maintaining privacy of medical records is certainly an issue in any of these proposals, and the version we're putting forth puts the consumer in charge of who may view his or her personal information.

The Greatest Danger

During a meeting with the CEO of one of the largest medical software companies in the world, he noted to me that the most dangerous instrument in the hospital is a pen. The reason is that when you start writing things with a pencil or pen, and it becomes difficult to read, you immediately put the life of the patient at risk. Maybe the physician has written 10 milligrams, but it comes out looking like 100. Or what if the doctor prescribes Digoxin to treat heart failure but, instead, they give you Amoxil, which is used to treat bacterial infections, because the nurse couldn't read his handwriting?

Doctors are notorious for bad handwriting. More than ninety thousand people die in this country each year from simple mistakes made in hospitals. There's no counting the number of patients who don't die but are nevertheless incorrectly handled. And how much is the current system costing us? I think this is one improvement we can make that would deliver important, immediate benefits.

Ask yourself, why aren't the airlines still using paper tickets and manifests with long lists of names that have to be checked off one by one? Because they have computers that can process data in a fraction of the time, with far fewer errors, and in a much more efficient and safe manner. Many frequent fliers these days book their own flights from their homes or offices, and the only paper they see is the boarding pass they're given at the airport or that they print out themselves.

People need to be more involved in their own medical decisions. Before a medical procedure is ordered or a prescription given, the patient and the family need to know what's being done and why, and they need to be consulted about the financial consequences of the care they're receiving. That alone would drive the costs of medical care down, and we would have a better system all around.

Some of my colleagues have used the following example, and I think it's a good one. Lasik eye surgery was advertised in a Kansas City store recently for fifteen hundred dollars per eye. Most major metropolitan areas have multiple Lasik eye centers. They advertise their service, so you know the price when you go in. You pay for it with your own money, and it's a competitive marketplace. If the quality of treatment is poor or if injuries occur, the surgeon is sued and the center goes out of business. That's how it generally works.

What happened with Lasik could be instructive for the rest of the health care system. First, Lasik has a market and price competition. It's open pricing, so we see what costs are involved, up front. Second, we're using our own money, so we shop for the best product at the best price.

The problem with the current health care system is that it's not generally seen as using our own money, and we have no price transparency. We don't know what we're paying for. We get a bill at the end of the treatment, and frequently a third party pays for it. At that point a major negotiation takes place between a big hospital and a big insurance company, and they decide what you received and how much they'll have to pay for it. People working in the system are frustrated with it. People getting care are frustrated. We can do better.

Under the current system, the patient is merely the person in the middle. The patient isn't the one directly paying the bills. The patient needs more information, and we need more price transparency.

One of the things I've cosponsored is a bill requiring the disclosure of the amount Medicare reimburses on typical procedures, and we would then distribute that over the Internet by zip code. By this system, what Medicare pays for services in your community could be available over the Internet. This, I think, is the first step toward getting the patient back into the decision-making loop with regard to his or her own medical care and pricing.

The second thing I'd like to see is a greater emphasis on Health Savings Accounts (HSAs). HSAs allow you to set aside your own money, tax-exempt. Individuals could buy a medical insurance policy with a high deductible of, say, 5 thousand dollars. The policy would pay for everything over that amount, but you would pay for everything up to 5 thousand dollars with your HSA.

That way you become more involved in the decision making. You decide when it's appropriate to seek treatment and how far you want to go with it.

You will be in a position to decide between various options and prescribed treatments, because you're talking about spending your own money. With the current system the patient is so far removed from the financial end of the transaction that he or she doesn't have much to say about what the patient is receiving or whether or not the price is fair. The changes I'm proposing would be a huge improvement over the current system.

A Socialized Nightmare

The big danger at the moment, however, is that the other side is pushing hard for more government control over health care and a bigger government-funded system. The big push for the Democrats is nationalized health care on the order of the failed Clinton health care proposals of the 1990s. The Democrat platform made a big push for socialized health care; I don't think they've lost the appetite for doing that now. In the 2004 and now in the 2008 presidential elections, we see some of the front-runners on that side pushing for major expansions of nationalized health care.

I don't think most Americans want more government in their health care system. They've heard about the difficulties and delays in socialized medicine in Europe and Canada. They recognize the limitations of those systems. The market-engaging solution is the one that can actually work. Our way is to restore market mechanisms to the system, not simply to have more and bigger government in health care.

Approximately 16 percent of the entire U.S. economy is health-care related, headed upward toward 20 percent at an astonishing pace. It's the largest single component of the economy. I don't think anyone wants to see government in charge of that. It will be more efficient and effective if we can keep health care and health care systems in the private sector.

I was told recently that the legacy cost on a General Motors automobile is fifteen hundred dollars. This means that for every GM car sold in this country, about fifteen hundred dollars of the price you pay goes simply to cover pension and health care costs of retired General Motors workers. That doesn't include anything for current employees of General Motors, only the retired workers.

This is an important problem. But if we get it right, we can live longer, healthier, better, and with lower cost. And we'll have more control over our own lives. This is going to be a big challenge for us to work with for some time to come, and that's why I've made health care and health-care systems a central focus moving forward.

17

MIRACLES OF SCIENCE

One of the most amazing scientific feats of the last hundred years was the discovery made by James Watson and Francis Crick of the double-helix structure of deoxyribonucleic acid, or DNA. In computer language this is the software of our bodies. It directs the operation of our cells. It is both elegant and complex. "The language of God," as Dr. Francis Collins, the head of the Human Genome Project, calls it.

Our genes and chromosomes via DNA transmit genetic information from parents to their offspring, like downloading a software program from one computer to another. Understanding how this system operates allows researchers to trace relationships and find many important connections and associations that have health, functionality, and quality-of-life implications. Understanding the way the DNA software works has allowed scientists to begin mapping their functions and "software" responsible for particular applications. The medical and pathological importance of this information is immeasurable. Plus, it's really cool science.

Second only to the work of Drs. Watson and Crick in 1953, is the work of the Human Genome Project, headed by Dr. Francis Collins, which in recent years has completed the map of the human genome. As a result, we now know the basic genetic structure of the human body. And if there was ever any question whether or not we are, as the Bible says, "fearfully and wonderfully made,"

I would challenge anyone to take a look at what the biogenetic researchers at the National Institutes of Health have achieved.

The United States Human Genome Project was launched in 1990 as a joint effort of the Department of Energy and the National Institutes of Health. Organizers predicted that the project would last fifteen years, but thanks to a series of technological breakthroughs, researchers were able to identify all of the approximately twenty thousand genes in human DNA in just thirteen years. Analysis of the estimated 3 billion chemical base pairs that make up human DNA, will go on for years. Scientists are now creating databases of vital information for future study, and they're in the process of transferring all this information to the private sector, which was a part of the original mandate of the Human Genome Project.

Francis Collins, who holds both an MD and a PhD in medical research, is the director of the National Human Genome Research Institute at the National Institutes of Health. He led the effort to complete the mapping of human DNA, and Dr. Collins has become a man I have relied upon for information and advice through the years. Dr. Collins stated that if we printed out the human genome on regular-sized paper, with the standard number of letters on each page, it would be a book the height of the Washington Monument. The Washington Monument is 555 feet high, which is just over fifty stories.

The DNA code involves four letters—A G T C, representing the four different types of amino acids strung together in differing combinations and order. Each of the approximately ten trillion cells in the human body carries the same genetic information. What an incredible, beautiful, and simple design! We now have it mapped, but we have only touched the tip of the iceberg in understanding how each section of DNA works. Like Lewis and Clark reporting back to President Thomas Jefferson, we have traveled to the end of the terrain and back, but we hardly know what all is there.

Someday we'll be able to discover proclivities toward certain diseases or other medical anomalies by examining an individual's genetic code at a very early stage. This new science comes with a number of ethical and moral concerns, as well as promise. How exciting it is to unpack this treasure trove of biological information. How important it is that we treat what we learn with care and wisdom.

SCIENCE AND THEOLOGY

Science, by it's very nature, has always involved ethical and moral questions. Science is magnificent. It has improved our lives and given us so much that we can be proud of. But there are some things that science must not do, no matter how noble the aims.

There are many people who believe that the cloning of Dolly the sheep in 1997 was a step too far, as well, because it opened a Pandora's Box for a type of experimentation—human cloning—that could lead to the cheapening of human life. So there are many important ethical questions at the intersection of science and theology, and the grander the discoveries of science the more critical the ethical questions become. Guided by moral principles, science is a gift of God for the benefit of humanity. But without moral guidance, it can be a tool for oppression.

There are some people who would say that ethics should have nothing to do with science, but I strongly disagree. In my view, science and theology are not in conflict. If they seem to, we need to check our science or check our theology. It's not unfortunate that these two great human pursuits seem to be at odds so often in our modern world. I propose that we stop the fighting and begin more constructive dialogue. People of goodwill on both sides should host conferences and write papers—with eminent scientists and theologians discussing the same topics from their different vantage points. Such discussions would be enriching for all of us.

We could discuss the origin of man—what we know physically about man's creation—and then cast our thoughts about why we exist. This could only aid our understanding and enrich our thinking. Scientists and theologians could discuss the nature of the universe or the human mind. We are made to need each other and are harmed by the failure to use all the resources of humanity in putting together the puzzle of understanding.

For most of human history, up until modern times, science has been considered the companion of religion. When the principles of astronomy and the physical sciences were being discovered in the sixteenth and seventeenth centuries, scientists such as Galileo, Copernicus, and Isaac Newton believed they were merely thinking God's thoughts after Him. They were thrilled to think that they were looking into the secrets of how the world was made. In every experiment they were finding out how the sciences revealed the majesty and power of the Creator.

WORDS OF WISDOM

Nicholas Copernicus made no secret of his belief in God. His study of astronomy was an attempt to find out how the heavens were made and how the stars and planets operate. Johannes Kepler, who succeeded him, wrote to a friend, "I have constantly prayed to God that I might succeed if what Copernicus had said was true." Kepler originally set out to become a theologian, but when he learned of the discoveries that Copernicus was making, he knew he had found his true calling. "For a long time I wanted to become a theologian," he said, "and for a long time I was restless. Now, however, behold how through my effort God is being celebrated through astronomy."[1]

By the same token, Robert Boyle, the founder of modern chemistry, began each day with a prayer that God would reveal to him the secrets of nature. He wrote, "When I study the book of nature . . . I find myself often times reduced to exclaim with the psalmist, 'How manifold are thy works, O Lord, in wisdom hast thou made them all!'"[2]

And Sir Isaac Newton, with his discoveries in optics, calculus, and the principles of gravity, argued that science should never attempt to discount the agency of God in the universe when His hand is so clearly visible there. "All sound and true philosophy is founded on the appearance of things," he wrote, "and if this phenomena inevitably draws us against our wills to such principles as most clearly manifest to us the most excellent council and supreme dominion of the All-Wise and Almighty Being, they are not therefore to be laid aside because some men may perhaps dislike them."[3]

The founders of modern science felt a genuine humility in their investigations because they understood that the advances they were making in mathematics, physics, chemistry, and other fields were, in fact, part of the infrastructure of the world God had created. For them, nature wasn't merely a puzzle to be solved but a book to be opened and studied. Einstein said that "God is a scientist not a magician."[4] All the early scientists agreed that the truths they were privileged to discover and describe were the work of a genius of the first order. The incredible majesty of our world, with all its fantastic creatures and complex systems, could not be explained in any other way.

When Albert Einstein became aware of the conflict between science and religion among by some of his peers, he said, "The real problem is in the hearts and minds of men. It is not a problem of physics but of ethics." The debate over the interrelationship of science and religion today often seems more like an all-or-nothing fight for supremacy rather than any discussion of complimentality. But the founders of modern science did not have a problem sharing the platform with the Creator.

True Humility and Greatness

The story of the great African-American scientist George Washington Carver provides a wonderful example of what can happen when we understand the interrelationship of science and faith. Born a slave during the first year of the Civil War, Carver started out in Missouri but spent much of his boyhood in Kansas at a time when there were both proslavery and antislavery factions still in the state. He lived for a time in a proslavery part of the state, but when he witnessed lynchings there he left and eventually settled in the town of Minneapolis, Kansas, which was an immigrant community.

The citizens of that area were all antislavery, so he did very well and finished his early education there. Later, Carver applied for admittance to the community college in Highland, Kansas, and was accepted. But when he showed up for classes, he wasn't allowed to enroll. The application didn't say that he was African-American, and the college didn't allow black students to enroll at that time. He was hurt by their decision, but he sent an application to Iowa State and was accepted and enrolled. He earned his bachelor's and master's degrees there, and showed incredible promise of becoming an eminent scientist.

George Washington Carver had been a gifted student from boyhood on, and he became one of the most important botanists and chemists this country has ever produced. While he was teaching and doing his research at Iowa

State, he received a letter from Booker T. Washington asking him to come to Tuskegee Institute, which Washington had recently founded in Alabama. Carver accepted the offer and became a distinguished researcher and professor at Tuskegee.

He was an example of someone who persevered and was used mightily. He believed that God had a calling on his life. He didn't see any conflict at all between science and theology; he saw them as completely complementary. In one of his most famous speeches, Carver said, "When I was young, I said to God, 'God, tell me the mystery of the universe.' But God answered, 'That knowledge is for me alone.' So I said, 'God, tell me the mystery of the peanut.' Then God said, 'Well, George, that's more nearly your size.'"

He saw science as a way to improve our lives and to relieve suffering. Having grown up in the Midwest, he also understood the importance of agriculture, and he applied himself to the study of peanuts at a time when farmers in the South were struggling with crop failures of various kinds. In time he found more than 325 applications for peanuts, and his discoveries helped restore hope and income to thousands of farmers. He helped to multiply many times over the benefits not only of peanuts but also of sweet potatoes and many other plants.

Carver's most overlooked accomplishment may have been his theories of crop rotation, which alternated nitrate-producing legumes, including peanuts and peas, with the major crop of the day, which was cotton. Without rotation, cotton would deplete the fertility of the soil. This would be disastrous for farmers, and could lead to blight and other crop failures. Carver found ways to restore the balance of nature and reduce the number of crop failures by planting peanuts for a season. Southern farmers were thrilled with these discoveries. Carver helped to make their lives better!

Among the other peanut uses discovered by Carver were products as diverse as milk, cheese, ink, facial cream, shampoo, and soap. And these were only his most-celebrated discoveries. His research was wide-ranging, and he literally changed the way botanical research was done in this country. Faith was always central to his work. He sometimes entered the laboratory with nothing in his hands and would say, "God, what are You going to show me today?" Carver said, "I love to think of God as an unlimited broadcasting station who speaks to us every hour, if we only will tune in."[5] His faith and his science went hand in hand.

SCIENCE AND ETHICS

The convergence of science and religion shouldn't be a source of conflict. I'm a strong proponent of science and scientific research, but I'm also a strong proponent of growing our souls. I believe these disciplines can and should work together.

Dr. Francis Collins is not only a world-class scientist and researcher in human genetics, but he is also a man of sincere faith. His view is that these two fields inform and reinforce each other. It gives us far greater understanding of the world when we can look at science and theology as being complementary rather than as being in conflict. Einstein saw the beauty in nature, and he often said he saw the majesty of God in the structure of the universe.

Senator Robert Byrd handed me a beautiful book that described how the laws of physics of the universe were perfectly calibrated for sustaining human life. If any one of the myriad laws of physics were off by the smallest degree, our planet would be uninhabitable and human life could not exist. When you think about phenomena such as gravity, the effect of the moon on tides, the growing seasons and how they differ in the northern and southern hemispheres, the importance of clouds and rain, the effect of cold and daylight, and so many other things of this nature, you can't help but marvel at the beauty and majesty of it all.

We should be saying, *Yes, we are fearfully and wonderfully made,* as the Bible attests. We are incredibly complex creatures of the living God, and we want to give Him the respect He deserves for His ingenious design. But at the same time we're going to search to find out how these things came to be, how and why this human machine operates as it does, and how the earth, the stars, and the planets interact with life in the universe as they do.

God didn't create us for despair or ignorance. He created us for love. We need to do whatever we can to find cures and treatments for maladies. We need to begin a new dialogue with people with honest and open hearts about this, and start from the premise that science and theology are not in conflict. They each ask different basic questions. Science asks, "How?" Theology asks, "Why?" The two together give us the big picture. We need to end the battle of words and begin a new discussion so that the best of both can be brought to bear on today's problems, and humanity can be enlightened and enlivened!

The Right-to-Die Debate

The debate over what's now referred to as "the right to die" is a complex one. If there was ever an area that demanded ethical and moral answers, this is it. It's your life, after all. Some suggest that you ought to be able to do with your life whatever you want. If a person finds things so abhorrent and life so difficult that he can't go on, or if he has a terminal illness and no possibility of recovery, the merciful thing to do is to let him take whatever steps he wishes to end it— or so goes the rest of the argument. Many have had similar thoughts.

One day in 2002, I was in the town of Pittsburg, Kansas, in the southeast corner of the state, where I met with people from a group called Hearts and Hammers. They were fixing up homes for people who weren't able to do it themselves. It's a community effort, and it's a beautiful thing. I had just stopped by to say thank you and applaud their efforts. The lady who owned the home they were working on came out to speak to me. I was happy to visit with her. Interestingly, after a few minutes she began telling me about the times she had attempted to commit suicide.

She had been at the bottom, she said. Life was bad, and her relationships weren't working out. Her family was in chaos, everything was terrible, and she was in despair. So she decided to end it all and took a bunch of pills. Somebody found her, and they were able to have her stomach pumped out just in time. During the next several months this happened again. The third time she was determined to finish the job.

She told me she planned to start the car in the garage, with the doors closed, and sit there until the carbon monoxide did its job. She got her keys and headed out the door, but as she was going down the steps to the garage, she was suddenly struck by the thought that "thou shalt not kill" includes yourself! She wasn't religious, so the thought was surprising and puzzling. But as she began thinking about it, she felt a warmth in her spirit. Broken and crying, she put the keys down and sat there and wept.

During the next several weeks she began to reach out to people of faith and to read the Bible and pray. She began to understand and feel God's love for us. Almost immediately things seemed brighter and her problems less severe. When I met her, she had joy in her smile, and to top it off, the Hearts and Hammer people were there to help put her house back into shape. It all started with the thought that the God who gave us life also told us not to take innocent life—even our own.

Many people endure levels of difficulty and pain that I can't even imagine, particularly when there is a serious illness or when the individual is elderly or weak and unable to care for him or herself. But I'm also convinced there are incredible, beautiful things that can happen at the end of life, even amid the pain and difficulty. The transition of the soul from a physical home to a spiritual one is a sacred time. One person's trial can be an incredible testimony to those around him who survive, particularly family and close friends. I think it would be a terrible tragedy for the government to legitimate the act of taking one's own life.

It's another one of those difficult debates. According to some reports, in the Netherlands, as high as 8 percent of all infant deaths are the result from doctor-assisted suicide. Tragically, not only can individuals opt for suicide, but also parents can choose it for their disabled young children.

In places where physician-assisted suicide has been legalized, there are people who wish their governments had never taken that step. It encourages people who are frequently depressed to end it all instead of receiving treatment. Family members are put at odds with each other in an emotionally charged setting, with one encouraging assisted suicide and another strongly opposed. A strain is created that often will never heal and remains a deep source of bitterness between family members or friends for the rest of their lives.

I spoke to a lady from the disability community who told me that for many in the disability community, the "right to die" begins to sound an awful lot like the "duty to die." This is doubly true for the elderly, who can come to feel like a burden on their families whenever illness or incapacity sets in. They know their medical care is expensive, and they feel that they're a drain on everyone. That awareness can cause them to believe that it's their duty to move on.

Neither the American Medical Association (AMA) or the American Psychiatric Association (APA) supports physician-assisted suicide. More than 90 percent of those who die by suicide suffer from depression or another psychiatric illness and need treatment. For the AMA, physician-assisted suicide is contrary to the Hippocratic oath and the pledge "First, do no harm."

AVOIDING DISASTER

Public policy should not legitimate and thus encourage such a diabolical practice as killing yourself. I have submitted a bill in the Senate that would prohibit the use of federally controlled substances for euthanasia and physician-assisted suicide. Recently, the Supreme Court ruled 6–3 in *Gonzales v. Oregon* that the Controlled Substances Act, as currently written, does not permit the federal government to prohibit physicians from using federally licensed pharmaceutical substances for assisted suicide. What they were saying, in essence, was that there is no law forbidding doctor-assisted suicide. Our bill would create that law and specifically allow the government to forbid the use of prescription drugs for that purpose. I'm afraid the bill is on a lonely path at the moment because there are a lot of opponents. A very similar proposal was put forth in the 108th Congress, the Nickles-Lieberman bill, but I expect it will be a difficult battle.

The center of the argument of those advocating for euthanasia is the attitude that it's *my right!* I am in control of my life, and no limits should be placed on me in that regard. If I want to end my life at any time, then I should have no restraint from doing it. Even though in the case we are talking about here, it would be the use of a federally licensed pharmaceutical substance for off-license purposes. But even more important, the law is a teacher. Certainly this is something we do not want in America! We're not God, yet we believe that we have the wisdom to make life-and-death decisions that are not our prerogative.

We really need a culture that fights for life, not one that encourages its end. Life is sacred—at the beginning and at the end and every place in between. How much better we will be when we treat all life and particularly our own lives that way!

☆ 18 ☆

THREATS TO
GOOD GOVERNMENT

Some people have compared the legislative process to making sausage. The sausage may be delicious, but you really don't want to see it being made. There are times when that metaphor seems very appropriate. I tend to think of the process as something like a three-level game. On one level you're playing football; on the next level you're playing golf; and on the third level you're playing chess. But the trick is you can move the pieces from one level to another! So you can tackle a player on the golf course or take a golf club to a chess piece. It's tough and complicated. You can never be certain what the outcome will be.

Furthermore, you never play the same game twice. Each game moves differently. It's packed with personalities that you have to play through. It's amazing at the end of the day that we ever get anything done.

Most bills never become law, and that's probably a good thing. The process is designed to be difficult and slow to move through. The framers of the Constitution meant for it to be that way. Sometimes the only way we can move legislation is for it to be a topic that is so important that it has to be dealt with or that it's something required, such as funding the government.

For a bill to have a shot at becoming law, it must go through the various committees of the House and Senate, pass both bodies, survive a conference committee of both houses before being reviewed by the executive branch, and, finally, signed into law by the president. There are many delay tactics that can take place in the House and the Senate. House members work by majority rule, while the Senate is designed as more of a consensus-building body in which the individual senators have more authority. By long-standing custom, a single member of the Senate can stop a piece of legislation in its tracks, at least for a while. The entire process is laced with traps.

The president is in a position to either sign or veto a bill when it reaches his desk, but the role of the Chief Executive is really bigger than that. The president and the administration can, and often do, become involved in legislation as it's moving through. If they feel strongly one way or the other, they can usually influence a bill along the way. Even though they don't have a vote, they do have a veto. A presidential veto means the end of the line for a bill unless the Senate and the House can override that veto by a vote of two-thirds of its members. That rarely happens.

INFLUENCE PEDDLING

In the Senate we have a thousand topics to deal with, and there are people and groups of all kinds, inside and outside of government, with an active interest in shaping the way our laws are made. In the Federalist Papers the framers expressed the belief that it would be best if all citizens were involved in government through groups that would either push or pull for their specific concerns. They envisioned a system in which hundreds or even thousands of actors would be trying to influence legislation, and indeed that is the case today.

You can find an organization operating in Washington, DC, representing nearly every group in America. You name it and it's there. The hotter the current topic, the more groups you'll find. They seem to multiply.

Many of these groups may lie dormant for a period of time or only take interest in a particular bill. Others may exist solely for defensive purposes. Companies hire lobbyists, as do industry associations, labor unions, nonprofit groups, and many others. A directory published in DC, called "Washington Representatives," listed 11,500 active lobbyists in its 2006 edition. But the total number of lobbyists, both active and inactive, is even larger. According to the Senate Office of Public Records, which monitors lobbying activities and maintains a list of active lobbyists on the Internet, there were some 32,890 lobbyists registered to work in Washington as of October 2005. That's a lot of lobbying!

According to a report from the Center for Public Integrity (CPI), which monitors lobbying organizations involved in the political arena, more than 1.85 billion dollars was paid to political consultants in the run-up to the 2004 general election. This was approximately half of the total spending by presidential candidates, national party committees, general election candidates for Congress, and the so-called 527 groups named after the section in the Internal Revenue Code that they come under.

According to the Congressional Research Service (CRS), which does legislative research for Congress, the cost of a political campaign has gone up more than twice as fast as the cost of living. In 2004, the average cost of a winning campaign for the House of Representatives was approximately one million dollars, and a Senate race cost each candidate closer to seven million dollars. That's eleven times more than the same races would have cost thirty years earlier. During the same period, the cost of living had gone up only threefold.

Other findings of the CPI survey indicated that roughly six hundred professional consultants were involved in planning strategies for the campaigns for national office in 2004. Media consultants were paid a whopping 1.2 billion dollars; direct mail consultants brought in another 298 million; and fund-raising consultants cost the candidates at least 59 million. A report from the Federal Election Commission cited by the study projected that candidates running for office at the national level in 2006 would be spending 12 percent more overall than candidates spent two years ago.[1] That's too expensive! I still believe there's room for idealists to run on passion and the power of their ideas. Campaigns should be less professional and more personal—for example, what is this candidate going to do for America?

An Amazing Trusteeship

When you consider that there are nearly forty thousand registered lobbyists who focus part or all of their time on campaigns for state legislatures alone, you realize how intense the pressures from outside interests can be. That's an average of at least five lobbyists for every office holder, and there are hundreds and even thousands of private groups and nongovernmental organizations who want to help determine how our laws are made.

These lobbying organizations have both Republican and Democratic lobbyists so they can connect more effectively with the members from both parties. It's a system where it's tough for a bill to make it through, but it's also a system in which we have to deal with an extremely wide variety of topics. When a man or woman arrives in Washington as a new member of Congress, that person has to decide what he or she is going to focus on, because it's obvious that person can't do everything. One person can't hire enough staff to do everything, yet he or she has been given this amazing trusteeship. That's how I view my office.

I am a trustee for the people of Kansas and the citizens of the United States of America. I will not be here forever, but while I'm in this job, I want to do everything I can to make America better. I've been entrusted with an incredible trusteeship, and I intend to give a good account of how I've used it.

The American people want their country to be used for greater things. It's startling sometimes to realize that many of the greatest speeches in American history call for sacrifices. They don't promise prosperity and unending rainbows of happiness. Think of John Kennedy's famous words, "Ask not what your country can do for you, but what you can do for your country." That would seem to be unwise rhetoric for a politician; you're asking the people to sacrifice, and you're not giving them anything in return. Yet it resonates with people, because I believe it speaks to what Abraham Lincoln referred to in his First Inaugural Address as "the better angels of our nature."

Think of Ronald Reagan standing at the Berlin Wall and calling on Soviet Premier Mikhail Gorbachev to "tear down this wall." Talk about a provocative speech! He was calling on the biggest nuclear threat to the United States to reverse course. He may as well have said, "OK, Soviets. Let's see what you've got. Put 'em up!" And there were, incidentally, many people in Washington at the time who were terrified that this was exactly what would happen—a nuclear confrontation.

Yet these words resonated with the American people. They created a new reality. Millions of Americans were thrilled to hear the president speak so passionately and honestly to the Soviets in words that the whole world would hear and understand. He was standing on the greatness of America to bring down an "evil empire." The people responded to that. The entire world was listening—and they responded.

You can speak to the flesh, or you can speak to the soul. The flesh responds to what it wants, but the soul responds to a higher calling. When you speak to the soul and the need for personal sacrifice, the people respond. I've seen this at times during my own speeches. I'll be talking about one problem or another, pointing out all the challenges, and sometimes it's about bread-and-butter issues and things the voters want me to accomplish, but then when the focus turns to the higher purpose and the sacrifices that will be required, the mood changes. You see the audience sit up, and you realize that this has touched them. It's amazing to see, and it has been very encouraging to me.

That's where we should be leading, in those areas where we're doing the right things for the right reasons, even when it may be more difficult for us. Those are also the areas that we're most pleased with when all is said and done. If all we do is deal with things that are self-centered and self-focused, nobody is satisfied at the end of the day.

LEGISLATING ON PRINCIPLE

What we try to do in our office is to target key areas and then assign a couple of key staff members to be responsible for each topic. They're the ones who will be on the offense, trying to move the bills through. They may file a bill or join another colleague on a bill that's already moving, and they will also have a number of areas to defend. If they see symptoms of erosion in an issue that we've championed, or if they find out that our opponents are presenting legislation that we believe will be detrimental to our constituents or to the nation as a whole, then their job is to muster the research, coalitions, and votes to help block that action.

Our job, then, is to pick the issues that the citizens of Kansas and the people of the United States would consider to be the most important. They may include issues of life, the expansion of liberty against tyranny such as the ongoing struggle against militant Islam, or issues of science that can find cures and treatments for serious illness. We will be interested in limiting taxes, working for greater efficiency in government, and supporting initiatives that will help the citizens to prosper. We may need to get involved in what's happening in cancer research or adult stem cell research. Or we may find ourselves knee-deep in foreign policy issues and wise uses of American diplomacy.

I want to use my platform to help spread liberty and democracy in Asia, Africa, Latin America, the Middle East, and many other hot spots around the world. I support the family and renewing the culture, encourage marriage and child rearing, honor what's good, and discourage what's harmful.

AVOIDING TEMPTATION

There's a real temptation in this business to focus on the big things and ignore the little ones. When I stop and think about all the work I have to do and all the demands that are made on my time, I sometimes think, *OK, I only have so much time and energy, so I'm just going to work on the biggest things and let somebody else handle the small stuff.*

The old saying is "Major on the majors." There's wisdom in that idea. But that's not always the best way in Congress, because if you fall into that mind-set, you begin to think, *I can't slow down for the little things, and I can't afford to be concerned about how people around me are doing, because I'm focusing on the big things.* That's another false choice, but nevertheless one that can be a temptation to someone in any walk of life, but particularly in the U.S. Senate.

I talk about family values, but if I'm not caring for my own family, then nobody's going to hear the words I say. I could easily say, "Look, it's far more important for me to give this speech urging passage of this legislation through Congress than to spend time with my wife and kids." Wrong! Our deeds need to match our rhetoric for our words to carry weight.

At the end of the day, I sometimes have to ask myself, *Which is more important, giving a speech that will affect my ability to pass an important piece of legislation, or attending the sporting event my son is playing in that day?* This is a very real problem that I have to wrestle with. I've found that if you do what you say you'll do, and live the way you talk, the big things will take care of themselves. If I honor and care for my family, particularly when I'm a man who says in public forums that we need to renew the family, that sends a powerful signal—more powerful than any words I could ever speak.

Mother Teresa always said, "Pay attention to the little things." To me, that means that I ought to pay attention to everyone I come in contact with and make it clear that I honor each of them as a beautiful child of the living God. If I treat people with courtesy and respect even when I'm in a hurry, that's what speaks loudest. I don't always get it right. Often I fail. But when I do get it right, it is a beautiful example of truth lived out in a practical way.

HARD CASES

I've learned some hard lessons along the way about relationships and priorities, and it has made me more sensitive to the personal nature of my job. I'm fully committed to doing the best job I can as a member of the United States Senate, but I never want the perks of the office or the demands on my time to become more important to me than the people I serve. I've mentioned that I have a number of Mother Teresa's maxims posted on the walls of my home and office. One of my favorites says: "At the moment of death we will not be judged according to the number of good deeds we have done or by the diplomas we have received in our lifetime. We will be judged according to the love we have put into our work." That's a wonderful truth, and it applies to the Senate, the family, and whatever else we may do in life.

It also applies to how I treat my colleagues, even those I absolutely disagree with on policy matters. No matter how far away they may be from my position on the issues, they're not the enemy. It's essential for me to treat people with dignity and respect, regardless of how they treat me. That's part of my calling, I believe, and it's also the best way to do business.

If there's one area where I'm continually challenged in this regard, it's in dealing with organizations who are working overtime to undermine the family and religious values of this country. I've run into them repeatedly through the years. One of the most recent dustups is happening now in their war against faith-based programs in the prisons in Iowa.

Iowa is one of six states with prison systems that offer, or plan to offer, the InnerChange Freedom Initiative or other faith-based programs established by Prison Fellowship and other faith-oriented organizations. As I wrote in chapter 6, Arkansas, Texas, Minnesota, Iowa, and Kansas already have these systems in place. Florida is on line for the next one. But in a case filed in Iowa, a federal judge gave Prison Fellowship just sixty days to get out of the prisons, and he ordered them to repay $1.5 million in public funds they had received from the state, which would amount to about 40 percent of the total cost of running the facility. The rest comes from private donations.

This is going to be a big threat. Antireligion groups are going after Iowa's faith-based prisons now, and our program in Kansas could be next. My hope is that Prison Fellowship will win this case on appeal. We need to recognize the danger that the constant undermining of faith is having on this culture. Faith is a good thing. It brings out the best in us. It is what powered Martin Luther King and Mother Teresa. It propelled George Washington Carver just as it does Billy Graham.

This faith-based prison program actually works. It works both for the inmates and for the state of Iowa. Inmates participate in these programs on a voluntary basis, and they can leave the program simply by asking to be transferred. Ask any of the participants, as I've done, and they will tell you that it's changing them from the inside out. Men who go through the IFI program don't want to return to crime. The program grows their souls and teaches them new skills and new ways of dealing with stress, and it gives them a bolder and better perspective on their lives.

THE ACTIVIST COURT

Most Americans don't agree with the attack on faith in this country, but they don't know how to fight back. Ultimately, I'm hopeful that either the Court of Appeals or the Supreme Court will allow these programs to continue. Absent this, I don't know how we're going to reduce the recidivism rates or reduce the family impact on individuals affected by crime.

I also think of the attacks by antifaith groups against programs like Teen Challenge, a faith-based program that helps to transform the lives of teens who become addicted to drugs or alcohol. The program has been written up numerous times in magazines, newspapers, and featured on broadcasts because it has proven to be so tremendously successful in stopping addiction and restoring young people to their families. It gives them a new lease on life.

Yet, even though every social measure shows that Teen Challenge works, the antifaith lobby is so dogmatic and so opposed to taking a faith-based approach to a social problem, that they would rather see young people remain enslaved to their addictions than to allow them to take advantage of the one hope they may ever have to restore peace and sobriety to their lives.

This doesn't make any sense to me. The passion of some to remove any mention of God from the public square is a growing problem for America. They're not after a separation of church and state but a removal of faith from the public square. Search the record of history. A country that walks away from God, walks away from its future. This is particularly true for America. We are a faith-based country. Our motto is "In God we trust." Must we change our motto too? We should encourage and embrace faith, not run it out of the public square and into a closet to be brought out in an emergency or for sentimental purposes. To be clear, I am adamantly opposed to a theocracy. It would be bad for religion and bad for government and bad for America. But let's end the war on faith in the West.

When Mother Teresa came to Capitol Hill to receive the Congressional Gold Medal she was with us less than an hour, frail and weak, yet her joy and faith were radiant. As I helped her into her car, she grabbed my hand and said three words, four times. She said, "All for Jesus! All for Jesus! All for Jesus! All for Jesus!"

That was her life and her faith, which empowered her to care for millions, even as a weak and frail elderly woman. That worn-out body could not diminish the brilliance of her soul. Faith, true faith, is a force for good. We need more of that, not less!

A Brick in the Road

I recently put forward a bill in the Senate to prevent the antireligion caucus from being awarded attorney's fees on Establishment Clause cases, such as where a small community is sued for having a nativity scene on the courthouse lawn at Christmas. I'm hoping there will be broad-based support for this initiative in the House. The cases could still be brought, but each side would have to pay its own legal fees.

We've had former and current ACLU lawyers testify that they do use the threat of legal fees to blackmail communities to take down a cross or Ten Commandments, even without a suit. The ACLU threatens a community by saying that if the citizens try to fight the suit and resist the ACLU challenge, then those communities will have to pay all the ACLU's attorneys' fees if the ACLU wins the case. The current law provides for that.

By using threats and intimidation, the ACLU has been able to intimidate school districts, small communities, church groups, and many others all across the country in many cases. Establishment Clause cases are complicated, and the law is in flux. If groups want to bring these cases, that is their right. But they shouldn't be given the incentive to do so by the promise of big legal fees.

Small community organizations simply don't have the funds to wage a legal battle on big Establishment Clause cases, even if they think the case is winnable and even when they know they're within their rights. They can't risk it, so why go into it if there's a chance they could lose. When the option is whether to take down the Ten Commandments or a Nativity scene or to risk a judgment that could cost them a half million dollars in legal fees, they generally give in to the blackmail and take down the religious objects. It's a national disgrace that a systematic stripping of the foundational beliefs and values of American society is taking place right before our eyes, and much of it is funded with public money because of the current law. This must change!

An Appeal for Sanity

I'm hoping the measure we've put forward will get some traction, and I believe that if enough people hear about our bill, it will get the support it needs. At this point in time, our bill is there to help start the discussion. The American people want to say that we're "one nation, under God." They believe in God, and they want our social and cultural institutions to reflect that fact.

According to a poll conducted by *U.S. News & World Report* and PBS's *Religion & Ethics Newsweekly*, America is still a very religious nation, despite the secularization of the past forty years. Nearly two-thirds of Americans surveyed said that religion is "very important" to them, and nearly half said they "attend church or synagogue at least once a week." That's the highest percentage since the 1960s. At the same time, voluntary giving to religious institutions, at more than fifty-five billion dollars annually, surpasses the gross national product of many nations.[2]

Findings like these echo the annual Gallup Survey of Religion, which reported that upward of 90 percent of Americans believe in God, 81 percent believe in heaven, and 84 percent believe in miracles. Furthermore, as Gallup reported, there's a deep desire among the majority of those surveyed for a return to their spiritual moorings. They realize that secularization has done its best to strip society of its basic beliefs and values. Yet there's a hunger for God among people of all religions, ages, and classes. Faith is alive in America. It will be the leading force in renewing our families and culture and giving us another American century!

CONCLUSION

THE ROAD AHEAD

There's no doubt that things have been different recently with Democrats in control of both houses of Congress, but no one should underestimate the strength and resolve of the conservative coalition or the political will of the majority of Americans who are conservative in their views. This coalition represents many different approaches. We have pro-growth conservatives, fiscal conservatives, social conservatives, libertarians, and a large body of people of faith, whose convictions span a fairly wide range of beliefs. While we've been shaken by the results of the 2006 midterm elections, these people aren't going away. They're in it for the long haul.

The Republican coalition includes some members who are focused on foreign policy but less interested in some of our domestic policy initiatives. We have a number of members whose positions on social issues would probably be questioned by some of the members who are fiscal conservatives. There are business interests who want to see lower taxes and a pro-growth economic climate but who are less enthusiastic with the social issues. They're all part of the coalition, a center-right majority that has hung together despite the challenges.

We also have a geographic base that is primarily Southern and middle American. While the heartland of America is primarily Republican today, the Northeast and West Coasts tend to be predominantly Democratic and more liberal in outlook. The conservative coalition is actively competing for additional votes, in all places and among all groups across America. We must reach out and invite others in, especially Asian Americans, Hispanic Americans, and African-Americans.

Despite our wounds and the loss of key leadership positions in Congress, we have a healthy and dynamic coalition, and we're going to see some important changes in the months ahead. As each new group and new member comes on board, the Republican party changes a bit. People tend to think that a political party is static, but that's not the case. Political parties are an amalgamation of groups of people, and as each group joins in, they shift the party's focus—not its principles, just its focus. The Republican party is built on principles, not personalities. We disagree on many things, but our core principles of growth, fiscal responsibility, compassion, faith, strength, family, personal responsibility, justice, and freedom are uniting ideas that hold us together.

One of the lessons of the 2006 elections was that a lot of people were unhappy with the increases in government spending during the Bush presidency and a Republican Congress. That's a valid criticism. Balancing the budget is a two-step process. First, we have to cut taxes and stimulate the economy in order to get it growing. Economic conditions at the end of 2006 were very good, with historically low unemployment, a dynamic stock market, and strong personal income.

The United States is a marvelous economic machine with a 12-trillion-dollar economy. When you get an economy that large up and rolling with a 3 or 4 percent rate of growth, that stimulates enormous revenues for individuals and businesses. It also kicks off a lot of tax receipts to governments at all levels. Next, and the most important step by far, is to grow the economy. That may be 80 percent of balancing the federal budget.

Building a robust economy dwarfs anything else in importance that we can do, and the GOP pushed that. We've pushed tax cuts through that have stimulated the economy. Under the Republican-controlled House and Senate, we got things such as the capital gains tax cut, the dividend tax cut, and the marriage penalty reduction. President Bush helped a great deal, and he deserves credit for it. And I believe strongly that we should ake all these tax cuts permanent, and then do more.

I think the current tax code should be taken behind the barn and killed with a dull ax! I also strongly support an optional flat tax as a means to offer

Americans a choice while we work to reform the current tax code. But step two of balancing the budget is to restrain federal spending to a pace below the rate of the economic growth of federal receipts. That has been a failure. The system is built to spend whether Democrats or Republicans are in office. The system must be changed to control wasteful spending! And it can be changed.

FISCAL AND POLITICAL REALITIES

I would like to see us cut federal spending not just below the growth rate but to reduce it below current levels as a percent of the economy. It's very difficult to cut federal spending. Conventional wisdom in Washington says that the best you can do is restrain it below the growth rate of the economy. Therefore, if the economy is growing at the rate of 3 or 4 percent, we need to hold spending to below that. I believe we can do much better than that and still meet the needs of our people and new priorities.

To reduce spending to that extent would require a change in the machinery. But it can be done. The problem is that once you create a federal program, it's almost impossible to kill it. President Reagan said that "there is nothing so permanent as a temporary government program." I'm afraid he was right about that. It's like the Energizer bunny: *It just keeps going and going.* And this is another reason why Republicans took a beating at the polls in 2006. We didn't do enough to stop those costly programs, and the people reacted.

The GOP got into trouble on spending, but before jumping to conclusions, we need to consider where a large part of that spending was going. In 2001, through no fault of our own, we suddenly found ourselves at war with a global network of terrorists. Considering the loss of life and the potential threat to our homeland, there was no option but to equip and deploy the military, and that costs a lot of money.

In August 2005, Hurricane Katrina blasted the Gulf Coast, severely damaging several cities in Louisiana, Mississippi, and Alabama, and causing more than 81 billion dollars of damage. The city of New Orleans was flooded and much of it destroyed. As we know only too well now from the news coverage that followed those events, there was a wake of devastation that covered tens of thousands of square miles across a three-state region. In response, President Bush asked Congress for 105 billion dollars to support the relief efforts, including 62.5 billion dollars for relief to families who lost homes and jobs.

Less than a month later, in September 2005, Hurricane Rita hit the Gulf Coast, causing more than 10 dollars billion in damage. Once again the federal government stepped in to help clean up the mess and relieve the suffering of the more than 750,000 people who lost their homes, and in many cases their livelihoods. It's hard to place the blame on Republicans for catastrophes beyond our control.

The country didn't fundamentally change in 2006, but the people have changed captains in Congress. Most of the exit polling I've seen suggests that the voters were primarily concerned about the war in Iraq and the charges of corruption in Congress. I believe the vote was mostly about the war.

Another lesson of this election cycle is that the Republican base—made up primarily of fiscally and socially conservative activists—wasn't motivated to get out and vote, and it was because they felt that their representatives in Congress weren't very motivated. I traveled to ten states in the weeks leading up to the November 2006 elections, and it was obvious that the base was less than enthusiastic. There were signs of reawakening in the last few days before the elections, but by that time it was already too late.

The United States remains a center-right nation, with the majority of voters supporting traditionally conservative positions on most issues. In fact, it was apparent that the Democratic challengers in many states were taking more conservative positions on the issues in order to be elected.

DIVIDED LOYALTIES

It would be unwise to see the losses in any of these races as a repudiation of conservatism. Actually, they show the strength and growth and affirmation of the conservative and pro-life movements on many fronts. The war in Iraq, corruption charges, immigration reform, and excessive spending were the key issues. Also the party in power almost usually lose seats in a midterm election. The party in power always takes a hit in off-year elections, and that's especially true for the second midterm elections of a two-term administration.

Some pundits call it the "sixth-year itch." *Congressional Quarterly* has called it the "sixth year swoon." In the sixth year of an eight-year presidential term, the party in the White House almost always loses seats in Congress, and this pattern has been consistent for more than 125 years. In the 2006 election, all 435 House seats and 34 Senate seats were up for grabs, along with 36 governorships. The Democrats won a majority in all three categories.

When the 110th Congress convened under new leadership in the first week of January 2007, Democrats controlled 233 seats in the House of Representatives, and Republicans held just 202. There was a 49 to 49–seat tie in the Senate that could be broken by the two Independents—one of which is Senator Joe Lieberman, who became an Independent during the contentious Senate race in Connecticut—who indicated their intention of voting with the Democratic caucus. That meant that Democrats would be in the driver's seat in both houses of Congress for the next two years.

An issue that needs to be discussed further, of course, is public reaction to the war in Iraq. This was the dominant issue. The fact that a week before the election spokesmen for the president said that the administration was going to "stay the course" may have added more fuel to the fire. For those who were already discontent with the apparent lack of progress in Iraq, the administration seemed to be saying that they had no intention of changing strategy. If we had appeared to be more open to new strategies, using language suggesting that we were looking for new approaches to the war, I think that could have changed the results in a couple of close races.

A WILDERNESS JOURNEY

As we well know, we are in a time of war. We are fighting against Islamic fascists who seek the demise of the United States, Israel, and the progressive Muslim states in the region. We are not simply fighting terrorism, which is a tactic, but we are fighting a group that practices a militant version of Islam and is bent on our destruction. For the sake of our children and grandchildren, we must not lose the will to fight and to win this war. We will win if we do not lose the will to fight.

If we lose the will to fight, our children and grandchildren will pay the price and, moreover, we would be abandoning the hope of freedom in the Middle East to fanatic fascists—a thought our forefathers could not bear. Victory in this part of the world requires a political solution to match our military presence there. We will have to maintain a military presence in that part of the world for some period of time, as we do in Bosnia and other parts of the world. But a military solution is not enough. We need to come to some kind of political equilibrium where we aggressively push a political solution in addition to our military presence.

In the near future, the situation in Iraq will be substantially different than it is today. We have to get our troops off the front line. We have to turn the security of Iraq over to the Iraqi people. And we've got to get a political solution in place. We cannot "cut and run." We can't extract our forces and leave the people and the region in an even more precarious position. That would leave Iraq in complete chaos and a breeding ground for terrorism.

I also think it's important to look seriously at the option of keeping Iraq together as a loose federation of separate states with a Kurdish area, a Sunni area, and a Shiite area—with Baghdad as the federal city. A unified capital won't be an easy proposition, since much of the fighting is taking place there. But a precipitous pullout by the United States would only empower the militias, and we can't allow that to happen. The day we announce our withdrawal is the day al-Qaeda declares victory. We need a combined political-military solution that recognizes sectarian divisions in Iraq. We need a strong military presence to provide a secure atmosphere for political solutions to work. Some sort of ethnic and religious division of the country seems to be a logical option. This model worked, so far, in Bosnia and the so-called "Dayton Accords."

Both of our political parties will need to be very responsible here, or we could see even greater carnage in the Middle East. On the eastern border of Iraq is Iran, the leading supporter of terrorism around the world. Many good things are happening in the move toward democracy in the region, but I think we have to admit that there are too many fires for us to fight all at once.

I do think there are people who are willing to listen to our concerns. It may mean that we have to go to some of these countries and say, "Yes, we've made mistakes. But this is a critical situation that will affect the region and the world for years to come, and we need your help." That's simply the reality of the situation as it is today.

The situation in Washington is that Republicans are going to be the minority in Congress. I hope our time in the minority will be short and will cause us to search again for what we stand for and to be able to come back with a strong agenda of hope and ideas for the future. "The party or person that offers the most hope and ideas for the future is the one that wins," someone once wrote. The candidate who offers hope and ideas is generally the one who wins. This should encourage us in the next election cycle.

Finally, as I have repeatedly pointed out, we must reclaim our culture at home in order to be able to engage in such a long term struggle. Our proposal to the world—a free and just society—can only take hold if we model that free and virtuous society here at home.

A PRACTICAL RESPONSE

This may turn out to be a very fruitful time for the Republican Party, a time for us to focus on what we stand for and then to return with a strong agenda that reinforces our core values and at the same time offers new hope and new ideas. Republicans held the Congress and a majority of governorships for more than a decade, and through the years I think focus on core principles was lost. New ideas, bold ideas, for implementing these principles were not brought forward.

The good news about the 2006 midterm election, however, is that our ideas and our philosophy were not repudiated. If anything, they were replicated by the other party. Now it's time to get back to basics, reassuring the American people that we are a pro-growth party with a strong commitment to fiscal restraint. We remain a pro-life, pro-family party, and we need to show genuine enthusiasm for those issues along with new ways to address them and accomplish our goals.

We need a robust military and a strong, realistic foreign policy. We should deal with the rest of the world as we try to operate at home—with wisdom and humility. Not all the answers are in Washington. At times we may have to work with people with whom we disagree strongly on certain issues. We need to stand strong in defense of our core principles, but we must nevertheless be realistic in how we do that. This can be especially challenging in places like the Middle East. We cannot forget other regions too, like Latin America, where challenges abound primarily because of the lack of progress in living standards and opportunities for most people. Government "of the people" must produce results "for the people."

We need to come up with hopeful new ideas on topics that hit people right where they live. People know that the basic family structure in this country has been fractured and fragmented. We need to rebuild the family and renew the culture. We need to talk about some of the specific things that we can do to restore these essential institutions. One of the things I've talked about is welfare reform with an emphasis on building strong family units. We need to follow up on that.

We also need to publish federal statistics on an annual and semiannual basis showing what's happening to families in this country and how well or poorly the culture is doing. This can be done on a state-by-state basis and in metro areas using important social data. What's happening in our families? What is the divorce rate? What is the rate of teen suicides? How many children are being born in various parts of the country, and how many of them are born out of wedlock? Regularly seeing this social data and the trend lines will help us understand where we are as a nation and where we need to focus our efforts most intensely.

We need to focus on vital health issues, such as cancer. I've written about this in chapter 17 in my discussion of health care initiatives. We need to make a formal commitment to finding ways to end death by cancer in ten years. It's doable, and it's something that will touch people where they live. This is an area where we need ideas and we need to follow through. This would electrify America with hope and ideas. It's an American-sized dream that can come true.

We need school choice and more local control of education decisions. I strongly support creating optional, personal savings accounts to offset and eventually replace a failing social security system.

We also need to move on energy security in North America. We can achieve this goal, but it's going to take a lot of effort and focus. This will help people in real and substantial ways, but it will require us to think creatively with our counterparts in Canada and Mexico about how to achieve these goals. Whether it's expanding oil exploration, using coal gasification, increasing the use of ethanol with cellulose-based and biodiesel fuels, or using more electricity in our car fleets, these are ideas that will help people where they live.

Obviously we need to cut wasteful government spending! I strongly support creating a commission to review all government programs, offering Congress an up or down vote to keep or cut wasteful or ineffective federal programs. On the topic of corruption, I hope we would come back with a renewed commitment to support term limits as a way of dealing with some of these problems. One of the key things that we can do is to regularly change the people who serve in Congress. I think this could be one of the most effective ways of dealing with corruption. We would have people who serve for twelve years in the House, and people who serve twelve years in the Senate. We should do the same thing with federal appellate court judges.

Of the more than three hundred million people in America, there are more than enough qualified Americans to have regular changes in the people who serve in these important positions. We'll get fresher ideas, better government, and less corruption if we do this. I hope this could be one of the issues we return to and push strongly in order to address the public's concerns.

A Lasting Difference

The great British parliament, William Wilberforce, wrote a powerful book that served as a guidepost for many people in an era of great transition. The title of the book is *A Practical View of Christianity*. Wilberforce wrote about how Christian principles can be used to improve conditions in society, and more directly, how they could be practically applied to the problems that existed in England at that time.

My hope is that this book may be a small effort in a similar vein, and that it will offer some thoughts on how traditional American values and historic Judeo-Christian principles can be used to address some of the fundamental problems this country is facing today. It is by no means an all-inclusive book. I've labored to keep the narrative informal and to the point. This book is by no means expansive enough to cover all the issues we're confronted with today. I hope it may at least stimulate discussion of what we can do, and how we can apply our principles in an effective fashion to the problems facing our society at this hour.

We have many problems, but we also have a marvelous nation blessed with many talented people of great heart. We have achieved much. We can do even more. It would be my hope that each reader will be moved to think more deeply about how we can use our resources to address our problems more effectively, using the time-honored principles that have guided Western civilization since its beginnings.

The answer, C. S. Lewis wrote in his final book in *The Chronicles of Narnia,* is "further up and further in." Moving up by moving in. Our path upward is an inward one. We improve by improving our souls. We increase in greatness by increasing in goodness. As we grow in our love of God and others, we will grow in stature and acceptance, as individuals and as a nation.

The path is an old one and hard to follow, for our very nature often pulls against us. Yet with resolve and aided by grace, the "narrow way" can be found and traveled. Can we afford to do any less? A great deal is riding on this generation of Americans. We must respond to the "better angels of nature," and I believe we will!

NOTES

Chapter 4
1. George Will, "Eugenics by Abortion: Is Perfection an Entitlement?" *Washington Post*, April 14, 2005; A27, www.washingtonpost.com/ac2/wpdyn/A516712005Apr13?language=printer (accessed September 10, 2006).
2. David C. Reardon, PhD, "The Abortion/Suicide Connection," *The Post-Abortion Review*: 1(2) Summer 1993, a publication of the Elliot Institute, www.afterabortion.org/suicide.html (accessed October 22, 2006).

Chapter 5
1. Steven Ertelt, "New Poll: Majority of Americans, Blacks, Students Pro-Life on Abortion," Zogby International, April 26, 2004, www.zogby.com/Soundbites/ReadClips.dbm?ID=8087 (accessed October 22, 2006).

Chapter 6
1. Bureau of Justice Statistics, Office of Justice Programs. "Prison Statistics." (Dec. 31, 2005), www.ojp.usdoj.gov/bjs/prisons.htm (accessed April 15, 2007).

Chapter 7
1. U.S. Department of Health and Human Services. Indicators of Welfare Dependence: Annual Report to Congress, 2005, Appendix C. Additional Nonmarital Birth Data, aspe.hhs.gov/hsp/indicators05/apc.htm (accessed April 15, 2007).
2. Linda J. Waite and Maggie Gallagher, *The Case for Marriage: Why Married People are Happier, Healthier, and Better Off Financially*, (New York: Doubleday, 2000), 148–49.
3. Stanley Kurtz, "The End of Marriage in Scandinavia: The 'conservative case' for same-sex marriage collapses," *The Weekly Standard* (9, no. 20), February 20, 2004, www.weeklystandard.com/Content/Public/Articles/000/000/003/660zypwj.asp?pg=2 (accessed November 8, 2006).
4. Francisco Vara-Orta, "Majority of Freshmen View Gay Marriage as OK," *Los Angeles Times*, January 19, 2007, www.latimes.com/news/local/la-me-freshmen19jan19,0,6657121.story?coll=la-home-headlines (accessed January 19, 2007).

Chapter 8
1. Ron Haskins, "Fathers' Role in Rearing Called Key: Poll results indicate strong support for healthy-marriage initiatives." *Washington Times*, November 18, 2005.
2. Barbara Dafoe Whitehead and David Popenoe, "The State of Our Unions: The Social Health of Marriage in America." The National Marriage Project, Rutgers, The State University of New Jersey, 2005, marriage.rutgers.edu/Publications/Print/PrintSOOU2005.htm (accessed October 12, 2006).
3. Testimony of Ron Haskins, Senior Fellow, Brookings Institution and Senior Consultant, Annie E. Casey Foundation, before the Committee on Agriculture, Nutrition and Forestry, United States Senate, July 19, 2001, agriculture.senate.gov/Hearings/Hearings_2001/July_19__2001/719has.htm. (See also the PBS *FrontLine* special: "Let's Get Married" www.pbs.org/wgbh/pages/frontline/shows/marriage/.)
4. National Center for Children in Poverty, at Columbia University. "Early Childhood Poverty: A Statistical Profile," March 2002, www.nccp.org/media/ecp02-text.pdf. (See also Robert E. Rector, Kirk A. Johnson, PhD, Patrick F. Fagan, and Lauren R. Noyes, "Increasing Marriage Would Dramatically Reduce Child Poverty," Heritage Foundation: Center for Data Analysis Report #03-06, May 20, 2003, www.heritage.org/Research/Family/cda0306.cfm; and Patrick F. Fagan, Robert E. Rector, Kirk A. Johnson, PhD, and America Peterson, *The Positive Effects of Marriage: A Book of Charts*, (Washington, D.C.: The Heritage Foundation, April 2002), www.heritage.org/Research/Features/Marriage/index.cfm.

Chapter 9
1. Report on Marketing Violent Entertainment to Children, Federal Trade Commission, November 20, 2000, www.ftc.gov/os/2000/11/violstudymccain.htm.

2. The findings are confirmed by a number of studies, including: Craig A. Anderson and Karen E. Dill, "Video Games and Aggressive Thoughts, Feelings, and Behavior in the Laboratory and in Life," *Journal of Personality and Social Psychology* 78, no. 4 (April 2000), 772 – 90, web.pdx.edu/~cqmv/anderson.and.dill.html (accessed April 16, 2007).

Chapter 10
1. Dr. Kevin Bales maintains an active assessment of statistics regarding slavery, involuntary bondage, and trafficking at the Free the Slaves Web site: www.freetheslaves.net.
2. Albert Mohler, "Pornified America: The Culture of Pornography," Crosswalk.com: Aug. 22, 2005, www.crosswalk.com/news/weblogs/mohler/?adate=8/22/2005 (accessed September 22, 2006).
3. The media are beginning to pay attention to this problem. One widely cited source on the impact of pornography on teens is: Bella English, "The Secret Life of Boys: Pornography is a mouse click away, and kids are being exposed to it in ever-increasing numbers." *The Boston Globe*, May 12, 2005, www.boston.com/ae/media/articles/2005/05/12/the_secret_life_of_boys?mode=PF (accessed September 23, 2006).

Chapter 12
1. "ASTMH Supports Neglected Disease Legislation," American Society of Tropical Medicine and Hygiene: May 10, 2006, www.astmh.org/press/neglected.cfm. (Accessed December 9, 2006).

Chapter 15
1. Nissan Ratzlav-Katz, "Iran´s President Calls for Destruction of Israel and the West," *Arutz Sheva* (Israel National News), October 27, 2005, www.israelnationalnews.com/News/News.aspx/91812 (accessed January 11, 2007). The report quotes: "The goal of a world without the United States or Zionism, Ahmadinejad said, is 'attainable and could definitely be realized . . . Our dear Imam [Ayatollah Ruhollah Khomeini] ordered that the occupying regime in Jerusalem be wiped off the face of the earth. This was a very wise statement.'"

Chapter 16
1. Ahmedin Jemal, et al., "Cancer Statistics, 2007," *CA Cancer Journal of Clinicians* 57, 43–46, caonline.amcancersoc.org/misc/cancerstats2007.pdf (accessed April 16, 2007).

Chapter 17
1. From a letter to Michael Maestlin, Kepler's former professor at Tübingen University. Cited in: Gerald Holton, "Johannes Kepler's Universe: Its Physics and Metaphysics," *American Journal of Physics* 24 (May 1956). 340–51.
2. Sir Robert Boyle, *Seraphick Love*, 1959 (Ann Arbor, MI: University Microfilms International, 1981).
3. Roger Cotes, Cote's preface to the second edition of Newton's *Principia*, *Sir Isaac Newton's Mathematical Principles of Natural Philosophy and his System of the World* (Berkeley, CA: University of California Press, 1962), xxxiii.
4. Cited in Freeman Dyson, *Disturbing the Universe* (New York, NY: Harper & Row, 1979). See also: Albert Einstein, *Ideas and Opinions Based on Mein Weltbild*, edited by Carl Seelig, and other sources. New translations and revisions by Sonja Bargmann (New York, NY: Crown Publishers, 1954).
5. Quotes from Dr. Carver, George Washington Carver National Monument, www.nps.gov/archive/gwca/expanded/quotes.htm (accessed January 7, 2007).

Chapter 18
1. Sandy Bergo, John Perry, Agustín Armendariz, "A Wealth of Advice." The Center for Public Integrity, www.publicintegrity.org/consultants/report.aspx?aid=533 (accessed October 10, 2006).
2. Jay Tolson, "The Faith of Our Fathers," *U.S. News & World Report*, June 28, 2004, www.usnews.com/usnews/news/articles/040628/28faith.htm (accessed September 15, 2006). See also: Andrew Kohut, "Anti-Americanism: Causes and Characteristics." A Report of the Pew Global Attitudes Project, December 10, 2003, pewglobal.org/commentary/display.php?AnalysisID=77. The report states in part: "Among wealthy nations, Pew has found, the United States is the most religious nation—in sharp contrast to mostly secular Western Europe. A 58% majority in the U.S. views belief in God as a prerequisite to morality—just a third of Germans and even fewer Italians, British, and French agree."